FROM ANDREWS TO ZASTUDIL features more than fifty sports figures chatting with *The Plain Dealer* sportswriter Dennis Manoloff about myriad topics. Here is a microcosm of what can be found inside:

Erin Andrews 2012:

"I always wanted to do this for a living, but, obviously, I never dreamed it would get like this." (page 1)

"I've got girlfriends who want me to be more girly. My friend is in the apartment talking about window treatments and a side table and I'm like, 'When is the Pro Bowl on?'" (page 3)

Dr. James Andrews, 2013:

"I want parents and coaches to realize the implications of putting a 12- or 13-year-old through the type of athletic work done by a 25-year-old ..." (page 11)

"... their kid needs at least two months off each year to recover from a specific sport. Preferably, three to four months." (page 11)

"Seeing these guys get back to doing what they do best, that's where I derive the enjoyment. I don't worry about how much money they might make in the future." (page 12)

Allison Fisher, 2005:

"If somebody thinks they can beat me, I say, "Yeah, you probably can." I'll leave it at that. Go ahead and think you can, if it makes you feel good." (page 105)

Tonya Harding, 2006:

"Highest high: being the first American woman to land the triple axel. Lowest low: Losing my career because of bad judgment." (page 115)

Padraig Harrington, 2005:

"I've played well when I'm paired with Tiger because he's an easy guy to play golf with, as good a guy as you could pick." (page 121)

Chad Johnson, 2006:

"If you're a good receiver, regardless of who's throwing the ball, the numbers will be there." (page 146)

"I'm not going to change what makes Chad, Chad. It makes me who I am. Look, everybody's different. That's what makes the world interesting." (page 151)

Kenny Lofton, 2010:

"The guys called me the igniter. Once I ignited the flames, everything took off. It was an exciting time." (page 188)

"... I know there are people who cheated, cheated to extend their careers, and it's not right." (page 189)

Kevin Millar, 2005:

"The road I've taken is laughable, really. I was never drafted — high school, junior college or college. I played one year for the St. Paul Saints of the Northern League and made $600 a month. Eleven years later, I was on the team that gave Boston its first World Series title in 86 years. You couldn't sell that script." (page 207)

Dominique Moceanu, 2006:

"You don't show signs of weakness in competition. You are trained to be tough like a warrior." (page 211)

"I didn't want to show that, at the Olympics, the biggest competition of my life, the injury was a factor." (page 211)

"The Olympics were a great chapter in my life, but I am level-headed. I knew it wouldn't be like that forever." (page 214)

Joe Montana, 2005:

"I wouldn't want to go to a Super Bowl and lose. Thankfully, I don't know that feeling. I can't imagine it feels very good." (page 217)

Danica Patrick, 2004:

"I didn't race Go Karts with the idea of one day being recognized as a female racer." (page 221)

"I work out all the time. I guarantee I'm more fit than a lot of guys out there. It's important for my racing and my marketability." (page 223)

Curt Schilling, 2002:

"Tell me, how on God's green earth did we get the word greedy attached to us, especially when it comes to negotiations between owners and players?" (page 245)

"I say what's on my mind. That shouldn't automatically mean I'm controversial." (page 248)

Venus and Serena Williams, 2005:

Serena: "Venus has a stone face on the court. She never gets mad. I'm always mad and angry and, like, "Ugghhh." Venus is like "Oh, well, I'll get her next time." (page 289)

Venus: "Serena does what she wants to do. She goes for it. She doesn't let the person next to her determine what she's going to do." (page 289)

From Erin Andrews
to Dave Zastudil

From Erin Andrews to Dave Zastudil

A Collection of *The Plain Dealer* Sportswriter Dennis Manoloff's Favorite Interviews via **D MAN'S** WORLD

THE WOOSTER BOOK COMPANY

Wooster Ohio • 2015

The Wooster Book Company
where minds and imaginations meet

The Wooster Book Company
205 West Liberty Street
Wooster, Ohio 44691
www.woosterbook.com

Printed and bound in the United States of America.

Articles reprinted here with the permission of *The Plain Dealer*

ISBN: 978-1-59098-250-1

To Grace

Contents

Introduction

One of my first attempts at a one-on-one interview with a prominent sports figure ended almost before it began. As a reporter for my college newspaper, *The Daily Northwestern*, I waited for Indiana coach Bob Knight after his team finished a workout in Evanston, Illinois. Our meeting during the 1986–87 season was scheduled, and I had the letter—with Knight's signature—to prove it.

Knight approached, asked who I was, and informed me that his time was short. I looked at my long list of questions and knew I was in trouble. Before I could say, "Bob Knight is an intimidating individual to a college sportswriter," the "interview" had wrapped.

My Fright Knight experience did not discourage me. Nor did my failed attempt, as a young sportswriter for *The* (Cleveland) *Plain Dealer*, to chat with Indians slugger Albert Belle in 1995. Belle was a danger zone for even the most seasoned reporter, so I didn't feel too bad.

Fortunately, my batting average got considerably better with time. I have interviewed hundreds of athletes and sports figures at all levels in my twenty-six years at *The Plain Dealer*, Ohio's largest newspaper. Scores of those interviews have been published under the column sig, "DMan's World," a form to present the news as I see fit. The majority of DMan's World stories are in Q-and-A format.

If not handled properly, Q-and-A interviews with any subject can be a bad read. They can be easy-bake journalism: simply ask questions, get answers and—presto—an article appears. I prefer to view the Q-and-A as a science of interpersonal communication, something that requires skill, ingenuity, and quick thinking to achieve the desired result. From my perspective, it is a challenge. I need to work hard to get the best out of the person sitting across from me, or on the other end of the phone, sometimes in a (very) compressed time frame.

Feedback from readers, colleagues, and the interview subjects allows me to humbly submit that my Q-and-A's are fast-paced and enjoyable. More readers have responded to my Q-and-A's than anything I have done. I recognize the importance of finding a good subject, then conversing with the person rather than following some sort of script. When readers finish my Q-and-A's, they feel as though they just listened in on a chat at the dinner table.

I never thought of compiling the work in book form until colleagues encouraged me to do so. They maintained I had something unique to offer even the casual sports fan. So I amassed all of my Q-and-A's, and other stories that centered on one-on-one interviews. Then I whittled the list to my favorites. I began with no set number. All of the Q-and-A's are from the pages of *The Plain Dealer*, as part of my daily or special assignments.

What comes through these pages is considerable star power. The interviews were conducted only if the subject had credentials and/or offered intrigue as a character in his or her vocation, with a periodic nod toward Cleveland. There are Hall of Famers and future Hall of Famers, or authors of Hall of Fame moments, throughout.

Baseball carries the load because my primary responsibilities at *The Plain Dealer* have been baseball-related. Baseball fans will want this book because of its lineup. Where else can they find under one cover interviews with Bob Feller, Roger Clemens, Derek Jeter, Rickey Henderson, Dennis Eckersley, Johnny Pesky, Johnny Damon, Jim Thome, Luis Gonzalez, Kevin Millar, Kenny Lofton and Curt Schilling?

Yet this book is about much more than baseball. Where else will sports fans, in general, find interviews under one cover with football's Joe Montana and Chad Johnson; auto racing's Danica Patrick; pool's Allison Fisher; gymnastics' Dominique Moceanu and Mary Lou Retton; skating's Tonya Harding; golf's Paula Creamer; and strongman's Phil Pfister? As much as the baseball Q-and-A's resonate, the Harding and Pfister interviews might be the most interesting of the crop.

I have been fortunate to write about sports for a living for nearly three decades. Part of the enjoyment has come from speaking with the subjects that comprise this book. My hope is that the reader finds the content entertaining and informative, thereby gaining an appreciation for what makes these sports newsmakers do what they do.

—DENNIS MANOLOFF
March 2015

Erin Andrews, *television*

January 2012

Erin Andrews is more than just a quality TV reporter. She is a brand.

Andrews will emcee the Greater Cleveland Sports Commission's annual awards banquet Thursday at the Renaissance Hotel downtown. The event is sold out. Plenty of recognizable names will attend, but Andrews likely will create the most buzz. How do we know this?

Twitter. In the twenty-first century, where social media reigns, Twitter serves as a strong indicator of popularity. Andrews had a cool 1.075 million followers as of Monday. Cavaliers owner Dan Gilbert, as big as he is in these parts, had 49,800.

Given that Andrews' assignments often put her on college campuses, starry-eyed students no doubt have played a large role in the name recognition. That is the innocent side.

Andrews also is well-known because of what happened to her beginning in 2008. Michael David Barrett filmed a nude Andrews multiple times through the walls of hotels; one of the videos went viral. Barrett pleaded guilty in December 2009 to interstate stalking and was sentenced in March 2010 to two and a half years in prison.

Andrews has tried to move on from the very public humiliation. It has not been easy. She remains an engaging, funny person—but some of the words come with an understandable edge.

DM: What do you make of the Erin Andrews phenomenon, where you have attained somewhat of a rock-star status?

EA: I always wanted to do this for a living, but, obviously, I never dreamed it would get like this. I kind of laugh about it, because I've never looked at myself like that. I wouldn't say it's been difficult adjusting to it, but it's been different. Unfortunately, there have been situations in my life over the past couple of years that have forced me to change the way I live, how I travel, things like that. There are precautions I've had to take. I've been burned as much as anybody. At the same time, I know I have a great job and I'm very thankful for all the fan support.

DM: How wild is it to walk into college venues and see giant pictures of your face in the stands?

EA: Honestly, I don't need to see my nose that big. I'm already very self-conscious of my nose, and to see it on a huge cut-out. .... It's fun, though. I'm really thankful because I've never played and I've never won anything. I think it's great that kids get so excited about it. I get it, too, because I'm still such a huge sports fan. I was like that at school.

DM: Unusual autograph request?

EA: Last year at Villanova, a kid took a dorm-room screen, blew up my picture and put it on the screen. He held it up with a big stick. I said, "Dude, where did you get a screen like this?" He said, "I took it from my dorm; I need to have it back tonight." I said, "Sounds good, I guess."

DM: A cursory Google search of your name uncovers such phrases as "arguably the most revered female broadcaster—"

EA: Oh, my gosh.

DM: And then there's this: "She's on the Mount Olympus of hot sports reporters—"

EA: Oh, God. Geez.

DM: How do you process those types of statements?

EA: When people say, "You're so hot," I say, "I've got a pimple on my face and need to work out some more." I don't take myself too seriously. I'm self-deprecating. The biggest thing for me is, I'm in a pair of sneakers every time I don't need to be dressed up. I'm such a tomboy, such a daddy's girl.

DM: On the college campuses, in particular, how do you handle the goofus— or 10—who yells, "Erin, will you marry me?"

EA: Unfortunately, it gets a lot nastier than that. It's why I would never bring my father or a boyfriend to the game. I've had security guards who followed me and said, "It's bad that you have to listen to this." I tell them, "I don't. I have earpieces."

DM: Undoubtedly, people try to catch you in "gotcha" moments.

EA: Sure. I had it happen to me at the College World Series, soon after the incident. A guy screamed in front of me, "Nice video!" I didn't need to listen to that. I feel like people will back down when you come up to them and you're not cursing or saying anything nasty. You're just saying, "Grow up. There's no need for that. There are kids around here."

DM: But have you ever wanted to spin on someone and drop a few expletive bombs?

EA: Of course. We all have. But that's when you need to remember that cameras and camera phones are waiting to catch it. I could lose my job if I were to lose it on somebody.

DM: How do you deal with the pro athlete who asks you out?

EA: Maturely. I'll leave it at that.

DM: Did you long ago concede that female sports reporters/ anchors—especially those who happen to be attractive—face a higher burden of proof than that of any male colleague?

EA: It's looked down upon, almost as if you can't do both. You can't look a certain way and know sports: She just got her job because of the way she looks. Are you joking? I've got girlfriends who want me to be more girly. My friend is in the apartment talking about window treatments and a side table and I'm like, "When is the Pro Bowl on?"

DM: Are you ever concerned that the Erin Andrews phenomenon obscures the quality of work, where you don't get taken seriously enough?

EA: In my career and in my life, I'm done worrying about what's on the blogs and message boards. I know that the players and coaches respect me and trust me; they know how invested I am in my job. Coaches return my calls, I'm privy to inside information, not because of the way I look but because of how I do my job.

DM: The players must have been impressed when, during a baseball telecast several years ago, you absorbed a line-drive foul ball to the jaw and lived to tell about it.

EA: I was working Dodgers-Mets in New York. I was recording what happened in the previous at-bat and, all of a sudden, somebody yelled, "Look out!" My spotter, the guy who was supposed to be protecting me, put his head down. I turned right into it.

DM: Ouch.

EA: My first reaction was, "Holy crap." I worried I might have lost some teeth. Then, I was embarrassed. When you work with men, you don't want them to carry your luggage. You don't want to be late for dinner because they'll think you're primping. I didn't want them to see me cry, and initially, I didn't. I told everyone to leave me alone. I grabbed a Diet Coke and took a sip. A couple of innings later, though, my dad called and I started bawling.

DM: Result?

EA: We eventually had it looked at. The surgeon said, "Your jaw should have shattered. We have no idea how it didn't." I had taken a clean hit, but there wasn't a crack and I didn't lose any of my teeth. I just had an awesome bruise, and I wanted to wear it loud and proud.

DM: Where are you psychologically re: Michael David Barrett and the incident?

EA: I think I'm going to be haunted by it forever, but it will be at different levels and in different phases. Instead of the crying/ I'm sad phase, I'm pretty much in the ticked-off phase at the moment. I'm mad that this is allowed to happen. I'm so angry that the hotel industry allowed this to happen so easily. And I'm mad that our government and our laws allow this to continue to happen. The penalty isn't tough.

DM: You are not running from the nightmare, though.

EA: I'm now in a position to help change and rectify, to reach out and be of assistance to other people. Not only did I deal with stalking, I dealt with video voyeurism. I'm working with lawmakers in my hometown in Florida for new laws against video voyeurism. What happened to me is still happening, and as technology gets better and better, it's going to get worse and worse. Right now, the laws for video voyeurism are an absolute joke. They're outdated.

DM: Are you worried about when Barrett gets released?

EA: I deal with it every day.

DM: On a lighter note .... When I say, "Cleveland sports," what is the first thing that comes to mind?

EA: Everything that has happened the past couple of years with LeBron. It has unfolded in front of everybody's eyes.

DM: You finished third, with partner Maksim Chmerkovskiy, on the tenth season of *Dancing With the Stars* in early 2010. Why did you do *DWTS*?

EA: I originally was asked to participate before everything happened with the stalker. I told them I would think about it, although I pretty much knew I would do it because I love dancing and love the show. We found out about the stalker video in July, and I went back to work in August but wasn't myself. After that college football season, *DWTS* came back and asked me to be part of the next season. I said no, turned it down right away, because I figured everybody was going to think I was doing it to try to profit from what happened to me.

Nothing could be further from the truth.

DM: What changed your mind?

EA: My agent, my parents, even people at ESPN like Mike Tirico and Chris Berman said, "We think you need to go do it. We need our girl back." I'd lost a ton of confidence, I was very embarrassed and felt awful about what happened. I was mortified knowing how many people saw that video. So I thought: If I would go dance, get away from sports and have fun, it would help me get my confidence back.

DM: Speaking of confidence: Chmerkovskiy took some hits this past season for projecting egoism and arrogance. Is he as cocky as he seems?

EA: Yes, he's very cocky. He's very proud. He's bossy and stubborn. We had fights, and I cried at times. But I loved having him as a partner. He was an awesome guy to work with, and he was so protective of me at a time when I really needed it. I had death threats, and he didn't let anybody get near me. He was my rock.

DM: The Hollywood rumor mill had you dating him. True?

EA: No. When you're with someone for three months, eight hours a day, seven days a week, you feel like you're married. But no, I'm not dating him.

DM: Smartest person(s) you've ever met?

EA: If not the kids I worked with at the National Spelling Bee, I'd say my mom and dad.

DM: Favorite athlete you've interviewed?

EA: I've got two: David Ortiz and Marty St. Louis.

DM: Favorite sport to cover?

EA: College football. At ESPN, we make it like the Super Bowl every week. There's such a buildup with the College Gameday crew coming to town.

DM: Thanks for your time.

EA: You're welcome. Now I do have to tell you, being hit in the face by the foul ball was bad. But my very first hockey game as a sideline reporter covering the Tampa Bay Lightning, we were in San Jose, for the morning skate. I was being a chatterbox, talking to our play-by-play man. He just said, "Look out," and swatted a puck coming directly for my head. It could have killed me.

DM: So the Erin Andrews phenomenon could have been over before it started.

EA: Either that, or I would have had a really nice shaved head with about 40 stitches.

UPDATE: Erin Andrews left ESPN in June 2012 to join Fox Sports, where she serves as a field reporter for most major sporting events and as an in-studio contributor to various shows. Andrews became co-host of *Dancing with the Stars* in March 2014. She had 2.57 million Twitter followers as of March 2015.

Dr. James Andrews, *sports medicine*
February 2013

James Andrews has seen enough.

Enough of coaches who mean well and try hard, but who really don't know what they need to know.

Enough of parents who think their son or daughter is the next superstar athlete and must be pushed and pushed and pushed.

Enough of youngsters who are forced to visit him and his colleagues around the nation.

Andrews has become so alarmed that he is issuing written and verbal warnings to anyone willing to read or listen. Why should the public care what Andrews thinks? Because when the "Dr." is placed in front of his name, he becomes a world-renowned orthopedic surgeon.

Andrews, who has practiced medicine for nearly 40 years, is most famous for his ability to put professional athletes back together. These athletes—notably, a who's who of quarterbacks—have signed contracts for a combined total well north of $1 billion after his surgeries. In 2010, Andrews was the only doctor to be named among the top 40 most powerful people in the NFL by *Sports Illustrated*.

Andrews' specialties are knees, elbows and shoulders. One of his recent patients was Washington Redskins quarterback Robert Griffin III, who needed the anterior cruciate ligament and lateral collateral ligament repaired in his right knee.

The work on athletes, while important, isn't the reason Andrews collaborated with Don Yaeger, a former associate editor at *Sports Illustrated*, to write, "Any Given Monday: Sports Injuries and How to Prevent Them, for Athletes, Parents and Coaches—Based on My Life in Sports Medicine." He felt compelled to write the book, then talk about it, out of fear for the younger generation.

"I started seeing a sharp increase in youth sports injuries, particularly baseball, beginning around 2000," Andrews told

The Plain Dealer in a telephone interview. "I started tracking and researching, and what we've seen is a five- to sevenfold increase in injury rates in youth sports across the board. I'm trying to help these kids, given the epidemic of injuries that we're seeing. That's sort of my mission: to keep them on the playing field and out of the operating room.

"I hate to see the kids that we used to not see get hurt. ... Now they're coming in with adult, mature-type sports injuries. It's a real mess. Maybe this book will help make a dent."

DM: What is the crux of the mission?

JA: The deal is, as sports physicians, we've all been amiss for years worrying about putting people back together and fixing things and new techniques. But we've largely ignored the real problem: prevention of injuries. Everybody now agrees that the time is right to keep these kids from getting hurt so often. That's been my mission for 10 to 12 years, and it's really come to the forefront that last three to four years, when I helped start a prevention program with the sports-medicine society that we call the STOP program: Sports Trauma and Overuse Prevention (in youth sports). All proceeds from the book are going to the STOP program. It's not an "I" thing, not a financial thing, for me. It's a passion.

DM: Why the spike in youth injuries?

JA: Multiple factors, but two stand out: specialization and what we call professionalism. Specialization leads to playing the sport year-round. That means not only an increase in risk factors for traumatic injuries but a sky-high increase in overuse injuries. Almost half of sports injuries in adolescents stem from overuse. Professionalism is taking these kids at a young age and trying to work them as if they are pro athletes, in terms of training and year-round activity. Some can do it, like Tiger Woods. He was treated like a professional golfer when he was four, five, six years old. But you've got to realize that Tiger Woods is a special case. A lot of these kids don't have the ability to withstand that type of training and that type of parental/coach pressure. Now parents are hiring ex-pro baseball players as hitting and pitching instructors when their kid is twelve. They're thinking, "What's more is better," and they're ending up getting the kids hurt.

DM: Is money at the root of the problem—e.g., the pursuit of college scholarships or pro contracts?

JA: The almighty dollar has a lot to do with it, yes. Some parents are putting a football or baseball in their kids' hands when they're three years old, and it's not just for a fun little photograph. Parents are projecting ten, twelve years. Don't get me wrong: I'm for sports. I love sports. I want these kids to reach their full potential, and if the potential is a college scholarship, great. If it's a pro career, great. But to think they're all going to be professional athletes is misguided. The odds against it are so very, very high. Even the ones who get college scholarships comprise a much smaller percentage than parents think.

DM: Can parents be put in a no-win position, as well?

JA: Yes, to this extent: The systems out there in youth sports, particularly travel ball, have been important financial resources for the people who run them. Parents spend a fortune keeping their kids in a year-round sport, with travel and everything else. What's happening is, the tail is wagging the dog. The systems are calling the shots: If your son or daughter doesn't play my sport year-round, he or she can't play for me. Never mind that your kid is twelve—I need year-round dedication.

Parents need to understand that we've got to correct the system. Unfortunately, it's easier said than done. It's a big problem. And it becomes a socioeconomic problem if they keep getting hurt in high school.

DM: The best advice you would give parents of a young athlete?

JA: The first thing I would tell them is, their kid needs at least two months off each year to recover from a specific sport. Preferably, three to four months. Example: youth baseball. For at least two months, preferably three to four months, they don't need to do any kind of overhead throwing, any kind of overhead sport, and let the body recover in order to avoid overuse situations. That's why we're seeing so many Tommy John procedures, which is an adult operation designed for professionals. In my practice now, 30 to 40 percent of the ones I'm doing are on high-schoolers, even down to ages twelve or thirteen. They're already coming in with torn ligaments.

Give them time off to recover. Please. Give them time to recover. I said in the book, I want parents and coaches to realize the implications of putting a twelve- or thirteen-year-old through the type of athletic work done by a 25-year-old. Parents and coaches, though they mean well, need to understand what the long-term effects of overuse can be.

DM: What are your thoughts on youngsters throwing curveballs?

JA: Throwing a curveball has a neuromuscular-control dynamic. In other words, it takes a lot of natural ability at a young age to throw that pitch. It's a complicated pitch. If you throw it with good mechanics, it doesn't have any greater force on your shoulder than throwing other pitches, but you've got to throw it correctly. It's misleading to say it's OK to throw the curveball with good mechanics because the rub is, most kids don't throw it with good mechanics. My rule of thumb is, don't throw the curveball until you can shave, until your bone structure has matured and you have the neuromuscular control to be able to throw the pitch properly.

DM: What advice would you give pitchers, in general?

JA: 1) Use proper mechanics. The number one problem in any specific sport is improper mechanics. 2) Don't play year-round. 3) Avoid the radar gun at a young age. Don't try to overthrow. A lot of kids are thirteen years old and checking the radar gun. That's going to get you in trouble. The radar gun makes you want to throw harder than you are capable of throwing. 4) Be very careful with showcases. I call them "show-off" cases because kids go there Saturday after throwing the football on Friday. They jump on a mound and overthrow because scouts are there. The next thing you know, the shoulder or elbow gets injured.

DM: On how many pro athletes have you operated in your career?

JA: I've had people ask me that, and I don't like to answer with numbers because it might sound like I'm bragging or self-promoting. So I don't go into a specific number. (*Chuckle*) What I like to say is, "Too many to count and not enough to quit."

DM: What percent of your total operations are done on pro athletes?

JA: About twenty percent. Now I'm getting to where I'm operating on the sons of ballplayers I had.

DM: Have you stopped to think about the money in player contracts for which you've been responsible by extending careers?

JA: (*Chuckle*) No. Seeing these guys get back to doing what they do best, that's where I derive the enjoyment. I don't worry about how much money they might make in the future. I wish them all the best, but it's nerve-racking just the same. Every play. In the NFC Championship Game a few years ago, the Vikings played the Saints. Brett Favre and Drew Brees were two of my patients. I was pulling for Drew on offense, then Brett on offense, so I couldn't lose. But I was nervous.

DM: It is easy to forget how many surgeries you do on non-stars.

JA: A huge joy for me comes from operating on kids in high schools near where I live, kids who were injured and didn't have insurance. We've had a policy through the years that, if you get hurt playing high school football in my area, we'll do the best we can to help. [Andrews has offices in Alabama and Florida.] To see these kids come back and get a scholarship, or even a pro contract, is a thrill. I once had a high school basketball player in Mississippi whom nobody would fix. The coaches brought him to me. Well, he eventually signed an NBA contract and has had several contracts and made tens of millions of dollars. He came back to see me with another injury. I told him, "This time I'm going to charge you." You'd be surprised in our part of the country how many kids get hurt. We've had kids playing in rural areas, great athletes who get hurt but never were able to get the proper medical attention.

DM: The most complex surgery you've ever done?

JA: Marcus Lattimore, running back from South Carolina—his leg. Drew Brees' shoulder. I'll say this about Drew: It's amazing that he's been able to come back and throw a football, let alone play at the level he does.

DM: What goes through your mind when players such as Adrian Peterson, whose knee you fixed, come back to rush for 2,000 yards in one season?

JA: I don't want to take credit for things like that. If you operate on the right athletes, the high-level athletes, they will make you look pretty good as a physician. If you don't have athletes who are motivated, who are so driven to come back, it won't matter. And the people who get the players after the surgeries—they're the ones who deserve the most credit. The physical therapy and rehab people. My time with them is a couple hours, then I become a cheerleader. As an example, the people who rehabbed Adrian were incredible. The combination of Adrian's motivation, his God-given ability and the help he got post-surgery gave you what you saw on the field in 2012.

DM: Which is the more complicated surgery—torn ACL or Tommy John?

JA: Even though they involve different parts of the body, they are similar surgeries. I've called Tommy John the ACL of the elbow. Throwing a baseball at 90 miles an hour with a reconstructed elbow is equally as impressive as a running back coming back from an ACL tear.

DM: Have you ever needed to tell an athlete after surgery that it doesn't look good?

JA: My rule is, the glass is half full, not half empty. One of the things you don't do is wake up an athlete in the recovery room and say, "That's the worst injury I've ever seen, and you're not going to make it back." You've got to be positive. I told Drew [Brees]: "I could do your operation 100 times and probably couldn't do it as well as I did it today. You are going to get through this, and you will be better than ever. Now go to work." At the same time, you have to be realistic. When you get to a certain point where you know they're not going to be able to make it, you let them down slowly. You don't tell them right away. You gradually work it in. As you get to know them better, you gradually let them know there is life after football.

DM: Because of your resumé, do you feel pressure to deliver every time?

JA: Yes, I feel pressure. A lot of it. But the bulk of the pressure is what all of us feel in this profession. There is extra pressure because people come to me who've had multiple surgeries. All of a sudden, you are inundated with people who have had failed surgeries. They come to you and expect you to put them back together again. So the pressure mounts, believe me. All of us in sports medicine operate in a fishbowl. If there's a failure, it's all over the place. But you can't be perfect with everything you do. You do the best you can. Unfortunately, the only results I ever really remember are the bad ones. Those are the ones you need to study in order to figure out what you can do better.

Thea Andrews, *television*

March 2004

Cable television viewers in the United States are discovering what Canadians have known for years: Thea Andrews is a serious talent, and she knows sports.

Andrews earned a promotion this week to co-host of ESPN2's *Cold Pizza*, a morning variety show with sports as the undercurrent that has soared in popularity since its launch last October. With due respect accorded the show's other on-air personalities, including Bowling Green product Jay Crawford, Andrews brings star quality to the proceedings.

How do we know this? Toronto-native Andrews has *Playmakers* on her résumé. She played sports reporter Samantha Lovett on the controversial ESPN drama series about a fictional pro football team. It lasted one season [August to November 2003] before being canceled under siege from the NFL.

And, no less noteworthy, the Andrews filmography includes *Prom Night IV: Deliver Us from Evil.*

DM: What is your favorite moment from the *Playmakers* series?

TA: Walking onto the field at SkyDome. I'd probably been to 500 Blue Jays games but never been on the field. It was a rush.

DM: So you filmed *Playmakers* in SkyDome?

TA: Yes. And we had a replica locker room at a studio in a suburb of Toronto.

DM: What was your most memorable line from the series?

TA: (*Pause*) I'll pass.

DM: Whom did you say it to?

TA: No, that wasn't the line. I mean, one doesn't jump out, so I'll skip it.

DM: Did *Playmakers* get a raw deal?

TA: No question, because it was a well-written, critically acclaimed series. It's too bad it got canceled.

DM: How do you react to executive producer John Eisendrath's comment on the show's demise after eleven episodes: "The decision is censorship, pure and simple. The NFL didn't like the show so it told ESPN to take it off the air, and ESPN dutifully took it off the air."?

TA: I can understand his disappointment.

DM: Your role as Samantha Lovett, who oozed sensuality, caused quite a stir. The Association for Women in Sports Media lodged a complaint to ESPN, raising questions about the depiction of women sports journalists and the potential conflicts of interest for ESPN by your appearance on *Cold Pizza* and *Playmakers*. Your response?

TA: I absolutely disagree, but they're entitled to their opinion.

DM: Did any actual NFL players ask you on a date after watching the show?

TA: (*Protracted laughter*)

DM: Well?

TA: Why would I assume it was related to the show? Just kidding, just kidding. Seriously, what has been surprising is how many players recognize me from *Playmakers*. Players I'd never met came up to me at this past Super Bowl and said, "Hey, Thea," like they knew me.

DM: I'm sure you are aware the ESPN brass is jittery about its employees discussing *Playmakers*.

TA: Well, I can't speak to that. But let me let you in on a little secret: A number of the players are huge fans of the show. I've had an overwhelmingly positive response from them about it. Even the guys who hated it, loved it. They say, "This was unrealistic, that was unrealistic, this would never happen"—but they watched every episode.

DM: You are a student of the sweet science. Favorite boxer, past and present?

TA: Muhammad Ali and Roy Jones Jr.

DM: What was it like on the set of *Prom Night IV*?

TA: Oh my gosh, that was so long ago. You've really dug deep into the vault, haven't you?

DM: What was the genesis of the role of Louise?

TA: The father of a good friend of mine from high school produced it. I lost a bet to my friend, who told me the payment was to get offered in his dad's movie. I think I had six lines. They said, "You get to be the school slut." I was like, "Why do I have to be the school slut?" You know how it is, the brunette always had to be the trampy one.

DM: What most underscores the popularity of *Cold Pizza*?

TA: People who come on the show now. We're getting most of the big-name guests we want.

DM: *Cold Pizza* brought you to the states full time. What is the biggest misconception Americans have about Canadians?

TA: That Canadians are so much nicer than the people in, say, New York. Canadians are more polite, but it doesn't automatically make us nice. And the people in New York are very friendly.

DM: Did you know Jay Crawford was arrested for stealing pumpkins as a prank while at Bowling Green?

TA: Yes, he confessed to us. I was very disappointed, but we talked it through, and I'm satisfied his pumpkin-stealing days are over.

DM: What don't we know about Jay?

TA: He's the sweetest, most generous guy in the world. And his tongue is longer than Gene Simmons'.

DM: Have you ever been asked out by athletes?

TA: You've come around to this question again after I tactfully avoided it the first time. Why are you asking?

DM: I'm wondering if you have a policy about it based on the heat you took for Samantha Lovett.

TA: Well, I guess I would say I do have a "policy"—even though I've never thought of it that way—because I don't date athletes. But Playmakers has nothing to do with that decision.

DM: Research indicates you are a voracious reader. What is your favorite book?

TA: Gabriel Garcia Marquez's *One Hundred Years of Solitude*.

DM: That's an intense work, isn't it?

TA: It's a novel about the mythical village of Macondo. It's magical realism, a genre of Latin American literature. The mind gets a workout.

DM: You have interviewed countless A-list stars in sports, entertainment and politics. Who is someone who remains on your interview to-do list?

TA: National Security Advisor Dr. Condoleezza Rice. From what I've read and heard, she's fascinating.

DM: Do you like pizza?

TA: Of course. Who doesn't like pizza?

DM: Do you like it cold?

TA: No. If I'm eating leftover pizza, it's going in the microwave first. Come to think of it, we don't even have a cold piece of pizza in the studio. I wonder why that is.

UPDATE: Thea Andrews has been a correspondent and host on *Entertainment Tonight* (November 2006–October 2009) and host of the first season of *Top Chef Canada* and the country music singing competition, CMT's *Next Superstar*. Since January 2013, Andrews co-hosts *The Insider*.

Phil Bova, *on refereeing*

November 2007

For the first time in decades, a college basketball season is underway without Phil Bova as a referee. Bova retired after last season.

A former three-sport standout at Cleveland West High, Bova was a referee for thirty years in the Big Ten and for twenty consecutive NCAA Tournaments. Bova, a longtime educator who lives in Westlake, is a member of the Greater Cleveland Sports Hall of Fame.

DM: What is one lesson aspiring referees cannot do without?

PB: Don't put basketball ahead of your family. Refereeing is a gift. Not everyone can referee a basketball game, and the higher you go, the more difficult it becomes. But when it's all said and done, you need your family. It was there when you started, and it needs to be there when you're done. Too many guys put the game ahead of the family because they want to work as many games as they can.

DM: Favorite arena?

PB: The Schottenstein Center [in Columbus, Ohio].

DM: Favorite referee of all-time?

PB: Earl Strom. He was a man's man. He controlled the game. Coaches wanted Earl Strom on the road because he was so fair. He was never afraid to make the "gut" call when it had to be made.

DM: Favorite game you refereed?

PB: Too many to single one or two out. I would say any of the Big Ten rivalry games and any of the NCAA Tournament games.

DM: What would you say to the hyperactive fans who constantly berate officials?

PB: They have a right to boo, they have a right to support their team. But they also need to understand that there are other people around, youngsters in particular, who shouldn't have to be exposed to abusive language or constant yelling. And they need to realize that the officials at the highest levels have high integrity. The best officials control the game as they see it without being influenced by the score, how much time is on the clock or how many people are in the stands.

DM: Three keys to being a top-flight referee?

PB: 1) You need to take pride in your physical condition. 2) You need to have a feel for the game. If you've played the game, I think you'll be a better referee. There are subtleties to basketball that you can't teach. As an example, I don't think I'd be much of a soccer official because I never played. 3) As I said earlier, family support.

DM: Biggest mistake young referees make within a game?

PB: Too much communication with the coaches. A lot of young officials spend too much time trying to appease the coaches. The best coaches will respect you more at the end of the day if you don't try to appease them all the time.

DM: Do too many twenty-first century referees think they are bigger than the game?

PB: I don't want to be negative, but too many guys today want to climb the ladder too soon. They're not patient. And if you're not ready to move, it's going to show. That's when you get labeled and maybe don't get a second chance. You have to set a realistic timeline to advance.

DM: Best part of being a referee?

PB: Coming off the floor knowing I gave it 2,000 percent.

DM: Worst part?

PB: Travel, especially in the Midwest.

DM: Of what are you most proud in your career?

PB: I had a basketball officials camp for twenty-five years. My staff and I trained more than seventy officials who are working Division I, II, III and NAIA today.

DM: What would you like your legacy to be?

PB: That I gave it everything I had every time I stepped out on the floor. That I did my absolute best to be fair.

Roger Clemens, *baseball*

Summer 2003

Roger Clemens has all but guaranteed he will retire at the end of the season. Whenever it happens, he will go down as one of the greatest, if not the greatest, ever at his position. He enters a start tonight against the Indians with a career record of 301-157 in 592 games (591 starts) for Boston, Toronto and the New York Yankees.

A six-time Cy Young Award winner, Clemens ranks third all-time with 4,301 strikeouts and has allowed 602 fewer hits than innings pitched (3,582 to 4,184-2/3).

Before his starts at Yankee Stadium, Clemens rubs the plaque of Babe Ruth for inspiration. Too bad the public never will be treated to that matchup.

DM: How would you pitch Bambino?

RC: I'd have to go after him. That's the type of pitcher I am, and the fans want to see power against power. I'm not going to nibble. It would be something, wouldn't it, to face The Babe? What's really been enjoyable for me over the years is the matchup with the big power guys — Mark McGwire, Jose Canseco, Cecil Fielder, Greg Luzinski, Jim Thome. It's not that fun for me when they hit the ball a long way, of course, but it's a win-win for the fans.

DM: You always have seemed cognizant of the fans' role in the game.

RC: When we played the Cubs last month in Chicago, I didn't feel good. I had bronchitis. But I had to answer the call for that start because people wanted to see the Yankees and the Cubs, and they wanted to see me face Sammy Sosa. I take pride in that. I turned those ball loose, and Sammy swung for the fences. Those are the times when you don't want to be at the concession stands. You want to be in your seat, watching.

DM: Would you knock down The Babe?

RC: I think I'd have to step off the back of the mound and really collect myself before facing him. Even with my experience I'd have to do it, because of who he is. I remember a start not long after I broke in. We were playing the Angels, and they announced Reggie Jackson. I had to step off and collect myself, because this was *Reggie Jackson*. Now, would I knock down Babe Ruth? Well, I couldn't afford to let him get too comfortable, that's for sure. I don't think I'd need to knock him down, though.

I could get him off the plate without knocking him down.

DM: Toughest hitter you've ever faced?

RC: I remember having trouble with Robin Yount. You know he must be a tough out when you get a phone call from your mother and she says, "He owns you." That's humbling.

DM: Who would join you at your dream pitchers' roundtable?

RC: I'd need to have three of them: Walter Johnson, Cy Young and Christy Mathewson from way back. Don Drysdale, Nolan Ryan and Tom Seaver from the recent past. Greg Maddux, Curt Schilling and Randy Johnson from the present.

DM: What is your dream batter-pitcher matchup, mixing and matching all eras?

RC: I'd want to see Ruth or Mickey Mantle against Mathewson, Johnson or Young.

DM: Have you stopped to think about how you rate among the all-time greats?

RC: In three or four months, I'll get a chance to sit back and really look at my career and ponder where I stand. I do think it's neat this past year when reporters have mentioned me with some of the legends. It's a huge compliment, and I'm awed by it. When I passed Walter Johnson to become the A.L. strikeout leader [with number 3,510], it was just awesome. Guys like Walter Johnson—you look at them and they don't even seem real, because you never had a chance to watch them.

DM: Yes or no—All-Star Game for homefield advantage in World Series?

RC: I don't have a problem with it this year. For us in the American League, it's a no-lose situation, because we weren't supposed to have homefield this year, anyway. So we can kind of steal it.

DM: What about all the controversy surrounding that decision?

RC: I think it came on kind of quickly. A lot of guys were surprised by how the voting went down, because some guys got to vote and other didn't. I'm as curious as anyone to see how it will play out.

DM: Are you upset about not being named to the All-Star team in what appears to be your final year?

RC: Not at all.

DM: What does it mean to be a 300-game winner?

RC: It means I stayed the course, I stayed true to myself, I put the work in. I'm proud of the fact that I got to 300 in rapid time, twenty years—and that's despite the injuries I've had. To finally get to 300 is a big deal because you get to be mentioned alongside the greats. You realize how much work you put in to get there.

DM: For all the effort, though, you still trail Cy Young by 210 victories.

RC: (*Chuckle*) Yeah. That number is unreal, just unreal. I can't imagine winning 500 games.

DM: You seem the like the type who could have taken the ball every third day, as opposed to every fifth. That would have put you closer to Cy.

RC: They look out for us so much now. I know that the money part figures into it; they have so much invested in us. I understand the reasoning behind it, but I dislike the fact that they baby us a little bit. Then again, when you've got a staff like we have here, with a rotation that's four, five deep, how can you argue? It's a joy to pitch here because you know if you have a problem, you've got some horses behind you to help out. I suppose it would be interesting to see which guys would hold up in today's day throwing every fourth day, or even every third. I hope I'd be one of them.

DM: If you were commissioner for a day, what is one change you would insist on making?

RC: That's easy—I'd enforce the high strike. I'd like to go back, way back, to the day when they really enforced the high strike.

DM: Does it go without saying that pitchers have gotten squeezed in an era where offense is king?

RC: I don't have a problem with not expanding the strike zone east and west, because the plate is clearly defined by measurement. But we're still not going underneath the armpits or the letters to make guys offer at that pitch.

DM: Have you contemplated how many more strikeouts—and, in turn, victories—you might have right now if the high strike had been enforced since day one of your career?

RC: Well, who's to say it would have happened? Maybe I would have pitched differently and not been as effective. But I do know that, at this stage of my career, I can still get the ball up there at a good rate of speed, so I can afford to pitch up in the zone and not worry about getting burned too many times.

With my split, I can get them looking down, and with the fastball I can get them looking up. The high strike gives me more room to work, to change the hitter's eye level. I'd like to think they'd have a difficult time with it.

DM: Best game you ever pitched?

RC: There are too many to narrow it down—and I'm not saying that to brag or anything.

DM: Trust me—you're not bragging, regardless.

RC: I appreciate that. My best games would have to be when things were magnified, in the postseason. There was the game against Seattle in the 2000 ALCS (nine innings, one hit, 15 strikeouts)....Game 4 of the 1999 World Series against Atlanta, when we clinched and I got my first ring. And the two starts in the 2001 World Series against Arizona, Game 3 and Game 7, even though we lost the series.

DM: What is the most pressure you've ever felt in one start?

RC: Probably Game 3 of the 2001 World Series [at Yankee Stadium]. The President came to throw out the first pitch, and you factor in all the emotion that was in the stadium after 9/11. Plus, we really needed to win that one.

DM: What about your two twenty-strikeout games [with Boston on April 29, 1986, vs. Seattle at Fenway Park; with Boston on Sept. 18, 1996, at Tiger Stadium]?

RC: They were great just for the fact that I didn't walk anybody.

DM: In which of the two did you have your best stuff?

RC: Probably the one against Seattle, because of the fastball command. My split and fastball were just as hard, if not harder, when I was younger. But the split really got devastating in 1996.

DM: Biggest change in the game since you broke in?

RC: The way the guys take care of themselves. On the whole, guys are stronger and in better condition than they were twenty years ago. And the ballparks are smaller.

DM: Your fitness regimen is legendary.

RC: It makes my career feel more complete when I get comments from a Kerry Wood or a Curt Schilling or somebody else talking about my preparation. I've talked to a lot of guys and tried to set an example. The key is, you have to follow through with it. You can't simply talk about putting the time in and figure everything will take care of itself. The guys who separate themselves are the ones who actually do what they say they'll do.

DM: How have you maintained the work ethic?

RC: It comes from my roots. Everybody in my family has worked extremely hard. My grandmother, for one, is a very stern lady.

We've never blinked an eye when it comes to work. We knew the only way to get where we wanted to be is by hard work.

DM: Yes or no—designated hitter?

RC: I don't mind having the DH because that's all I've known. The only thing I don't like is, when we play interleague games in N.L. parks, I don't get to practice as much hitting as I'd like. So I'm not as good of a hitter as I want to be. I realize I'm not going to be great at it, but I want to be able to hold my own.

DM: Have you contemplated what your strikeout total could have been if you had pitched exclusively in the National League, with all those pitchers swinging in vain against you?

RC: No, not really, but I can tell you there was a different feeling to Game 3 and Game 7 of the 2001 World Series, for example. In Game 7 in Arizona, when I didn't have the extra hitter to deal with, and instead had the pitcher batting ninth, I felt like I could handle it. It's a totally different lineup and a totally different approach to pitching.

DM: Any regrets about your career?

RC: Of course there are some things you'd like to change, but regrets? No. I'll take this career and feel blessed.

UPDATE: Roger Clemens' twenty-fourth and final MLB season unfolded in 2007. He played for four teams and finished with 354 victories, a 3.12 ERA and 4,672 strikeouts. He won the AL Cy Young Award seven times, the MVP once (1986) and the World Series twice. Because of his link to PEDs, he was named on just 37.5% of the ballots in the 2015 Hall of Fame voting (his third year on ballot).

Jason Couch, *bowling*
November 2003

Jason Couch is one of the best professional athletes you've never heard of. That is because bowling, while making inroads at the highest level recently under new Microsoft-alumni ownership, remains a largely overlooked part of the pro landscape.

Couch understands this, but knows all he can do is continue to validate his status among the world's premier bowlers. He has won eleven PBA National titles and eighteen Regional Tour titles. Most impressive, he is the three-time defending champion of the Tournament of Champions—his sport's equivalent of The Masters. No one had ever won three consecutive Tournament of Champions.

DM: How many career 300 games?

JC: Including pot games? Seventy-two.

DM: What is your highest career average in a league?

JC: In the summer a few years ago, I averaged 253. But that's pretty much how it goes for everybody on tour. To put us on league conditions is silly.

DM: Career 7-10 conversions?

JC: Four.

DM: Highest series ever?

JC: An 866 at a PBA event in Austin, Texas, in the late 1990s. And I didn't shoot 300. It went 289-289-288.

DM: What is the most money you've ever made in a pot match?

JC: Ten thousand. We bowled a lot of games over two houses. You don't want to challenge me over the long haul.

DM: What is the biggest misconception about pro bowlers?

JC: Everybody knows it: That we're old, out-of-shape cigar smokers and beer drinkers with towels hanging out of our back pockets. Did I mention out-of-shape?

DM: How can the PBA Tour member combat the stereotypes?

JC: All people have to do is come out and watch us from the beginning of a tournament to the end, and they'll find out that stuff is nonsense. They'll realize what a grind it is, physically and mentally. If they still aren't convinced, the fruit salads and vegetable juice are on me.

DM: You reside in Clermont, Florida. How close are you to the Tiger Woods estate in Windermere?

JC: Ten minutes.

DM: Does Woods have an open invitation for a bowling lesson?

JC: Absolutely. He'd probably pick things up quickly, he's such a great athlete. But I've got to take [PGA Tour standout] Chris DiMarco first. We've got a private lesson set up through a radio station in Orlando.

DM: On November 17, 1999, you stood on the approach and needed two strikes plus count to win your first Tournament of Champions and $100,000. What is a moment of truth such as that like?

JC: Nerve-racking, of course. It wasn't the money, honestly, even though that's a ton on our tour, because the money will be gone one day. It was the fact that my dream since childhood was to win a T of C.

DM: What advice would you give to the youngster who wants to be a pro bowler?

JC: First, I would tell them to stay in school and get set up for a career, because there are very few guys who get an opportunity to do what they want for a living in pro sports. After that, it's about basics: Make your spares. You've got to make your spares.

DM: Strangest autograph request?

JC: A woman asked me to sign in the chest area. She pulled the shirt down a little bit and pointed.

DM: Did you sign?

JC: Yes. I didn't want to be viewed as a snob.

DM: As with most PBA players, you drive to most tournaments. How many miles have you logged since becoming a tour member in 1991?

JC: Easily 750,000. Probably closer to 1 million.

DM: How do you do it?

JC: Sit down, fasten the seat belt, turn the ignition…

DM: Touché.

JC: I'm not going to lie: It can get monotonous. And the miles go on forever after you've had a bad tournament.

DM: How many speeding tickets?

JC: None in about four years.

DM: That wasn't the question.

JC: I racked them up pretty good in the early days. Probably 10 that I've paid for.

DM: Best line to wriggle free from a ticket?

JC: I got pulled over in Florida, and the cop recognized who I was. He asked if I had any pictures. I said, "Picture? I'll give you a signed bowling ball if you let me off with a warning." He said, "Sure." So we went to the back of my truck, I signed a ball and was on my way.

DM: You never have been afraid to run smack at your fellow pros. One example?

JC: I stated in my PBA program bio that I can't stand losing to Pete

Weber. They quoted me as saying I'd rather eat rocks than lose to Pete Weber. It's true. I can't stand losing to him—any time, anywhere.

DM: Ouch.

JC: He came up to me a couple of weeks ago and called me out on it. I said, "Well, dude, that's the way it is. If you don't like it, then beat me in a match." I'm not going to back down.

> **UPDATE:** Jason Couch has won 16 PBA Tour titles and rolled more than forty perfect games in PBA events. He was inducted into the PBA Hall of Fame in 2012 and USBC Hall of Fame in 2013.

Paula Creamer, *golf*
August 2005

Paula Creamer, budding LPGA superstar, is an engaging nineteen-year-old with a sunny disposition.

But beware when asking her about teeing it up against the men. "I have no desire to play in a men's tournament," she said, her eyes suddenly steely. "None."

At least not yet. "Maybe down the road, I'll be interested," she said, "but my focus is the LPGA Tour. I have so many goals I want to accomplish on the LPGA Tour."

That's the L-P-G-A Tour, in case you missed it. The tour stops in Dublin, Ohio, this week for the Wendy's Championship for Children. Creamer will be in Dublin, the only place she wants to be.

Leave the sponsor's exemptions to others, notably Michelle Wie, arguably the most celebrated women's amateur ever. Wie, fifteen, has failed to play the weekend in three exemption attempts against the professional men.

Paula Creamer
photo by Gabriel Roux

Given that Creamer—along with amateurs Morgan Pressel, seventeen, and Jane Park, eighteen—has been projected as one of Wie's principal foils in the coming years, she can be excused for snickering. Won't happen. Creamer is too respectful of Wie's skills and too savvy, in general, to take the bait.

What does rankle Creamer is the notion that a woman making the cut in a men's event rates as a glorious achievement. "Why would any of us just want to make a cut, no matter what tour it is?" she said. "I don't understand that thought process. I've always been taught to play to win, not to make cuts."

Creamer speaks with no trace of cockiness or arrogance, which is part of what makes her a fascinating study. She knows precisely how to convey a high level of confidence without coming across as insufferable or overstepping her bounds. It helps, of course, to have the talent to back it up. Before she began this, her rookie season, Creamer set three principal goals: win a tournament, win a major, make the U.S. team for the Solheim Cup. Is that all?

Never mind that Creamer still had homework as a high school senior, or that she would only have one year, not two, to amass Solheim Cup points. She did not author a magnificent amateur career by setting the bar low, or simply settling.

If any of her competitors chalked up such goals to youthful exuberance, they were way off-base. Creamer bagged her first pro tournament, the Sybase Classic in May, at 18 years, 9 months, 17 days—youngest in LPGA history to win a multi-round event. Four days later, she graduated from The Pendleton School in Bradenton, Florida.

Creamer won again at the Evian Masters in July, cruising past a top-notch field. Posting a 15-under 273, she beat Wie and Lorena Ochoa by eight strokes and all-everything Annika Sorenstam by 13. Creamer's check for $375,000 enabled her to surpass $1 million in earnings at 18 years, 11 months, 18 days—the youngest LPGA player ever to do so, by more than two years. She needed fewer than five months on tour to pocket $1 million, also a record.

Entering the Wendy's Championship, Creamer is on target to make the Solheim Cup. The Wendy's event is the last opportunity to secure an automatic berth. The major victory, though, proved elusive. Her best finish was tied for third, at the McDonald's LPGA Championship. "One of my goals was to win a major, and I didn't do that, so I'm disappointed," she said. OK, so she has something to keep her busy in her second year.

Meantime, Creamer ranks second in LPGA earnings with $1.15 million and owns seven top-ten finishes in eighteen official events. She is crafting one of the tour's finest rookie seasons, and it does not include her victory two weeks ago at the NEC Karuizawa 72 tournament in Japan. But huge success on the course might not even be half the story where Creamer is concerned.

The ears and eyes of her agent, Jay Burton of IMG, ache from fielding all the calls and sifting through the messages. "I've been representing professional golfers for 20-21 years, I've worked with Paula since January, and she's as solid as I've ever seen," Burton said. "She's doing things that simply amaze me."

Creamer has made Burton's life simultaneously difficult and easy by being a marketer's dream. She already comes with a nickname from her amateur days ("Pink Panther") and a surname whose pronunciation invites a slogan ("Creamer rises to the top"). "Paula is trailblazing in terms of the charisma, the look, the game, the attitude, the competitive spirit," Burton said. "She has a knack for presentation to go with a reputation of being cordial, gracious, grounded and genuine."

Burton attended an early-August appearance by Creamer in Slavic Village for the First Tee of Cleveland program. One of Creamer's endorsement deals is with Royal Bank of Scotland, which sponsored the visit. Burton watched as Creamer, though tired from recently having been overseas, enthusiastically interacted with several dozen youngsters for hours. She took particular delight in working with the golfers individually on their swings. She put on no airs. "If she's not the same at twenty-nine as she is today, I'll be shocked," Burton said.

Burton's favorite vignette comes from the Weetabix Women's British Open in late July. After the first round, Creamer headed to her car in a downpour, but reversed field and scurried fifty yards back toward the clubhouse because she had failed to thank the walking marshals. "I didn't witness it," Burton said, "but one marshal told the head of the marshals, who told the tournament operations manager, who told the sponsor, who told the tournament director, who told me."

Later at the Open, Creamer caught the eye of onlookers with a snazzy outfit that included high socks.

"Word spread through Royal Birkdale about what Paula Creamer was wearing," Burton said. "It wasn't about sex appeal, it was about classy presentation. By the time she got to the second tee, there were thirty photographers—no kidding."

The marketing of Creamer, a native Californian, does have its limits. Natalie Gulbis, another talented young LPGA star, also has gained attention with a couple of swimsuit calendars. Burton and Creamer's father, Paul, guaranteed Creamer will steer clear of anything that could be interpreted as risque. "Paula won't be somebody she's not," Paul Creamer said. "She won't be doing a swimsuit calendar."

Paul and Karen Creamer have watched their only child embrace the game virtually from the moment she first took her swings, at the relatively old age of ten. Even if they had an urge to push her, it was not necessary. "Golf made a special connection with her," Paul Creamer said. "She never practiced anything but golf in her free time." Paul Creamer made one request of Paula as she tabled her acrobatic-dance aspirations and began to blossom from tee to green: Have your work ethic match your expectations. "A lot of people say they want to be really, really good, but they aren't willing to work hard to do it," he said.

Paula Creamer must be willing to put in the time. Otherwise, she would not mark her ball with one of several 1958-issue quarters, a constant reminder of her desire to become the first to shoot a competitive round of 58. The preference would be at an LPGA event.

DM: Favorite golf movie?

PC: Probably a tie between *Caddyshack* and *Happy Gilmore*.

DM: You and Michelle Wie, head-to-head at Augusta National for 18 holes of match play....who wins?

PC: I have no idea... really... come on... Seriously?

DM: Seriously.

PC: Who do you think would win?

DM: Uh, well, you.

PC: (*Chuckle*) You're probably just saying that because I'm here and she's not. But thanks, anyway. I'll say this: It would be a great match.

DM: Dream foursomes—you and three other LPGA players, you and three PGA players?

PC: LPGA—Juli Inkster, Dottie Pepper, Annika [Sorenstam]; PGA—Tiger [Woods], Luke Donald and Sergio Garcia.

DM: Favorite course you've ever played?

PC: Courses on which I've won.

DM: Which would you take—ten victories, no major; or, one major, no other victories?

PC: Ten wins.

DM: Your favorite color is pink and your nickname is, "Pink Panther." How many Pink Panther items have fans sent you?

PC: Quite a few. I've got Pink Panther clothes, socks, sweatshirts, head covers, hats, shirts...I love them all.

DM: Worst rule in Rules of Golf?

PC: Fourteen clubs in the bag. I'd like to have as many as possible, especially because I don't have to carry them.

DM: Do you run smack on the course?

PC: Never on the course. Only in fun off it.

DM: You seem so put together in all aspects, particularly for someone so young. Do you have any vices?

PC: Oh, well, I don't know—sure, I do lots of things wrong. I always try to do the right thing, but of course I'm going to make mistakes. I'm human.

DM: You have a very solid support system around you, beginning with your parents and your agent. What have they taught you most?

PC: To work hard and to be humble while you're doing it.

DM: You are often referred to as one of the LPGA's "hottest" young stars. Do you mind the "hottest" part?

PC: No. I'd like to think they're talking about "freshness" as much as physical appearance. But even when they aren't, the bottom line is, you have to perform. You have to produce results on the course.

DM: Having said that, given your ever-growing popularity on and off the course, are you ready for the full-blown marketing of Paula Creamer? And are you concerned it might wear on you?

PC: No, I'm not concerned. It's fun to do photo shoots and other things off the course. That's when I get to be a girl. I enjoy it. I embrace it, I don't fight it. If that stuff didn't happen, we'd have something to worry about, you know? That would mean I'm not being successful at what I do.

DM: How many 1958 quarters in your possession?

PC: Three. Fans gave me all three.

DM: Would you ever paint one of the quarters pink?

PC: I never thought of that. I guess I'd have to say, "No. I'm not going to mess around with George Washington."

Paula Creamer, golf
July 2007

Paula Creamer, one of the best female golfers in the world, expressed zero faith in me, greenhorn caddie.

"You're not going to make it," she said. When we spoke the night before I was to handle her bag in the pro-am July 11 at the Jamie Farr Owens Corning Classic in Sylvania, Ohio, Creamer cited weather and my inexperience as the primary reasons for her pessimism. If conditions got too steamy, she said, I easily could go down.

Creamer knew the closest I had come to caddying was two years ago, when I zipped around in a cart with men's pro Padraig Harrington.

"Do you realize how heavy that bag's going to feel by the turn, especially if I make it even heavier just for you?" she said, a sinister grin from ear to ear. As it turns out, I did almost faint. The weather, pleasant after a front moved through, was not the problem. Weight of the bag was. Too light. Too light by one 7-iron.

After Creamer's shot on the par-3 sixth hole, I waited for her to hand me the club. But she became engrossed in conversation and began walking with it. By the time we reached the green, however, her hands were free.

She turned and asked for the putter.

"Uh, Paula, where's the 7?"

"I put it in the bag, as soon as we left the tee box," she said. "I went to give it to you, you were talking to someone, so I put it back myself."

A nervous count revealed thirteen, not fourteen. "Uh, Paula, I don't see it," I said.

"What?" Creamer said. "How could that be? You mean you lost the 7?"

Creamer's real caddie, Colin Cann, approached. Cann was doing most of his usual duties in preparation for the tournament,

Dennis Manoloff caddying for Paula Creamer
photo courtesy of Paula Creamer

including yardage marking and green reading, while trying his best to baby-sit.

"The 7-iron's missing?" he said. "Dennis, are you saying you lost the [expletive] 7? How does that happen?"

Cann, typically as genteel as they come, stared a hole in me. The expletive sold his anger. Creamer seemed annoyed. I thought about what Paul Creamer, Paula's father, might do to me on the nineteenth hole. When he and agent Jay Burton signed off on my little adventure, they basically issued one command: Don't do anything stupid. That would include allowing a club to disappear from under my nose.

"You probably dropped it somewhere along the way," Paula said. "We'll wait."

Now that I think of it, there was the one moment when I stumbled. …

Approximately fifty yards into my trudge, Creamer's voice pierced the air. "Oh, Dennis," she said. "Are you looking for this?"

I spun and saw her waving the club. Laughter and knee-slaps all around. Creamer and Cann had cooked up the mischief, slipping the 7 into an amateur's bag instead.

"You look a bit pale," Creamer said, putting her arm around my shoulder. Indeed. But at least I got the club back.

Being able to caddie for Creamer gave me a glimpse into her multilayered sense of humor, part of what makes her enjoyable to be around, even as the punch line. One of the amateurs in our group, a good player and class act named Sheree Bargabos, said Creamer's nickname should be changed from Pink Panther to Pink Prankster.

Being a caddie-for-a-day taught me how difficult a job it is at the highest level, and it had nothing to with lugging a sixty-three-pound bag for several miles. As long as fourteen clubs were in the bag, that was the easy part.

Breadth of responsibility, much of it largely unnoticed by the gallery or TV viewer, makes caddying for a pro a grinding mental exercise. I gained an appreciation for the diligence of Cann, a multiple-major winner with Annika Sorenstam and Se Ri Pak before eventually hooking up with Creamer.

Cann, as his colleagues do, constantly jots down notes and numbers in a book and sees breaks in greens I would not notice for an hour. When I stepped into Cann's role, pared down as it was for the pro-am, I felt obligated to think along with him on each shot. I had a headache by number fifteen.

I also felt a sense of power underneath the caddie's bib. I'm not sure what it would have been like on the bag of a mediocre player, but I felt I had certain rights working for a budding LPGA superstar. Foremost among them: the right to be a bad-ass—otherwise known as being Steve Williams. Tiger Woods' caddie Williams scares birds into not chirping when his man is at address. On the tee at the par-3 eighth, I think Williams would have approved.

After Creamer hit her shot, she was asked to do promotional shots with the Pink Panther mascot. As Creamer departed, a PR person asked me to stay back with the bag in order for the cameraman to shoot video of it.

I agreed. The cameraman used a few too many seconds for my liking, then he wanted shots with the mascot and the bag. Meanwhile, Creamer and Cann were on the green with the rest of the group sizing up their putts.

After a minute that seemed like fifteen, I had had enough. Funny what happens when the journalist always looking for extra time from subjects ends up changing hats. "Sir, I've got to move," I said. "Let's wrap this up."

No wimpy suggestion here. The words were crisp, the tone decisive.

The stunned cameraman looked up at me and snapped, "She has her putter, doesn't she?"

"Yes, she does," I barked. "That's not the point, though. I need to be up there."

"I'll drive you if you need me to," he said.

"Just wrap it up," I said.

On the ninth tee box, Creamer asked what took so long. I explained that I tangled with a cameraman.

"You did what?!?" Creamer said. As I explained, I figured she would be proud of me for holding firm.

She was anything but. "No, no, no," Creamer said, putting her hand on her head and rolling her eyes. "You can't do that. Those are the sponsors. They have jobs to do. It's the pro-am. You can't do that. …. Colin, guess what Dennis did?"

The churning in the pit of my stomach returned full force. "I truly apologize," I said. "Am I in your doghouse?"

"Yes," she said, her face as straight as her drive.

On the apron at the ninth, I gingerly approached.

"Am I still in your doghouse?"

"No," she said, smiling. "Of course not. I don't have one. Besides, I know your heart was in the right place. Thank goodness you didn't call him any names—you didn't call him any names, did you?"

She could rest assured I did not.

After the round, Creamer thanked me and said she was happy to have me along for the walk. Paul Creamer, the smartest golf mind I know, said the reports he heard were favorable, and that I might have earned a return engagement next year. The pleasure was all mine.

Paula Creamer, *golf*
February 2008

Paula Creamer finished 2007 as the fifth-ranked women's golfer in the world. Rather than provide a source of satisfaction, it left her hungry for more.

Creamer used the off-season to set changes in motion. She also improved her game simply by bumping into a certain high-profile neighbor at Isleworth in Windermere, Florida.

As the LPGA season got underway in Hawaii the previous two weeks, "The Pink Panther" allowed for a peek into her world by phone.

Creamer won the Fields Open last Saturday, one day before Tiger Woods closed out the Accenture Match Play Championship in Arizona.

DM: How close do you live to Tiger Woods?

PC: A few par-5s.

DM: How often have you seen him?

PC: A number of times at the [Isleworth] course. He's been out there putting and chipping. We haven't been able to play a round yet.

DM: Has he given you any tips?

PC: A couple. The main thing he always tells me to do is swing harder, but that's almost unfair given how hard he swings.

DM: What do you admire most about Woods?

PC: Everything. What's not to like? If I had to pick one part, it would be his work ethic. I'm not sure people realize how hard he works on his game. If anybody would have an excuse to slack off every once in a while, it would be Tiger. But he keeps putting in the time to make himself better.

DM: What advice would you give young girls who want to be you?

PC: Practice. You will have a lot of sacrifices to make, but it's all worth it when you're standing on the 18th green kissing the trophy.

DM: If you were LPGA commissioner for a day, what is one change you would make?

PC: Hmmm. Let me get back to that one.

DM: What are your goals this season?

PC: My goal every season is to be the number one player in the world. But I also have objectives pertaining to my fitness.

DM: Did you identify fitness as a problem from last season, or do you just want to get stronger?

PC: Both. If I wanted to take my game to another level, I knew I needed to get in better shape. My fitness, if I was going to be honest with myself, was a question mark. At my age [21], I should be able to go out and have a lot of energy throughout the year. I felt like I wore down a few times.

DM: Did you overhaul your diet?

PC: I made changes, yes. More protein, less bread.

DM: Favorite meal?

PC: Every one of them. I love food. That needs to change.

DM: The kicker is, at first, second or third glance, you don't look anywhere close to being out of shape.

PC: It's not being out of shape, it's getting in better shape. There's always room for improvement. The thing is, I'm probably not going to see changes right away. I'm going to have to be patient because it might take a year or two.

DM: What is one part of your game on which you worked in the off-season?

PC: Getting longer off the tee. Strength will help, but I made some technical adjustments, as well.

DM: Have you ever played a golf video game?

PC: Yes—Tiger Woods. The one I'm in. It was fun to be myself.

DM: What do you do to relax?

PC: It's hard for me to relax because I have so much energy. I like to watch movies and shop. It's kind of therapeutic to go to the mall—not necessarily to buy stuff, but just to look at the fashions.

DM: Your father, Paul, is known as a golf savant. What is the best tip he has given you?

PC: There are too many to single one out. If I had to, though, it would be: Control what you can, and don't worry about anything else. I don't watch what other people are doing on the course.

DM: As popular as you are in the States, you are even more popular in Asia. Why?

PC: (*Laughs*) Aren't I allowed to be popular in Asia?

DM: Of course.

PC: Well, I've had a great time each time I've gone. And I've won over there, so that helps.

DM: Yes or no to mandatory drug testing?

PC: Yes. It's good for the game. You have to be very aware of what you put in your body.

DM: Thanks for your time.

PC: What about being commissioner for a day?

DM: Oh, yes—what about it?

PC: I'd change the logo's color to pink.

UPDATE: Paula Creamer has won ten LPGA Tour events, including the 2010 U.S. Open at Oakmont. She has been ranked as high as No. 2 in the Women's World Golf Rankings. Entering the 2015 season, she ranked eighth on the LPGA's all-time earnings list with $11.1 million. She was married in 2014 to Derek Heath, an Air Force Academy graduate who now flies C-17s and is on active reserve status. She had 188,000 Twitter followers as of March 2015.

Ben Curtis, *golf*
July 2003

Ben Curtis won the British Open in his first attempt at a major, and he owes it all to the "Birdie Dance."

Well, at least part of it. Whenever Curtis birdied at Royal St. George's those four glorious days in Sandwich, England, his posse celebrated. Cousins Torri Hamilton and Angie Hamilton, alongside his finacée, Candace Beatty, danced. A series of hip movements and arm flaps, it happened quietly and quickly, just long enough to be acknowledged by wide-eyed contact from Curtis. "We eventually got some of the crusty old Englishmen to do it," said Torri, a former Chicago prosecutor. "Their version was, shall we say, a little more uptight."

The play of Curtis turned uptight on the back nine Sunday, as he suffered four bogeys in a six-hole stretch to relinquish the lead. But Thomas Bjorn cooperated by flailing in the bunker at number sixteen, and other notables such as Vijay Singh, Tiger Woods and Davis Love III failed to muster enough. The next thing anybody knew, Curtis, pride of Ostrander, Ohio, and the Mill Creek Golf Club, clutched the coveted Claret Jug. But when it came time for a victory dance, the posse froze. "We couldn't dance because we were in shock," Torri said.

A redux came Saturday at Mill Creek, when the rest of the extended family joined in welcoming home their 26-year-old champion. Curtis need not have birdied this time, and thank goodness for that: He was almost too tired to stand up. A post-championship whirlwind, which included a David Letterman appearance in New York City, could be seen on his face. But he refused to complain, recognizing the fun involved and knowing there is plenty more on the plate—notably, a trip to Washington for a scheduled meeting with President Bush this afternoon.

DM: On a scale of 1 to 10, with 10 being sensational, rate the "Birdie Dance."

BC: Definitely a 10. It's something to see. It helped keep me loose.

DM: Which will turn out to be more nerve-racking: The 18th tee on Sunday at the British, or meeting the president?

BC: The 18th tee at the British.

DM: What will be your first question to the president?

BC: I haven't thought of that yet.

DM: Speaking of big-wigs, has Tiger Woods called since the Open?

BC: Yes, he did, last Monday. I was walking to the gate to fly home and his agent, Mark Steinberg, was with us. Tiger called him and asked Mark to give the phone to me.

DM: What was discussed?

BC: He just wanted to congratulate me, then we joked around a bit. He asked how I felt on Sunday, and I said, "Having you guys chasing me was nerve-racking." He laughed. I told him that being able to compete against him and the other guys was an honor, and that it was fun. I appreciated the call, and I really respect him for it. He was a true gentleman.

DM: In one of your first television interviews after winning, you spoke of being a Browns fan. How intense?

BC: I'm a big Browns fan. I've followed them since I was a kid.

DM: Favorite Browns, past and present?

BC: Past—Bernie Kosar and Earnest Byner; present—Kevin Johnson.

DM: Hobbies/interests?

BC: Movies, hanging out with family, attending sporting events.

DM: Favorite golf movie?

BC: *Dead Solid Perfect*, with Randy Quaid.

DM: Have you seen *Caddyshack*?

BC: A couple of times.

DM: And you'd take *Dead Solid Perfect* over *Caddyshack*?

BC: *Caddyshack* is good, no doubt, but *Dead Solid Perfect* is hilarious.

DM: Mill Creek Golf Club/Ben Curtis shirts and caps are on sale in the clubhouse. Is a bobblehead next?

BC: (*Chuckle*) I doubt it. If they ever made one of me, great. If not, I'd survive.

DM: What food did you pack for England?

BC: Welch's fruit snacks, granola bars, caramel chews, Twizzlers.

DM: Favorite meal in Sandwich, England?

BC: Beef stew and roast beef with rice.

DM: Did you ever opt for the fish and chips?

BC: Yes. They leave the skin on the fish, though. You don't really taste it, but it's tough to look at.

DM: Chess or checkers?

BC: Checkers.

DM: The fish or the chips?

BC: The chips.

DM: Critique the Sandwich cuisine.

BC: It's not as bad as everybody says. It's actually good.

DM: At the British, you wore a cap with a familiar name [Titleist] but a shirt with a seemingly unfamiliar one [Kenda]. What is Kenda, and how long has it sponsored you?

BC: It's a manufacturer of tires and tubes that makes specialty tires for tractors, golf carts, bicycles, race cars. Kenda USA is based in Reynoldsburg, Ohio. I've been with them for three years.

DM: Suffice to say the Kenda folks were a tad thrilled with your performance?

BC: Oh, I would say so. Being on the cover of newspapers all over the world made them happy, I'm sure.

DM: Presumably, you now have a lifetime deal with them.

BC: (*Chuckle*) Well, I don't know. It's up to them. Hopefully, it will go that way.

DM: By all accounts, you are laid-back. What do you do to cut loose?

BC: Just hang out with Candace.

DM: You were quoted as describing yourself as cheap. Accurate?

BC: It's more that I'm careful with money.

DM: Car you drove pre-British?

BC: Toyota Camry.

DM: Car you will drive post-British?

BC: Toyota Camry. It's a good car, gets me from "A" to "B".

DM: What will be your principal indulgence from the British Open winner's check of $1.1 million?

BC: A nice, exotic honeymoon.

DM: But before the honeymoon, you'll have to finish the NEC Invitational [at Firestone Country Club, August 21-24]. August 23 in particular will be busy.

BC: I'm looking forward to fitting it all in.

DM: How many friends have come out of the woodwork since you won?

BC: Just a few. There haven't been too many I hadn't talked to in 10 years, which is a nice surprise.

DM: Does it bother you when some suggest you needed Thomas Bjorn's bunker misfortune to win?

BC: Yes and no. What happened to Bjorn is the way majors are—anything can happen at any given time. I feel bad for Bjorn. He played well enough to win, just like a lot of the other guys did. But I hope people will say that I won it rather than he lost it, because I know I earned it.

DM: What did you do to relax the night before the final round?

BC: I went with Candace and my two cousins to the house where I was staying. I had a beer. We sat and talked and didn't think about golf. Then Candace and I read a little bit.

DM: It is 2005, and you are the two-time defending British Open champion. You lead the tournament after two rounds when you get a call from the states that Candace, who had been expecting, is going into labor. What do you do?

BC: Fly back, without hesitation.

DM: Strangest thing you saw in the four days of the tournament?

BC: At one of the greens on Saturday, three guys were pretty drunk. They tried to be my best friends, but at the same time, they were out of control. They were trying to make jokes, but everybody was laughing at them instead of with them. I just waved and moved on.

DM: Best golf course/hole you've ever played?

BC: Pebble Beach, and number eight at Pebble. It's a par-4. You hit a 3-wood or 2-iron on top of a hill, then a 180- to 200-yard shot over a cliff. The most beautiful hole in the world.

DM: Candace is a a former Kent State golfer. Best tip you've received from her?

BC: Keep the head still while putting.

DM: Best part of the David Letterman experience?

BC: To see how the whole thing works. You don't even meet him before you go on. When you do go on, that's when you see him. I did a conversation with a lady on the phone for background—that's it. I didn't get to talk with him afterwards, either.

DM: The guest before you was Sylvester Stallone. Did you encounter Rocky?

BC: Yeah. It was pretty cool. When he was coming off, I got to talk with him for thirty seconds. He said it was nice to meet me, that I played great and that hopefully we'll get a chance to play sometime.

DM: Best / worst part of links golf?

BC: Best part—it's something I don't get to play every day, and it's where golf began. Worst part—you don't know which way the ball will bounce.

DM: Favorite athlete?

BC: Jack Nicklaus. He's a great role model, on and off the course. I've always looked up to him. Growing up thirty miles from where he did made it even more special. It's awesome that I get to have my name on the Claret Jug with his.

DM: Who joins you for two dream PGA foursomes—three from past, three from present?

BC: Past—Nicklaus, Bobby Jones, Gary Player; present—Tiger, Ernie Els, Charles Howell III.

DM: Rank these British Open champion perks in order of importance to you: play British until 65; five-year exemption to Masters, U.S. Open, PGA Championship; five-year exemption on PGA Tour.

BC: British Open exempt; three majors exempt; Tour card. I think that, no matter what, I was going to get the Tour card, because I had been playing better.

DM: Strangest request you've received post-victory?

BC: To do an interview with Russian TV. I have no relation with Russia at all. They were going to send a crew over, but I told them to talk to my agent. We haven't heard from them since.

DM: How did you transport the Claret Jug from England to Cleveland?

BC: It was on the floor between Candace and me on the flight home.

DM: You didn't store it in the overhead bin?

BC: Uh, no.

DM: Does it bother you to hear "fluke" attached to your accomplishment?

BC: Time will sort that out. I'll do my part to try to make sure it doesn't fit. I'm going to continue to work, continue to improve.

DM: What advice would you give Phil Mickelson on how to win a major?

BC: (*Pause*) To be less aggressive. Sometimes he tries to do a little too much, but that's his style of golf, and I don't think he'll change. If he's playing well one week, I think he'll have a chance to win, because he's a great player.

DM: What is one golf tip you would impart to up-and-comers even younger than yourself?

BC: To be themselves. Don't get caught up in the swing gurus, the nutritionists, the specialty coaches. You need a little guidance, but you have to rely on yourself more than anybody. You have to trust your instincts.

DM: Will you have an entourage now?

BC: (*Chuckle*) Gosh no.

DM: Fifty-four-hole match play, Curtis vs. Woods, Mill Creek Golf Club, next month. Who wins and what's the final tally?

BC: (*Pause*) Oh, man. Wow. I think I would have a chance.

DM: Have a chance? You just beat him in the British Open, and it's your home course.

BC: I'd say it would end in a tie.

DM: You can't get off that easily.

BC: OK, if I had to make a pick, I'd get him on the first extra hole.

Johnny Damon, *baseball*
June 2004

Athletes let their hair grow long. Athletes grow beards.But few have featured a combination that can match that of Red Sox center fielder Johnny Damon. The distinctly grizzled look has created a sideshow wherever he goes, his celebrity extending beyond baseball.

DM: Has it gotten old yet?

JD: Yes, but I still don't mind talking about it.

DM: So you really are at ease talking about your base stealing?

JD: Right.

DM: When did you decide to let both go?

JD: The hair was getting long last season, and I liked it, so I didn't cut it. The beard started getting thick in the off-season, and I didn't feel like shaving it. To be honest, I didn't feel like doing much of anything in the off-season.

DM: The lethargy was traced to the concussion you suffered in the playoffs last season [Red Sox infielder Damian Jackson drifted into the outfield in pursuit of a fly ball and KO'd Damon in a division series game at Oakland].

JD: I was pretty much in bed for a month, month-and-a-half. I had migraines every day. I only started to feel better in December, after a chiropractor adjusted me.

DM: Do you remember anything about the play or the aftermath?

JD: Not really. I thought it was 2001 and I was walking off the field as a member of the Oakland A's, waving to the fans.

DM: Any lingering effects from the concussion?

JD: I've forgotten how many outs there were twice this year. That never happened to me before. My short-term memory is faulty at times. In spring training, I would forget what I had for lunch. Heck, you can ask me now what you asked me a couple of minutes ago, and I'll be like, Uh … OK.... yeah.

DM: Well, then, when did you decide to let both go?

JD: Funny.

DM: Did you ever imagine your hair would get this much play? Was the look calculated in any way?

JD: Absolutely not. I had no idea people would become fascinated by this. I thought I was just like anybody else who has facial hair. Now I'm dealing with "The Damon Disciples" and things like that. It's bizarre.

DM: Have there been any offers for your locks?

JD: A lot of people want to cut my hair for charity. I'm all for raising money from this for a good cause, but it's gotten a little too fanatical. They want the exclusive to be there when my hair gets cut. Huh? My hair is not here for an exclusive, not for the spotlight. I'll cut my hair and I'll shave my beard when I feel like it. I'm just trying to live my life like a normal human being.

DM: It's difficult to be normal when fans look at you and conjure images of Jesus.

JD: As a Christian, that makes me very uncomfortable. There's the thing with The Damon Disciples, and fans in some ballparks have yelled, "You're no Jesus! You're no Jesus!" Well, no kidding. Those fans are smart, aren't they? Jesus is amazing to me and a lot of others. I can't fathom a comparison. In no way would I ever have long hair and a beard just to look like Jesus.

DM: What is your favorite Manny Ramirez story?

JD: I have two: We're on the road in Texas, and I'm wearing a cowboy hat and boots. I come up to him in the lobby and try to talk with him, but he blows me off while fans are trying to get his autograph. The next day, I come into the clubhouse and, half-kidding and half-serious, I say, "That's a lot of crap that you didn't talk to me." He says, "When did you want to talk to me?" I say, "In the lobby. I was the guy wearing the cowboy hat and boots." And he says, "That was you? Oh."

The second comes from when he had his baby. We ask him in spring training last year how everything went, and he says, "Great. I had twins." But we keep seeing him with only one kid. So we're like, "Where's the other kid?" He tells us he only has one. So we're like, "Fair enough."

DM: Does Manny make up a lot of stuff?

JD: I'll say this: He's a great hitter and a great storyteller.

DM: Was the Jackson concussion the most severe you've ever experienced?

JD: By far. I had a smaller concussion while playing high school football in Florida. Warren Sapp gave it to me.

DM: The Warren Sapp of NFL renown?

JD: That Warren Sapp. He was playing tight end and I was playing safety. He hit me instead of me hitting him.

DM: When healthy, what do you like to do in the off-season?

JD: Cruise around in a yacht, fish, jet-ski, dirt-bike …

DM: Does your contract allow you to jet-ski or dirt-bike?

JD: I would think it's all right, as long as I'm not doing anything really dangerous. The closest thing to me getting wild on the jet-ski is when I pull up to the dock and try to spray everyone.

DM: What's the wildest thing that's happened to you on the field?

JD: I hit a ball into a beer cup in right field a few years ago, when I was playing for Oakland. I had a chance for an inside-the-park home run, but they sent me back to second because the ball got stuck in the cup.

DM: You also had three hits in one inning last season—a single, double and triple in the first against the Marlins.

JD: That was strange. I ended up 5-for-7, but I didn't get the cycle. They didn't give me anything in my wheelhouse.

DM: Because you're such a nice guy, it's difficult to imagine anyone not liking you in the game.

JD: My ex-wife told me Chuck Knoblauch hates me. Supposedly it's because I once slid hard into second base and took him out. But I'm not sure if it's a true story, because that's an ex-wife talking. She's probably trying to get me going.

DM: Do you think people realize how good of a player you actually have been over the years?

JD: I can't worry about that. I'm not somebody who gloats or calls attention to myself. I just want my team to win games.

DM: The World Series ring has eluded you.

JD: The ring is the only thing I'm playing for. And if I get that ring this year, you might not ever hear another word from me. I might just disappear.

DM: Even with one year left on your contract?

JD: Even with one year left. I'll seriously have to think about it, but don't be surprised that, if we win, the next time you see me I'm in the woods, with an even bigger beard and a bald head.

UPDATE: Johnny Damon played eighteen MLB seasons (1995-2012) and won two World Series. He played for seven teams (Kansas City Royals, Oakland Athletics, Boston Red Sox, New York Yankees, Detroit Tigers, Tampa Bay Rays and Cleveland Indians.) He batted .284 with 2,769 hits, 235 homers, 1,139 RBIs and 408 stolen bases. At the outset of 2015, he was one of the contestants on *Celebrity Apprentice*.

Dennis Eckersley, *baseball*
July 2004

By the end of the 1986 season, Dennis Eckersley was teetering, on and off the field. He appeared headed to the Hall of Good Players Who Never Became Great For Any Number of Reasons.

Eckersley had gone 6-11 with a 4.57 ERA in 32 starts for the Chicago Cubs. It was the twelfth year of a career that began with the Indians in 1975. His neck ached from watching baseballs rocket past him at Wrigley Field and from throwing back cold ones on Rush Street.

Eckersley knew he had a problem on the field because hitters repeatedly squared up his pitches. Off the field was different. The adversary kept tricking him by offering no resistance

"The writing can be on the wall with alcohol, but you don't see it," he said.

One night during the winter that year, Eckersley got drunk while visiting his sister-in-law. His young daughter was in the house. Eckersley's behavior so alarmed his relative that she flipped on the video camera.

"I saw the tape the next morning, and it was ugly," Eckersley said. "Extremely painful to watch. I thought it was somebody else."

The necessary synapses finally fired. The homemade horror

show proved to be the intervention he desperately needed. It set into motion a plan to get treatment for alcohol abuse.

"I'm very fortunate," he said. "It was a spiritual thing, the grace of God. If I hadn't gotten sober when I did, who knows where I would have ended up."

A journey that began that winter has taken him to Cooperstown, New York, this week. Dennis Eckersley, superior ballplayer and recovering alcoholic, will be inducted Sunday into the National Baseball Hall of Fame.

No question Eckersley earned an immeasurable victory by saving himself from himself. But sobriety, as wonderful as it is, cannot put a fastball on the corner at the knees. As the 1987 season approached, Eckersley still needed to deal with a decline in performance that had been seven years in the making. The Cubs saw enough after his three seasons with them. They traded Eckersley, along with minor-leaguer Dan Rohn, to Oakland for three minor-leaguers on April 3, 1987. What little the Athletics gave up smacked of indifference, underscoring the fall of the cocky right-hander who won twenty games at age twenty-three in 1978.

"They probably thought, 'Maybe he's got a little left in him, maybe not,'" Eckersley said. "I wondered the same thing."

Because Oakland's rotation was set, Eckersley moved to the bullpen. He had not made more than one relief appearance in a season since 1976. Manager Tony La Russa slotted him for setup/long man, but an injury to Jay Howell created an opening at closer. With nothing better to do, Eckersley assumed the role.

No one—notably, the pitcher himself—could have foreseen the dominance that soon followed. After the All-Star break, Eckersley worked 43 $^2/_3$ innings. He struck out fifty-one and walked five as part of thirteen saves.

"I'm glad I wasn't stubborn when they asked me to come out of the 'pen," Eckersley said. "I didn't like it initially, but if I had said, 'I'm a starter, I've got to start,' I more than likely would have been done."

Instead, Eckersley saved 370 games over the next ten seasons, the peak performance coming with powerful Athletics clubs. He parlayed pinpoint control with a swashbuckling demeanor to set down hitters with ridiculous ease. Then he was required to unwind from the inherent pressure of being a closer by bypassing the watering holes.

"The temptation always was there, and it continues to be," he said. "You've got to work at it every day."

Eckersley, squeezing every ounce out of his second chance at life and the game, retired in 1998 with 390 saves and a record of 197-171. From 1975 through 1977, he went 40-32 with the Indians, including a no-hitter, before being traded to Boston. His resumé also features Cy Young and Most Valuable Player Awards and a World Series ring.

The body of work made the decision easy for voting members of the Baseball Writers Association of America in January. They listed him on 83.2 percent of the ballots for the Hall of Fame, easily securing election alongside Paul Molitor (85.2 percent). A candidate needs 75 percent.

"To be named on that many ballots is humbling," Eckersley said. "I keep telling myself, 'You can't sneak in at 83.2 percent.' I came in through the front door." The BBWAA had voted 15 players, including four starting pitchers, into the Hall since the last reliever (Rollie Fingers, 1992). As much as Eckersley hopes to see the likes of Rich Gossage and Bruce Sutter make it one day, he understands why he received the nod.

"I'm in because of everything, the uniqueness of two careers, really, as a starter and a reliever," he said.

Regardless, Eckersley is best remembered for his effectiveness as a closer. He only recently began writing his induction speech and has consulted with a writer to help him fine-tune it. Eckersley does not anticipate having the final version ready until moments before he walks to the podium. For Eck, that is as it should be.

"I like to take things down to the last minute, to get all nervous and feed off it," he said, chuckling. "It's what closers do."

However long the speech, there will be no mention of regrets. Eckersley refuses to reflect on his career and feel bad about the down times. How can he? He finished in Cooperstown, New York.

"I was lucky enough to play long enough to get through the regrets," he said. "Going through what I did has made me who I am, and I like who I am. So it's all OK."

DM: Do you think Pete Rose deliberately stole the spotlight from you and Molitor by having his book released near the time of your Hall of Fame election announcement earlier this year?

DE: Deliberately? I guess I'd have to say yes.

DM: Are you upset with him for it?

DE: No, because I understand. When you're somebody like Pete … it's obvious that he's not the classiest of guys. He's got some character issues, and this was mild compared to what else he's done. It was all about his book. Maybe he didn't have control over the timing of the release, but you'd think he could have stopped it.

DM: So you don't buy Rose's claim that he wasn't trying to detract from your moment?

DE: Who's he kidding? Honestly, though, it really didn't bother me because, who gives a [expletive]? We're going to the Hall of Fame, regardless.

DM: Should Pete Rose one day join you and Molitor in Cooperstown?

DE: No. I would have said yes a couple of years ago, but you know something? After a while, his denial … it just wears on you. Now I can see how character issues can outweigh 4,256 hits. And I wouldn't be surprised if a lot of voters have changed their opinions, as well.

DM: How would you respond to Rose defenders who might say that you're not in a position to judge character?

DE: It's a matter of not being in denial. Fans would have accepted Pete if he had admitted his problems, because people are forgiving. I admitted my faults.

DM: Have other players come to you for help, re: alcohol?

DE: Not necessarily for help, but I've had players come to me and say, "Thanks for giving me hope." It means a lot.

DM: After just three seasons in the majors, you were traded by the Indians to Boston on March 30, 1978. Your reaction?

DE: Shocked. I cried like a baby. I loved being an Indian.

DM: During your days in Cleveland, you had a falling out with good friend Rick Manning. What happened?

DE: Everybody knows by now what happened. Rick fell in love with my wife, Denise, and they got married.

DM: Were you traded to defuse, at least in part, the Manning situation?

DE: Absolutely not. [The front office] had no idea what was going on.

DM: Have you made peace with Manning?

DE: Oh, gosh, yeah. It was devastating at the time, but all is forgiven.

DM: Who are three eligible players you think should be in the Hall but are not?

DE: Bert Blyleven, in a heartbeat. Look at his numbers. Also Goose Gossage and Bruce Sutter.

DM: One of your teammates in Oakland was the incomparable Rickey Henderson. Describe him in twenty words or fewer.

DE: Wow.... I don't want to hoot on him. I'll say he probably was the greatest player I ever played with, because he could change a game.

DM: Was he a great teammate?

DE: He could wear on you—and not just because he cheated in cards. He was so good, you overlooked a lot of things. I don't think he's a bad person at all; he simply was Rickey being Rickey.

DM: Favorite Rickey nugget?

DE: There are so many. We were at old Memorial Stadium in Baltimore, and Aretha Franklin's "R-E-S-P-E-C-T" is playing on the sound system. I'm walking up the runway with Rickey and he's yelling, "R-E-P-C-T-S-E, find out what it means to me." I doubled over.

DM: What is your opinion of another former teammate, Jose Canseco?

DE: Tremendous talent, one of the most prolific home-run hitters ever, but also an ego gone wild. Jose had this chip on his shoulder. For what reason, I don't know. It worked for him, I guess, but as a teammate, it sort of bothered you. When he came toward me, I'd back out of the way because he used to have to take up the whole hallway.

DM: Did you ever witness Canseco, an admitted steroid user, inject himself?

DE: No, but it was pretty obvious without seeing him actually do it.

DM: Do you believe steroid use/abuse is a problem in baseball?

DE: I'd like to think not. At the same time, maybe I'm naive. Something's not right when they tell everybody there's going to be a test—and players still fail.

DM: Did you ever consider cheating/bending the rules?

DE: No. If the ball was handed to me scuffed, I wasn't going to say,

"Excuse me, Mr. Umpire, there's a problem with this ball." But as a control pitcher, it's dangerous to doctor the ball, because you're not sure where it's going to go.

DM: On Oct. 15, 1988, Kirk Gibson homered off you with two outs in the bottom of the ninth to win Game 1 of the World Series...

DE: He did? (*Chuckle*)

DM: Check. Anyway, as you know, the two-run homer that won Game 1, 5-4, is one of the most replayed moments in baseball history. Does it haunt you?

DE: No. Not at all. I'll tell you what: I'd give up that homer any day to be in the Hall of Fame. Heck, I'd give up a couple of those to be in the Hall.

DM: If you could do it over, would you stay with the 3-2 backdoor slider?

DE: Yes, as long as I didn't throw a strike with it. I committed to the slider for the right reasons. I thought he would pull off it because I'd been throwing him fastballs. But it got enough of the plate, and he didn't pull off.

DM: You largely have escaped the "goat" label for your role in the Gibson heroics. Why do you think that is?

DE: Because of the drama surrounding Gibby. It's his great moment more than my bad one. He comes out of the dugout as a pinch-hitter, limping around the joint. He looks terrible during the at-bat. He can't catch up to the fastball, then he flips the breaking ball out—way out. It's like, "What was in the barrel of that bat?"

DM: You're kidding, right?

DE: Of course I'm kidding. Magic was in that bat, same as Roy Hobbs [with "Wonderboy"] in *The Natural*. It was meant to be.

DM: Toughest hitter you ever faced?

DE: There were many, but I'd have to say George Brett. He was a powerful Rod Carew.

DM: Gil Flores, the last batter of your no-hitter with the Indians in May 1977, was one of countless players over the years on the receiving end of your smack. Why did you do it?

DE: It fueled me. It was in there to begin with, and I played on it. It helped me when I wasn't feeling all that good.

DM: Didn't you leave yourself vulnerable to sniping in the event of failure?

DE: I'm going to be miserable, anyway, so what difference does it make? You take me deep to win a game, go ahead and jump up and down. Do anything you want. I'm feeling so bad at that point, you can't make it any worse.

DM: Who joins you at your dream pitchers' roundtable?

DE: Juan Marichal, Sandy Koufax, Bob Gibson and Jim Palmer.

DM: Three teams for which you pitched were the Indians, Red Sox and Cubs. Do you believe in the respective curses of Colavito, The Bambino and The Billy Goat?

DE: No.

John Farrell, *baseball*

January 2014

In 2013, John Farrell won a World Series ring in his first season as Boston Red Sox manager. He owes it all to his work as Cleveland Indians director of player development from November 2001 through 2006. OK, not all—but some. "The experience was invaluable," Farrell said. "I often reference things I learned as farm director. It affects how I address problems and deal with certain situations today. I'm indebted to Mark Shapiro, Chris Antonetti and the Dolans for the opportunity."

During most of Farrell's tenure, I covered the Tribe farm system. Farrell and I spoke at least once a week throughout the season, and during those interviews, I often brought up two subjects: 1) His ending Paul Molitor's hitting streak at 39 games while a starting pitcher for the Indians in 1987; 2) His future as a major-league manager. Of the former, Farrell said he was happy to be linked to Molitor in some way; of the latter, Farrell said he was focused on being the best farm director he could be. Farrell became Red Sox pitching coach under Terry Francona in 2007. They won a World Series that year. Before he left Cleveland, I told him I wanted a one-on-one after he won his first World Series as manager. "Deal," he said with a chuckle.

When Farrell did, indeed, become a manager, it was in Toronto. His Blue Jays went 81-81 in 2011 and 73-89 in 2012. The Blue Jays sent him to the Red Sox in a deal that involved Mike Aviles, now with the Indians. Farrell did not accomplish much in his first year in Boston—other than guide his club to a 97-65 record in the regular season and victories over Tampa Bay in the ALDS, Detroit in the ALCS and St. Louis in the World Series. I let the calendar flip before seeing if Farrell would make good on his "promise." He got back to me the next day by phone from Fenway Park.

DM: Why didn't it work out in Toronto?

JF: We were building in 2011 and, in 2012, we were contending in the middle of June but got ravaged by injuries, particularly to the starting rotation. Injuries took away from a core group that was very promising. That's not an excuse; just fact. I am very thankful for the opportunity provided by the Blue Jays.

DM: When did you begin to think you had something special with the 2013 Red Sox?

JF: I knew when I got the job that the Red Sox had a very strong group, guys who had been successful. But injuries, much like in 2012 with the Blue Jays, were a huge factor. So I thought the key was to get guys healthy and back to their normal levels of performance.

DM: As you began to have success, then sustained it, how did you handle the comparisons to Bobby Valentine? Given Valentine's three-ring circus as Red Sox manager in 2012, you were viewed as the anti-Bobby V.

JF: Those are your words, not mine. From the first day of spring training, we set out to return the focus to the field. The most important thing every day was the game that night. That would drive our preparation and performance.

DM: Good dodge.

JF: I wasn't with the Red Sox in 2012. It didn't do any of us any good to revisit the past.

DM: Red Sox players became known for the lengthy hair on their heads and faces. What was the genesis of the sideshow?

JF: Guys came to spring training with varying lengths of growth. It turned into a bonding mechanism; if someone trimmed his, he probably would hear about it from teammates.

DM: I don't recall seeing you with a beard.

JF: Correct. I've never had one.

DM: Did players ask you to wear one?

JF: Multiple times.

DM: Why decline?

JF: For one, I'd never had a beard and wasn't going to start. Most importantly, though, I felt like this was something that connected the players. I firmly believe this game always will be about the players. The players came up with the idea and had the freedom to do with it what they wished—as long as it didn't adversely affect their preparation and performance.

DM: You could have scored points with the players by going along. How do you toe the line between being a "players' manager" and being their boss?

JF: Baseball is a very difficult game to play, especially at the highest level. Having played it, what I've always tried to keep in mind is: Players are doing their best. So when they struggle, it's important to show some compassion. But I also know—and I learned this my first day as pitching coach under Tito—that players want some form of direction. They want to know where the boundaries are. Finding that balance isn't too difficult if you're open and honest from the start.

DM: Do you have an open-door policy? If so, is it legit, or do you quietly hope the players don't keep coming in and overstaying their welcome?

JF: I'm a firm believer in inclusion. If you don't invite that inclusion—from players and coaches—then you limit their ownership of a given situation. In this position, I can't just be a good listener; I've got to be a great listener. I'd be shortsighted if I didn't encourage feedback. And in my experience, even when the door is open, players won't abuse the privilege. They've got more important things to do than hang with the manager.

DM: As you watched the Rays-Indians wild-card game, did you allow yourself to think what it would be like to face Tito's Tribe in the division series?

JF: You're preparing for both, and you know full well that if it's Cleveland, it's going to be something. There are so many relationships, so many connections, just as there were when we played Cleveland in the ALCS in 2007. Tito is probably the best at what he does, he is the most successful manager in Red Sox history, and he is revered. There would be a lot of attention paid to him—and deservedly so. I'd be one of those paying the attention.

DM: What is the most important lesson you learned from Francona?

JF: Tito has such a unique ability to connect with all types of people, from clubhouse personnel to players to those in the front office. What I appreciated above all else was how he handled players directly, never in the public eye, informing them of something face to face rather than having them find out through the media.

DM: How have you dealt with the legendary Boston media?

JF: I've been genuine. I've made them aware that, if something came up about a given player, please respect the fact that maybe I hadn't talked to that player before the question was asked. I want to be accessible, but there are built-in limitations to the access, and I think they understand that.

DM: The Rays defeated the Indians, then gave the Red Sox a decent test in the division series. Then came what turned out to be an epic ALCS against Detroit.

JF: Thank God David Ortiz hits a grand slam in the bottom of the eighth inning in Game 2, or we're going to Detroit down, 2-0, and things are looking bleak. Ortiz's swing changed the complexion of October for us.

DM: Thank goodness you didn't pinch-hit for him.

JF: You're a funny guy.

DM: The ALCS had a World Series feel. How did you get your players and staff to recalibrate for the Cardinals in the actual World Series?

JF: One of the primary strengths of this team is its ability to not take yesterday's results into today. We had a very competitive group that had a burning desire to go as far as we could. We knew the season wasn't over. And I've got to believe that the intensity of the Detroit series helped us against the Cardinals. I don't know if the World Series was a classic, but classic moments were inside of it.

DM: You made a bold move by sitting catcher Jarrod Saltalamacchia in favor of David Ross for the final three games. It paid big dividends. Explain the thought process.

JF: Decisions will be made that are not popular. You know that going in. I felt like David was swinging the bat better than Jarrod at the time and I felt like, as a team, we were responding with David and Jonny Gomes in the lineup—even if it might go against the numbers. I thought those two guys gave us an intangible and make us a better team, for three games, against St. Louis, in the World Series. Not over the course of the season, but at that moment.

DM: I take it Salty was upset.

JF: He took it the way I expected he would. He was disappointed. He had been our number one catcher and had his best year offensively. If he hadn't been disappointed, he wouldn't be the player I thought he was.

DM: When you reflect on the night you clinched the World Series, what is the first visual that comes to mind?

JF: Forty minutes after the final out, Fenway Park was basically full. The fans didn't want to go home. I was privileged to be a small part of something that special.

DM: In the manager's office that night, did you ever kick back when nobody was around and say, "I can't believe I just won the World Series?"

JF: I'm not sure there ever was a time when nobody was around. I don't think I left the ballpark until 3:30 A.M. It was surreal. So many things flashed through my mind—from the first day of camp to the final out of the World Series. I thought about how so many people had given so much of themselves to achieve the ultimate goal.

DM: Second baseman Dustin Pedroia is the heart and soul of the Red Sox. What is it like to manage him?

JF: An honor. He's one of the most driven people I've ever been around, regardless of profession. He would be successful at anything he does because of how much he prepares and how much he cares. You see the passion and energy with which he plays, and it's incredible. You can't teach it, you can't fake it. And only one thing matters to him: winning. Everybody feeds off that.

DM: Recognizing that you are watching from afar, do you think Jason Kipnis can be Francona's Pedroia in Cleveland?

JF: I don't know Jason Kipnis that well, but I know enough of him to recognize he's a very good player who has a similar style: all-out. On every team, you're looking for that one guy to lead by example, give of himself and put the team goals ahead of individual goals.

DM: How many meals have you needed to buy in Boston since the Series?

JF: I don't go out much, to be honest. When I do, I'll gladly pay. My daily life hasn't changed since the Series.

DM: On August 26, 1987, you stopped Paul Molitor's hitting streak at 39 games—

JF: (*Chuckle*) I did? Really?

DM: You're a funny guy.

JF: If it weren't for you, nobody would know.

DM: So people don't stop you on the street and say, "You're the guy who ..."

JF: Uh, no.

DM: Do you still remember that night?

JF: Like it was last night.

DM: Details, details.

JF: Well, as you know, I wasn't supposed to start. Five days earlier, Rich Yett and I started a doubleheader against the Tigers. Rich rolled his ankle, and by the time we got to Milwaukee, he couldn't go. During the day, we didn't know if we would play because the weather was bad.

DM: That Detroit start was your first in the majors and second appearance.

JF: I debuted August 18, 1987, against Milwaukee in the twelfth inning. I gave up hits to Molitor and Robin Yount on the first two pitches I threw in the big leagues, but somehow got out of it and got the victory. Three days later, I threw a complete game and we beat the Tigers. Then came the Molitor start.

DM: You gave up three hits in nine innings, holding Molitor to 0-for-4 with zero balls out of the infield, before Doug Jones relieved in a scoreless game. As Tribe fans know well, Brewers pinch-hitter Rick Manning drove in the winning run off Jones in the tenth as Molitor stood on deck. Manning was booed.

JF: When the fans booed Rick Manning for getting the game-winning hit, I thought, "This is unbelievable. Is this really happening?"

DM: Molitor's streak is the seventh longest in MLB history, fifth longest in the modern era. No major leaguer has matched Molitor since. How cool is that?

JF: It speaks to how hard it is to put together a long hitting streak. So many things need to go right for an extended period. Paul Molitor is a Hall of Famer. To have been able to end a streak of that magnitude, against a player of his caliber, is a source of pride, sure.

DM: Summarize your tenure as Indians farm director.

JF: Awesome. We had so many good people. Mark Shapiro held us accountable; he told us we needed to better the situation for everyone we were responsible for. Looking back, it's incredibly rewarding to see how many guys from the Cleveland farm systems in those days have had success in the majors. Not just as players—as coaches, trainers, front-office executives. When the Red Sox played the Indians in the 2007 ALCS, it had a strange feel in part because of how many players on the Cleveland roster had spent at least some time in the system. The '07 Indians were a testament to a lot of great baseball people—Mark Shapiro, Chris Antonetti, guys like that—in the organization.

DM: Your close friend, Francona, won AL manager of the year in 2013 after guiding the Indians to a 92-70 record and the wild-card berth. You couldn't have been surprised by his success in his first year in Cleveland.

JF: Not one bit, because he gets the most out of his players. They are his focus. And he has such a good understanding of how the game is played.

DM: In communicating with him during the season, did you sense that he was re-energized after not having managed or coached in 2012?

JF: No doubt. He's at home in the dugout. It was very clear that he loves where he is and loves doing what he's doing.

DM: Did Francona have unwrapped bubble gum in a jar waiting for him in the dugout before each game in Boston?

JF: He chewed a lot of gum, but I'm pretty sure he needed to unwrap each piece. I can't believe they're already unwrapped for him in Cleveland.

Bob Feller, *baseball*

March 2010

As I crept along the unfamiliar road in Gates Mills attempting to find Bob Feller's residence, I couldn't help but notice a pickup truck glued to my bumper. With no room to pull over, I nervously waved it past.

The truck stopped and the driver got out. I thought it might be a plain-clothes officer, and I was prepared to explain myself.

Before I saw who it was, I heard who it was.

"You've got the right place—but you're early," boomed the familiar voice of Feller.

I was, in fact, thirty minutes ahead of our scheduled interview time that afternoon in February of this year.

"I'm not ready for you," he said while standing next to my car. "You're going to have to wait in the kitchen while I change into different clothes."

It certainly wasn't a problem for me, but I couldn't help but feel I was in the doghouse before asking a single question.

Upon returning to his truck, Feller cautioned me that his driveway can be difficult to navigate in benign conditions; at this point, plenty of snow was on the ground and the pavement was slick.

"I'm going to follow you in," he said. "Just make sure you don't go right. No matter what your eyes tell you, don't go right."

I eventually went right—and got stuck, about 30 yards from his garage. Feller pulled next to me.

"I told you not to go right," he said.

"Sorry," I stammered, the doghouse having added a floor.

"Don't worry about it," he said, the voice still booming. "We'll deal with it later. Just turn off the engine and come in."

After a quick tour of his home, we got down to the business of my first extensive interview with the baseball legend. Feller and I had conducted dozens of quick-hitters over the years, mostly from the ballpark, but never anything multilayered. Never anything that involved Feller serving me coffee in his family room as deer scampered in the backyard.

The interview far exceeded my expectations, Feller answering all of my fifty-plus core questions and repeatedly going off on classic Feller tangents. Sometimes he growled, sometimes he grumbled, but he always kept it hopping.

"That's all you've got?" he said at about the two-hour mark.

"No," I said.

"Good," he said, "because I didn't have you come out here to go home right away. We'll take a break, then keep moving."

The break consisted of a visit to the barn in the back of his lot, a barn that housed several ancient tractors. He told me the story of each.

"You see this one?" he said.

"Yes."

"This one is going to get your car out of the ditch."

"Are you serious?"

"Of course I'm serious."

No need to ask who would be at the controls.

The second part of the interview lasted about 90 minutes. I was the one who called it.

"Did you get enough?" he said.

Feller asked the rhetorical question about five minutes after he had demonstrated a chair dip and finger-tip push-up, which were keys to his bionic right arm.

I was content. Little did I know that the truly gripping exchange had not even taken place.

As I got up to shake the 91-year-old Feller's hand, I decided to mention that my late father was a big fan, and that my father also had fought in the Pacific Theater of World War II.

The comment prompted a thirty minute discussion, my recorder safely packed in the computer bag. Most of it concerned, for a variety of reasons, kamikaze planes, the Marianas Turkey Shoot and Hiroshima and Nagasaki.

Thanks to my father, I knew enough so that the student could make it interesting for the teacher. It felt like my father was sitting with us.

Feller walked with me to the car. He told me to gun it a couple of times to see if I could get out of the ditch without his assistance.

Somehow, I managed to get enough traction. I thanked Feller for a fantastic afternoon and began to negotiate the other side of his driveway toward the street.

"No matter what your eyes tell you," he yelled, "don't go right."

*   *   *

Bob Feller's mind tells him he still can throw the speed ball by you. Or, if necessary, buckle your knees with a nasty curve.

Feller's body disagrees. He has been forced to make concessions that come with being 91 instead of 19.

"My best pitching weight was 183," he said. "I was exactly six feet tall, but I've lost an inch and a half, two inches, already because of age."

Already?

Feller spoke from a room with a view in his Gates Mills home, days before he left for Indians' spring training in Goodyear,

Ariz. The franchise's greatest player was just getting warmed up—figuratively and literally. He poured coffee for his visitor as deer scampered in the backyard behind him.

In June 2009, Feller was a starting pitcher in the inaugural Baseball Hall of Fame Classic in Cooperstown, New York. He played a significant role in the formation of the classic, which he and others hope will fill the void created by the cessation of the Hall of Fame Game.

The first Hall of Fame Game was played in 1940. Hall of Fame officials said Major League Baseball decided that keeping the game was unrealistic because of the complexities of the major-league schedule.

To Feller, a 1962 inductee, it sounded like an excuse—a weak one at that. He thinks MLB simply wanted to wash its hands of the game, in large part because players from the two teams were not thrilled about coming.

"All Major League Baseball players should visit Cooperstown [New York] and walk the Hall of Fame," he said in February, repeating what he said last summer and the summer before that. "When you go there, you see you're not the greatest thing on earth. There were people before you. Too many of the players today, I think, don't know what the Hall of Fame looks like or why it's there."

When the Indians open the regular season on Monday in Chicago, Feller will be there. He is being honored for his no-hitter against the White Sox on Opening Day 1940. It remains the big leagues' only Opening Day no-no.

Feller went 266-162 with a 3.25 ERA in an eighteen-year career, all with Cleveland [1936-1956]. He missed almost four seasons because of military service. Even with the time lost, Feller ranks on any credible list among the greatest pitchers ever.

Feller burst onto the scene as a seventeen-year-old fireballer out of the Iowa cornfields. Seventy-four years later, the words, not the fastballs, bring the heat:

Bob Feller
photo by Chuck Crow/*The Plain Dealer*

DM: When you hear the term "living legend" used to describe you, what does it mean?

BF: I owe baseball everything I am today. Whatever I may or may not be, I owe to baseball. I think of a young kid who had great parents, teachers, coaches and a scout, Cy Slapnicka, who signed me and took me in almost as his son. Living legend? It's a term I respect and appreciate because I started out as a kid with no idea what might happen in the game. Thanks to Cy having a lot of confidence in me, I was able to pitch for Cleveland.

DM: Which of the nicknames most attached to you do you prefer: The Heater from Van Meter, Bullet Bob or Rapid Robert?

BF: I don't like any of them that much, to be honest. To me, Bullet Bob is Bullet Bob Turley [1958 Cy Young winner]. Rapid Robert is the most popular, but I don't care for it. Anne, my wife, doesn't like it, either. I prefer to be called Bob. If they call me Rapid Robert, well, so be it.

DM: In official baseball records and on your statue outside Progressive Field, you are listed as Robert William Andrew Feller. What is behind the two middle names?

BF: My father's name was William. My grandfather—his father—was Andrew. Andrew's widow, when I was born in 1918, wanted me to have her husband's name. She asked right in our home in Iowa. So my parents said, "Yes, we're going to name him Robert William Andrew Feller." They didn't. She never knew it when she went to her grave. My legal name at the county recorder's office in Dallas County, Iowa, is Robert William Feller. Robert William Andrew Feller is not my name, legally.

DM: But you don't mind the two middle names?

BF: I don't mind at all.

DM: Growing up on the farm in Iowa, what was your least favorite chore?

BF: Cleaning out the barns on Saturdays, taking the manure out from the horses and livestock, was work we didn't want to do.

DM: Favorite chore, if that's possible?

BF: Sure, it's possible. I enjoyed feeding the hogs, shelling the corn to the hogs. Mostly, I enjoyed being with my father, especially when we'd feed the livestock, milk the cows and play catch in the hog lot. If not for my father, I would have had a lot more trouble staying in condition, because he would catch me at dusk every day. He'd hit grounders to me, I'd throw to him. He pitched batting practice.

DM: So Bob Feller got his start in a hog lot.

BF: We finally built a ball diamond in the pasture. We cut down twenty trees, put the post in the ground, put up the chicken wire and built the ballpark. We peeled the infield and fenced off the outfield to keep the livestock off. We started building in 1931 and by 1932 my dad had a team out there, a bunch of farm kids. We played all the time. When the seams on the balls would break and the stitching would come out, we used to take the covers off and sew them back up with harness thread. It was 108 stitches if you did it the way we did, 216 if you did it the other way. We'd run the harness thread through a big ball of bee's wax and put the covers back on.

DM: It sounds like you had the original Field of Dreams.

BF: More than fifty years before they built one in Dyersville. I've been up there. It's a waste of time.

DM: The field from the movie doesn't cut it?

BF: Oh, no. They never had a team up there. All they ever had was a movie. We played games for four years before I came to Cleveland.

DM: Is your dad's field still in play?

BF: No. It hasn't been there for years. It's soybeans and corn.

Nothing on it would make you think a ball diamond was ever there.

DM: Did your dad teach you how to pitch?

BF: No. He didn't teach me, he caught me. I learned how to pitch by trial-and-error method.

DM: What were some other chores growing up?

BF: Fixing fence, fixing harness, currying the horses, shoveling grain, castrating the hogs.

DM: Castrating hogs doesn't sound like much fun.

BF: First we had to catch them. Then I would hold them and my dad would castrate. Otherwise, they'd turn out to be boars. Once you'd castrate them, they'd gain weight faster. We always sold them. They weighed about 225 or 235 pounds.

DM: Your fastball is the stuff of legend. Were you a freak of nature?

BF: No. Let's just put it this way: There's an old saying: "If the good Lord didn't put it in you, you can't get it out." God gave me gifts. I was very lucky to have good coordination and good rhythm. But I had to develop what I was given.

DM: Growing up, what exercises did you do not related to chores?

BF: Finger-tip pushups. I hit the speed bag a lot. I had a 125-pound barbell and 25-pound dumbbells. My right arm and left arm were about the same, strength-wise.

DM: Could you have pitched lefty if you wanted?

BF: Oh, hell no. I'm 100 percent right-handed. I'm not at all left-handed. About twenty-five years ago, I tore my left rotator cuff and never had it repaired. It bothers me to this day. It bothers me when I try to catch the ball coming back.

DM: The right/left thing almost sounds personal. What gives?

BF: I never tried lefty. I was right-handed from the day I was born.

DM: What exercises can young pitchers do to help with the curve?

BF: I did finger-tips pushups. And I put my palms on a bench or chair and let the butt come near the ground. Up and down, like this [Feller demonstrates]. Doing things like that will strengthen the ligaments around the ulnar bone and ulnar nerve in your elbow. I'll say this: You can't keep your elbow in shape by sitting there eating popcorn or watching a video or reading a book.

DM: When did you begin doing finger-tip pushups?

BF: At eight or nine.

DM: Smartest person you've ever met?

BF: My father. I've been around this country a lot and I ask a lot of questions. I'm going to ask you this question: If you have a person with a great education or great intelligence or great common sense—which would you choose?

DM: Common sense.

BF: I've asked 1,000 people that. They all say the same thing you said. That was my dad. He went to eight grades of school, but he had great common sense and insight. He knew human beings very, very well. He was honest. He paid cash for everything. He worked hard for forty years. He never took a vacation for over forty years. My father was a very successful Iowa farmer. He didn't give me money, he gave me time.

DM: I read where you also built up strength carrying buckets of water.

BF: It was dry and dusty in Iowa in the early '30s, although the dust storms didn't hit Iowa as much as they hit Nebraska, Dakota, Kansas and Oklahoma. We bailed water out of the Raccoon River, which runs right through Van Meter. The farm was a little northeast of Van Meter. We carried five- to seven-gallon buckets out of the river, up the bank and dumped them in a tank in the back of our Dodge truck or a wagon with horses. And we hauled it to the cattle.

DM: Favorite player growing up?

BF: Rogers Hornsby was number one. My father liked Hornsby. Walter Johnson and Babe Ruth were up there.

DM: Do you remember the first pro game you ever attended?

BF: The first one that comes to mind wasn't a major-league game. It was when I saw Babe Ruth and Lou Gehrig play on their barnstorming tour—the Larrapin' Lous and the Bustin' Babes. They came through Iowa when I was a boy. I got a ball signed by both. Babe pitched one inning. Ruth and Gehrig batted once each inning. They had their own uniforms.

DM: What is your greatest achievement as a baseball player?

BF: My best decision in life was joining the Navy two days after Pearl Harbor. Getting back to my achievement as a baseball player, it would be being the first president of the Major League Baseball Players Association, in the 1950s. I started the baseball players association; now it's a union.

DM: But you don't get credit for that in the game's history books.

BF: Nobody knows it. ... Not many people know it. I took over when some other guys retired. You had to be on the active roster to represent the players. I organized the first convention, at a hotel in Key West, Florida. I've spent my entire baseball life fighting for players' rights, standing up for players. I'm proud of that.

DM: You also advanced the integration of baseball, having organized Bob Feller's All-Stars against Satchel Paige's All-Stars in a barnstorming tour in 1946.

BF: We put on a great show. Satchel Paige would have been one of the top five-to-ten pitchers in history if he had pitched in the big leagues during his prime.

DM: When did you first hear of the attack on Pearl Harbor?

BF: While I was driving to Chicago. I made up my mind right then and there that I was going to enlist. When I got to Chicago, I called Gene Tunney, head of the Naval Physical Fitness Program. I told him I was ready to sign up to join the Navy. He told me what I needed to do.

DM: Gene Tunney, the boxer?

BF: Yes. And Jack Dempsey was with the Coast Guard's physical fitness program during the war. I knew them both.

DM: Did you ever think about what you were giving up to enlist, and that you might lose not only your career, but your life?

BF: As soon as the war broke out, I was in, no matter what I was doing at the time. I wasn't concerned about anything but trying to do whatever I could to help my country.

DM: You went on to serve with distinction from 1941 to 1945. How does it feel to be a war hero on top of being a Hall of Fame player?

BF: I'm no hero. Heroes don't come home from wars. Don't get this wrong: Heroes don't come home from wars, survivors come home from wars. I'm a survivor.

DM: You were a gun captain on the USS Alabama in the Pacific theater. What did that entail?

BF: I was in charge of twenty-five guys—twenty-four on the guns, one guy standing beside me. I pulled the trigger.

DM: Were you ever afraid to die during combat?

BF: Never gave it a thought. You always knew that if a bullet had your name on it, you were going to get it. But when you're young, everybody thinks it's got somebody else's name on it. That's why we have wars. There was always a little panic, sure. Everybody had different emotions. But you had a job to do, and you needed to have a clear head. What they teach you in war college is, when you're on the guns, kill the other guy before he kills you. We had a few gutless people aboard, yes, and we got rid of them.

DM: What do you mean by "got rid of them?"

BF: Shore duty or something else way from the ship.

DM: Did you ever have someone next to you die?

BF: No. On the other side of the ship, several got killed by friendly fire. One of our five-inch guns fired right into the back of another one during the night and killed everyone in there.

DM: Did you shoot down kamikazes?

BF: Oh, hell yes. We had Variable Density goggles, which I have in my museum in Iowa. Kamikazes would come out of the sun at high noon, and you supposedly couldn't see them. We could use the goggles to block out the sun and see the plane and splash it with the barrel straight up. We fired eight rounds a second out of the 40-mm quad.

DM: How many planes did you, personally, shoot down in the course of the war?

BF: It's hard to tell whose bullets hit which targets because everybody's firing. But we splashed a lot of them.

DM: How close did an enemy plane get to you?

BF: A "betty bomber" got pretty close one time. It came in about ten feet above water, at dusk. The betty bombers would weave around, trying to get by battleships and cruisers to get to the carriers, which were full of aviation fuel. This one was coming right at us, where my battle station was. It got pretty close, maybe 1,000 feet—it's hard to judge distance on the water. It was dead ahead. Everybody was firing, all the 20-mm and 40-mm.

DM: Your 1946 season was unreal: 26-15, 2.18 ERA, 371-$^1/3$ innings, 277 hits, 348 strikeouts, 36 complete games. Do you consider it your best ever?

BF: By far.

DM: How did it happen?

BF: Barnstorming was only supposed to be for ten days after the '45 season ended. I made a deal with (Commissioner) Happy Chandler to go thirty days so guys could make some money they lost in World War II. I had a baseball clinic for returning servicemen for one month in Tampa, Florida. I worked out every day. I was in exceptional baseball condition by spring training.

DM: Other than salaries, what is the biggest difference between players of your era and today?

BF: A large percentage of them don't know the fundamentals, or don't work at them. I respect the abilities of today's players; there's a lot of very good ones. But I don't think these ballplayers, as a whole, practice and review the fundamentals like we did.

DM: Why do you suppose that is?

BF: It's a different game. It revolves around money. No secret there.

DM: Do you blame today's players, though, for grabbing as much cash as possible?

BF: Absolutely not. More power to them.

DM: If you were MLB commissioner, what is one change you would push for immediately?

BF: I would promote baseball more in the United States and not worry so much about promoting it around the world. They're trying to expand baseball to countries that don't even want it. I would increase spending on promoting the game in this country's grade schools, high schools, colleges. Each ball club should increase its support of local sandlots, junior highs, high schools and colleges. That's more important than the steroids, the DH or some of the other issues people talk about now. I mean, how often do you drive around and see a father playing catch with his kid in the yard? Not often. It's sad. I don't think the game's fast enough for people nowadays. They want to see action. They don't have the patience to watch something develop.

★   ★   ★

It had not happened in a major league game before Bob Feller took the mound Tuesday, April 16, 1940.

It has not happened since.

The Indians' right-hander no-hit the White Sox in a 1-0 victory in Chicago.

Feller was twenty-one. Seventy years later, Feller is surprised that he remains alone in the column for Opening Day no-hitters. At the same time, the ultra-competitive Feller is not eager for anyone to join him.

"I don't want anybody to pitch another no-hitter Opening Day as long as I'm alive," he said, chuckling, last week by phone from Phoenix, Arizona.

Feller will be honored Monday when the Indians open the season against the White Sox at U.S. Cellular Field. His younger sister, Marguerite, will be there. When Feller threw his no-hitter in 1940, Marguerite and his parents were among the 14,000 who witnessed history that afternoon.

"My sister and I might be the only two in the ballpark Monday who saw that game," Feller said. "I don't know if that's true, but it's possible."

Feller had not pitched well in spring training that year and got rocked in a final tuneup the previous weekend.

The day's conditions were more conducive to reading a book in front of the fireplace.

"Cold, windy and Norway-gray," Feller said. "The wind was blowing off the lake, coming in from center field."

Feller was wild early. He struggled to maintain his curve-ball grip in the low temperatures, so much so that he scrapped his second-best pitch in the third inning. He used mostly fastballs the rest of the way.

"I didn't have no-hit stuff that day," he recalled. "I've had much better stuff. But it was such a cold day, if you hit a ball on the fists, it was like you had a handful of bees stinging you."

The first two White Sox went down quietly, bringing up the ultra-dangerous Luke Appling. Feller walked Appling in a 10-pitch confrontation.

"At 2-2, he kept fouling pitches off," said Feller, who walked five and struck out eight. "He was timing me pretty good. He had hit a shot off me in the third.

"I threw the last two outside on purpose — even though nobody knew it but me. Even my catcher [Rollie Hemsley] didn't know."

Left-handed batter Taft Wright, a Feller nemesis, took a ball before grounding sharply toward the hole at second. Ray Mack lunged and knocked the ball down. He scrambled to pick it up on the outfield grass, spun and fired to Hal Trosky.

"Wright was out by a step," Feller said. "It was close, but it wasn't bang-bang. Ray made a very good play."

After the game, Feller singled out Mack, third baseman Ken Keltner and right fielder Ben Chapman for "pretty fancy support."

"If you don't strike out 27, there's probably going to be some luck involved in no-hitters," Feller said last week. "I had good defense behind me."

The no-hitter was one of three career for Feller, who added a staggering twelve one-hitters. They are part of a legendary career that began as a phenom on an Iowa farm and continues today as an ambassador for the Indians and the game of baseball.

Bob Feller
photo by Chuck Crow/*The Plain Dealer*

DM: On June 13, 1948, terminally ill Babe Ruth used your bat as a cane during his farewell speech at Yankee Stadium. How did that come to be?

BF: He just picked it out of the bat rack at random when he came up the steps into the dugout. There was one runway leading to the field. It could have been anybody's bat.

DM: What was going through your mind when Ruth spoke?

BF: I was warming up to pitch that ballgame. I couldn't hear him. I didn't know until later, when I couldn't find the bat, that he had used mine. Now it's in my museum in Iowa. It cost me $95,000 to get that bat back. One of my teammates had sold it to Barry Halper, who was a big collector. Halper eventually sold it, Upper Deck purchased it, and a guy in Seattle won it [in a sweepstakes]. I contacted the guy and told him I'd pay $95,000 for it, because I wanted it for my museum. He said he wanted $150,000. I said, "Good luck." Later, I called him back and said, "I'll give you $95,000—take it or leave it." He said, "OK, I'll take it." I flew out there and picked it up at the All-Star Game.

DM: Is the bat your favorite piece of memorabilia?

BF: No. My favorite is my father's original catcher's mitt, the one he caught me with back on the farm. It's also in my museum. It has a big, leather patch in the middle where I wore it out.

DM: What kind of a hitter were you?

BF: I averaged about .151 [He did, in fact, average .151]. I was a right-handed batter and had a little power—I hit eight home runs. I could bunt; that was my best attribute at the plate. I could hit Eddie Lopat with my eyes closed at midnight and the lights out. But I was the only guy on our team who could hit him.

DM: Any of the eight homers especially memorable?

BF: My first homer, in 1940, was the [go-ahead] run in St. Louis in the first-ever night game at Sportsman's Park. We won, 3-2.

It went over the right-field wall. Sportsman's Park is where I watched games in the 1934 World Series.

DM: If you could have one pitch back from your entire career, which would it be?

BF: The one I threw to Tommy Holmes in the eighth inning of Game 1 of the 1948 World Series. He singled with two outs to drive in the game's only run. [It was one of two hits off Feller in eight innings of a loss to the Boston Braves' Johnny Sain.]

I was trying to work him high and tight but didn't get the pitch high enough and left it too far outside. He hit a little bloop over third base to score the runner from second. The runner, Phil Masi, shouldn't even have been there because we had him out by three feet on a pickoff play. Somehow, the umpire called him safe.

DM: Elaborate.

BF: My mistake was walking the leadoff man [Bill Salkeld]. Masi pinch-ran, then they sacrificed him to second. Boudreau wanted me to walk Eddie Stanky. I didn't want to walk Stanky because he hadn't done anything against me that day. But Boudreau didn't like Stanky. It was personal. He hated Stanky. He didn't want to give him a chance to break open the game by getting a hit. Boudreau told me that the next batter, Johnny Sain, would probably hit into a double play. So we walked Stanky. Sain didn't hit into a double play, though. He popped to right. That brought up Holmes. We did the pickoff play, where I jumped and twirled and threw the ball about belt high. It's something we practiced a lot. The throw was on the money and Boudreau tagged Masi. I've got a photo of the tag, and it's plain as day he was out. It's in the books as one of the more infamous gaffes by an umpire in World Series history. Moments later, Holmes got the hit.

DM: Would you want back any one of the pitches that led to hits in your twelve one-hitters?

BF: No. Those one-hitters were meant to be, no matter what type of hit it was.

DM: Is anything about you misunderstood?

BF: I try to tell it like it is. If they don't like it, so be it. It's my opinion. I'm not always right; nobody is. If you never did anything wrong, you never did anything. Misunderstood? I probably get too much to the point. I'm not that much of a B.S. artist. Nowadays, in order to be a manager or coach, in order to run a business, you have to be full of horsemuffins and talk a lot.

DM: How do you respond to the criticism you get for being an "easy" autograph?

BF: If you don't want my autograph by now, you don't ever want it. If you don't want my autograph, don't ask me for it. Simple as that.

DM: Critics also have tweaked you for charging money for autographs.

BF: When I do card shows now and I get paid, I raise money for my museum. That's why I charge. Some people don't charge for autographs, but an autograph is a commodity. It's your property. It's your own. Do with it what you want, and it's nobody's business. Right?

DM: Right.

BF: Right. Just because you bought a ticket to see a guy play a ballgame doesn't mean he has to go out to dinner with you.

DM: Have you ever had arm surgery?

BF: Never.

DM: That's hard to fathom. How much pain did you ever feel in the arm?

BF: I hurt my elbow my first start in 1937, April 24 at League Park, and didn't start again until July 4. I threw a curveball, it was raining and muddy, and I slipped. I struck out 11 in six innings but had to leave the game. It didn't tear all the ligament off the bone, but I couldn't get my arm straightened out. A bunch of doctors couldn't figure out why. Slapnicka took me to a guy, a "bone setter." He put the elbow on his collarbone, popped it and broke up the adhesions. He said he wouldn't want me to pitch tomorrow, but that I could go the day after that. He charged $10.

DM: What was the key to your filthy curve?

BF: A lot of it is in the wrist, the forearm.

DM: Advice to youngsters, or coaches of youngsters, about throwing the curve?

BF: To throw a curveball, you have to keep the elbow away from the body. It's up and down. I tell the kids to get a pillow, take the ball in the bedroom ... up and down, up and down. Keep the elbow away from the body and snap—pull down the window shade or crack the whip.

DM: Yes or no—designated hitter?

BF: I would prefer not to have it, for the simple reason that it rouses up the records of the pitchers. It interferes with their records, which are important to the history of the game. Most pitchers nowadays are All-American outs. You might as well leave the bat in the dugout and stand up there and take three strikes.

DM: Yes or no for Hall of Fame—Pete Rose?

BF: No way.

DM: Mark McGwire?

BF: No. I don't believe a word he says.

DM: Barry Bonds?

BF: Yes—if he's never convicted or admits to using [performance-enhancing] drugs. He was never suspended. Nothing's been proven. There's a lot of circumstantial evidence, but nothing's been proven. If he's not convicted of anything, I'd vote for him.

DM: You and Rose have had a running feud for years. How intense is your dislike for Rose? Is it hatred?

BF: It's not hatred. He's a self-admitted liar, right?

DM: Correct.

BF: I hear people say, "What's wrong with betting on baseball if you want to bet on your own team to win?" You've heard that dumb question, haven't you? So if you bet on your team, and you want to ensure your bet, you're going to go to the other team and say to the manager or some of his players: "I've got $50,000 or $100,000 on this game. You see to it that I win and we'll meet in the hotel tonight and split the cash." It doesn't matter whether you bet for your team or against your team—you bet on the game, and it cannot stand.

DM: What is your reaction to Rose's criticisms of you —?

BF: Such as?

DM: That you always have axes to grind, among other things?

BF: Listen: If it weren't for baseball, no one would have ever heard of Pete Rose—or Bob Feller. The game made him what he is today. And lying also has made him what he is today.

DM: If, by some miracle, Rose were to call and say, "Bob, I just want to bury the hatchet with you on everything, and I apologize for what I've done to the game." Would you bury it?

BF: I probably would. But that's not going to stop me from disapproving of what he's done. Anybody who bet on baseball should be permanently banned from the game.

DM: What about the Black Sox?

BF: Judge Landis did the right thing by throwing out all of them.

DM: Even Shoeless Joe?

BF: Yes. Great ballplayer, great hitter, but he took the money. He was illiterate, but he never should have taken the money. I met him once. We shook hands. That's it. He didn't speak much. He was very quiet. He didn't know me from a bale of hay.

DM: What do you think of the twenty-first-century pitcher?

BF: I'm not sure a lot of pitchers right now are doing the proper exercises for their position. I think it's too standardized. You should take everybody as an individual and set up the mechanics accordingly. Pitchers must be able to figure out some things for themselves. I pitched in grade school, American Legion, high school and semipro. The more you play, the more you learn.

DM: Do you think pitchers would be better off if they threw more outside of games?

BF: Yes! Absolutely! In the off-season, during the season. The pitch count, to me, is ridiculous. It means nothing. It's a lot of horsemuffins. You might go out and throw ten pitches and they might get ten hits and it's time to take a shower and play a round of golf. What did the pitch count mean then? Or you might go out and dominate for eight innings but because you threw 100, 105 pitches, the manager takes you out and the bullpen gives up the game. What did the pitch count mean then? I think pitch counts have put artificial limits on pitchers' arms. The problem is, pitchers have been conditioned on pitch counts. That's all they know. Managers and coaches believe in pitch counts, so that's how they're going to play it.

DM: Ted Williams once said you were the fastest and best pitcher he ever saw and that you had the best fastball and curve he had ever seen.

BF: Ted Williams was a great, great hitter. I never faced Ty Cobb, Babe Ruth or Lefty O'Doul—but Williams was the best I ever faced. I don't know what his average was against me, but I'm pretty sure he hit ten homers against me.

DM: How did you pitch to him?

BF: I tried to throw sliders on his fists, tried to keep the ball inside so he couldn't get the fat part of the bat on the ball. Williams was so tough because he would not swing at a ball unless it was a strike. Amazing eye. And trying to throw a fastball by Ted was like trying to get a sunbeam by a rooster in the morning.

DM: How did you pitch to Joe DiMaggio?

BF: (*Chuckle*) Usually bad. He was pretty tough for me when I first came up. He had that big, wide stance. He couldn't get out of the way of the ball, so I had to be careful when I pitched him inside. I didn't go in there because I didn't want to hit him. When I finally started pitching him inside, I was able to get him out.

DM: What did you do to pass the time on the train during trips?

BF: I read books and magazines, talked to other players about the next opponent. I didn't play cards very much. Never was a card player. I'm still not.

DM: You endorsed numerous products as a player. Favorite?

BF: Wheaties. When people ask me if I took steroids, I say, "No, I ate Wheaties instead."

DM: Do you still eat Wheaties?

BF: If [wife] Anne buys them, yes.

DM: The only products you refused to endorse were alcohol and tobacco, correct?

BF: And patent medicines. I don't believe you should be advocating any medicines not given by prescription. I don't think you should be advocating medicines, period. I never used tobacco. I'll have a drink when I feel like it, but I'm not going to advertise it.

DM: Were you ever tempted by alcohol or tobacco endorsement offers?

BF: Big-time. I turned down a lot of money from Chesterfield cigarettes every year.

DM: Any regrets about your baseball career?

BF: Oh, I've made a lot of mistakes off and on the ball field. Show me a person who didn't make a mistake and I'll show you a person who didn't do anything. I probably could have worked harder. I walked too many hitters when I first came up.

DM: Why the walks?

BF: Lack of concentration. Carelessness. I talked to Slapnicka about it after the '38 season. I began to concentrate more in '39. That's when I became a decent pitcher. Before that, I was just a thrower.

DM: If you needed a hit and had one of these four from whom to choose —

BF: Lou Boudreau.

DM: I was going to ask you to pick from Ted Williams, Lou Gehrig, Babe Ruth or Joe DiMaggio.

BF: Lou Boudreau.

DM: Boudreau, it is.

BF: He was a great clutch hitter, a great player and the best manager I ever had. He didn't over-manage. He understood human beings and he instilled confidence in his players. He wasn't afraid of anybody.

DM: Mike Garcia?

BF: Very good, live fastball. Mediocre curve. Great guy, good teammate.

DM: Early Wynn?

BF: Good, live fastball. Threw strikes. Pretty good hitter. Very good teammate.

DM: Bob Lemon?

BF: The best as a teammate. Very good curveball, excellent sinker. Very good fielder.

DM: The 1948 World Series?

BF: We had a better ballclub than Boston.

DM: The 19—

BF: The American League was much tougher in '48 than it was in '54. Our ballclub in '48 was much better than it was in '54.

DM: But your club went 111-43 in 1954, as opposed to 97-58 in 1948.

BF: Doesn't matter. It wasn't that great of a team.

DM: The 1954 World Series?

BF: The first thing that comes to mind has to be the Dusty Rhodes bloop home run.

DM: Not the Willie Mays catch against Vic Wertz?

BF: A lot of center fielders could have caught the ball Mays caught. He put on the act pretty good; he always did. He let his hat fly off, then threw the ball back to the infield. The ball was hit into a small wind. The ball came down like a popup. He was playing shallow, but Vic Wertz was the hitter, so he should not have been playing shallow.

DM: So you're not impressed by the catch.

BF: Not at all. Not at all.

★   ★   ★

Bob Feller will talk pitching anytime, anywhere. During a lengthy interview with *The Plain Dealer* recently, Feller offered some advice to aspiring pitchers:

- Throw strikes. Keep an eye on the spot where you're trying to throw. You're not going to get it there all the time. It's going to take years and years to get that hand-eye coordination.

- Develop the fastball. Everybody wants to throw the off-speed pitches, but the pitch you have to have is the fastball.

- Learn to pitch from the stretch because you're going to have men on base.

- Make sure to follow through.

- Keep the glove ahead of the elbow, so if the ball comes back at you, you can knock it down. Don't ever let your glove get behind you.

- Develop your triceps. Biceps get the attention, but it's your triceps, your extender muscle, that helps you as a pitcher.

- Work on shoving off the rubber. I hear some of the pitching coaches say, 'Don't shove off.' Well, some of those pitching coaches were not too successful in their own careers.

- Build your upper-body strength. You hear people talk about how pitchers need their legs, and they do, but sometimes the upper body gets forgotten. You've got to have upper-body strength to be able to throw with your elbow away from your body. If you throw with your elbow against your body, you're going to ruin your arm.

- Be careful with weightlifting. Light weights are OK. But too much weight can be a problem, because it's going to restrict your motion. You're not trying to be Mr. America or Charles Atlas. You're not trying to be on the Santa Monica beach. You don't want to be on the cover of *Muscle Magazine*.

UPDATE: Bob Feller passed away on December 15, 2010.

Jennie Finch, *fast-pitch softball*
May 2009

Jennie Finch, perhaps the most recognized name in the history of women's fastpitch softball, will be at Baldwin-Wallace College, Friday and Saturday to conduct a pitching and hitting clinic. She will be the guest of Explosive Fastpitch, a Strongsville-based instructional entity whose founder is Jeanette Howard, a former four-year pitcher at Baldwin-Wallace and Strongsville's current coach.

Finch, who was a superstar at La Mirada (California) High School and the University of Arizona, pitches for the Chicago Bandits of the National Pro Fastpitch League. She also has been a cornerstone of the national team, helping Team USA to a gold medal at the 2004 Athens Games and a silver medal in 2008 in Beijing.

Finch is married to Casey Daigle, a pitcher for the Houston Astros' Class AAA affiliate. They have a son, Ace.

DM: Favorite part of doing camps?

JF: Meeting young girls and, hopefully, inspiring them. I want to share the dream with them. I once was dreaming of being a major-league baseball player and here I am today, a professional athlete. I play softball for a living. I think it's good for young girls to know the opportunity is out there.

DM: Do you want to coach major-college fastpitch at some point?

JF: I love camps, I love working with kids, but I don't know. Maybe on a volunteer basis. Maybe once our family has settled in somewhere.

DM: Sum up your experience at the 2004 Athens Games, when the USA softball "Dream Team" rolled to gold.

JF: Everything I could have imagined, and more. Here I was, standing with women I looked up to as role models, getting a gold medal around my neck. The whole experience was awesome. You couldn't have scripted it any better.

DM: As a correspondent for *This Week in Baseball* earlier in the decade, you traveled the country and pitched against various major leaguers. Talk about that.

JF: It was an amazing experience just getting to go to the ballparks, because I'm a big baseball fan. I'd interview a guy, then challenge him to hit off me. Getting to pitch was icing on the cake.

DM: You made most of them look bad. Very bad.

JF: It was a thrill to go against the best of the best. I think it helped give exposure to our game and prove how fast our game really is. When you watch our game on TV, it's hard to appreciate how quick and fast-paced it is.

DM: Wasn't Barry Bonds one of your victims?

JF: I faced him—but he wouldn't swing.

DM: He wouldn't swing?

JF: He just stood in the box.

DM: That's nice of him.

JF: Yeah. (*Chuckle*)

DM: Who was your most notable swinging-strikeout victim?

JF: Probably Albert Pujols. It was cool. Talk about somebody with some thighs.

DM: Best advice for youngsters who want to be you?

JF: Believe in your dreams and play hard. I tell kids, "You want to be able to look in the mirror every night with a big grin and be proud of what you are and what you've done."

DM: Favorite athlete?

JF: My husband.

DM: Besides your husband.

JF: Lisa Fernandez.

DM: Favorite historical figure?

JF: Jesus.

DM: You have turned down numerous offers for photo shoots in men's magazines. Explain your thought process.

JF: I've been blessed to be able to be a role model. I take that very seriously. So with everything I do, I try to consider what young girls would think about it, what parents would think about it. My family is truly how I stay grounded. They help me make certain decisions and let me know what's right. They make sure I'm not influenced by the moment or money, that I stay true to the bigger picture.

DM: Fitness tip for young and old?

JF: Compete at whatever you're doing. If you walk for five minutes one day, walk for six the next. Compete with yourself to do a little better each time.

DM: What does the National Pro Fastpitch League need to gain traction in the American sports landscape?

JF: Money. Money and marketing. We have an incredible product, it just hasn't broken through yet. Every league has its struggles. I'm happy to be part of it right now.

DM: You were a contestant on a recent *Celebrity Apprentice*. What was that like?

JF: Pretty wild. To be in New York City in a business suit and heels, to be around Donald Trump and his whole aura, in the board room—it was intense.

DM: Smartest person you've ever met?

JF: That's a tough question. I'd say my dad, or Casey for marrying me. (*Laughs*).

DM: If not a softball player, what would you be?

JF: Probably a health or physical education teacher.

DM: Hobbies/interests outside of softball?

JF: Right now, motherhood has taken over. But I love being outside, going to the beach. And I like to shop.

DM: Shopping? Seriously?

JF: Oh, yeah. It's relaxing, and I'm pretty good at it. Even the grocery store. I like going to the grocery store, because it means I've been in one place longer than a week. It's a highlight.

DM: What is left for you to accomplish in the sport?

JF: Something all of us involved need to do: Continue to make sure the game grows—not only nationwide, but worldwide.

Allison Fisher, *pool*

December 2005

At age seven, Allison Fisher got hooked on pool, having watched snooker matches on television at home in England.

By fifteen, she won her first national title in snooker, a variation of the game of billiards that uses a cue ball, fifteen red balls and six of other colors. Two years later, she was a world champion.

Fisher attained pool royalty in the United Kingdom before taking her act to the United States in 1995, where she commenced a career in 9-ball. Fisher owns four world and six national 9-ball titles and has won more than fifty professional 9-ball tournaments. In so doing, she has become a regular on ESPN and arguably the face of pool in the United States, regardless of gender.

Fisher was one of a select number of women chosen to compete on the fledgling International Pool Tour, which boasts the largest prize funds in the game's history.

Fisher, quite simply, is the best women's pool player in the world.

DM: When did you set your mind to dominating at pool?

AF: I knew when I was fourteen that I would make this my profession, even though no women to my knowledge were making a living at it. When they asked us in school what we wanted to be, I'd say, "A professional snooker player." And they'd say, "But what do you really want to be?"

DM: Why pack up in your late twenties and leave a comfort zone to move across the ocean?

AF: I had a great career at snooker, I loved it, but I didn't see any more I could do. I had eleven world titles but no sponsors. Prize money for women wasn't very good, so I just decided to go to America and play 9-ball. My ambition was to be champion in another game.

DM: Did you have your family's blessing?

AF: When I first told my mum, she said, "You must be out of your head."

DM: You have been praised for having a superior mental game. Innate or developed?

AF: I've had a good mental side from the beginning. It's not something I've consciously worked on.

DM: Part of it is, you never seem to get the least bit fazed during competition.

AF: I will only get mad if opponents are playing head games.

DM: Is there gamesmanship in pool?

AF: With some people, sure.

DM: Have you ever gotten into it with an opponent behind the scenes?

AF: Yes. Somebody was accusing me of something I wasn't doing. I said, "Don't ever do that again. Don't ever insult me again." I play professionally, and I pride myself on being honest.

DM: Where would the male have an advantage over women in pool?

AF: The power in the break. Even that's not always an advantage, though.

DM: Why are pool players huge celebrities in Asia but not in North America?

AF: Participation-wise, pool is big over here, but that doesn't mean everyone watches it on TV. There's too much competition for the sports viewer.

DM: How are you and the other pros able to put so much English on the ball?

AF: The amateurs can, too, if they just know a few little things. It's about how you hit the ball—the follow-through, the timing. It's about a slow backswing, then accelerating on contact. I could teach anyone to do it within minutes. After that, consistency depends on practice.

DM: I read where you don't practice much.

AF: I've been doing this all my life; I put in so many hours at the table growing up. When I go to play tournaments, I want to be fresh, I want to be motivated. I don't want to be fed up with the game.

DM: What are your thoughts about playing against men?

AF: In snooker, I played with the men. Gender separation in pool didn't occur to me until I got to America. I've got no problem with playing them—as long as they're good sports.

DM: Elaborate, please.

AF: From my experience, men don't take it too well when women beat them. Men have rather large egos. I've played in open tournaments, I've won open tournaments, and I've been sitting there with the trophy when one of the backers of the guy I beat comes up. And he says, "OK, now do you want to play for money? And he'll give you the 7-ball." And I've been like, "You've got to be kidding." I'm a tournament player, I won, fair and square, and now they want to gamble with me? It's rubbish.

DM: Do you let that type of smack roll off your back?

AF: Sure. If somebody thinks they can beat me, I say, "Yeah, you probably can." I'll leave it at that. Go ahead and think you can, if it makes you feel good.

DM: What do you think of the celebrated pool movies, *The Hustler* and *The Color of Money*?

AF: Well, unfortunately, an image of pool that keeps getting presented involves hustling. In my snooker career, I never, ever, was exposed to anything like gambling or hustling. So it was a big awakening for me coming over here.

DM: Are you ever tempted ....

AF: Not at all.

DM: .... to walk into the neighborhood pool hall or bar and take on the townies?

AF: No. I have enough money of my own.

DM: You seem a bit agitated by the question.

AF: Look, I'm a tournament player. I wouldn't hustle somebody—it's not in my nature. I couldn't hustle somebody, because I can't miss on purpose.

Luis Gonzalez, *baseball*

May 2002

The irony never will be lost on Luis Gonzalez. It always will prompt a chuckle. A 57-homer slugger in the 2001 regular season, Gonzalez realized his childhood World Series dream with a ... bloop over shortstop.

It happened with one out and the bases loaded in the bottom of the ninth Inning of Game 7 against the Yankees and ace closer Mariano Rivera. The RBI single scored Jay Bell and secured a title for the host Arizona Diamondbacks in their fourth season. "I really muscled up, didn't I?" said Gonzalez, who went 0-for-4 last

night in Arizona's 4-2 victory over the Indians. "The Bambino would have gotten a kick out of that one."

For all the glory those few seconds brought, Gonzalez never even expected to bat. He was convinced the batter before him, Craig Counsell, would deliver with runners on second and third. Counsell had a history of timely postseason hits; Tribe fans know him all too well as one of the Marlins antagonists in the 1997 Series. Before Gonzalez could begin celebrating, however, Rivera plunked Counsell. Your turn, "Gonzo."

"As I walked to the plate, I said, 'Oh, my gosh, this is the scenario I played out millions of times playing in the back yard or playing stickball,' " Gonzalez said. "Every kid who loves the game thinks bases loaded, bottom of the ninth, Game 7. And I guarantee they envision a home run on a big swing. I know I did, every time." Reality, however, called for a choke-and-poke. After fouling off a pitch, Gonzalez picked out a Rivera cutter and drove it high and deep over the head of a drawn-in Derek Jeter. The ball traveled barely more than 100 feet.

As pandemonium erupted in the desert, Gonzalez refused to believe he had ignited it. "I'm a sports fan, and I've watched on TV as Joe Montana made the touchdown passes in Super Bowls and

Michael Jordan made the big shots in the NBA Finals," Gonzalez said. "So I'm running down the line thinking, 'There's no way this happened to me, because I'm supposed to be the one watching on TV as it happens to somebody else.'"

In the ensuing weeks, Gonzalez allowed himself to reflect on Arizona's run. His thoughts had a theme: how truly difficult it is to win the ring. That, in turn, caused him to feel the pain for those who had come so close—among them, Jim Thome, one of his favorite contemporaries. "Thome's a guy everybody in our clubhouse respects immensely, for his professionalism and the fact that he's an all-around great guy," Gonzalez said. "I remember '97, when Cleveland had the one-run lead in the ninth in Game 7, and I can't imagine how those guys felt afterward. I know Thome had those shirts made, about how it doesn't mean a thing if you don't have the ring. You know how badly he wants it. If anybody deserves to win a championship, Thome does."

Gonzalez did not fully grasp the impact of Arizona's feat, and his role in it, until attending Super Bowl XXXVI between the Patriots and Rams in New Orleans. Everywhere he went, it seemed, New England fans saluted him for beating the hated Yankees. "They were shaking my hand as if I were one of the Red Sox," Gonzalez said. The Super Bowl was decided by a field goal from the Patriots' Adam Vinatieri in the final seconds. Gonzalez watched the drama unfold from the stands, surrounded by people who kept looking at him. Some pointed and nodded. "They were saying, 'You know what this feels like,'" Gonzalez said. "I thought that was pretty cool—first, to be recognized; second, to be recognized for coming through in a pressure spot on a big stage."

It would have been easy for Gonzalez to let all the adulation go to his head, breeding complacency. He could have conceded that a redux of 2001—.325 average, 142 RBI, 128 runs in the regular season, 60 total homers—was entirely unrealistic. But that would have been contrary to Gonzalez's makeup. The ultimate professional is producing at a high level again. He is batting .290

with 16 homers, 57 RBI and 46 runs in 79 games. He has played in 406 consecutive games, the longest active streak in the majors. "What we did last year has me hungry," Gonzalez said. "I want to experience that thrill again."

If it comes in the form of another 100-foot single, so be it.

DM: Last year, you hit 57 homers — twenty-six more than your previous career-best. Did you hear the whispers?

LG: Sure. After I hit thirteen homers in the first month, an article accused me of using steroids. Well, look at me: I weigh maybe 200 pounds. If I'm in a photo lineup with the top five home-run hitters and somebody picks me out as the guy using steroids, then that guy's the one who needs to take a drug test.

DM: Have you ever seen someone using steroids or cheating?

LG: No. And even if I had, I wouldn't tell you. There are unwritten rules where that is concerned.

DM: Does it rankle you when former players make allegations about current players using drugs or cheating?

LG: Absolutely, because the innocent players should not be forced to defend themselves. It's unfair for somebody to make a comment, to take a shot, when he doesn't really know what's going on behind closed doors in somebody else's clubhouse.

DM: What's the biggest change in the game now from when you debuted in '90?

LG: Everything's about power — power hitting, power pitching. And the young kids are more spoiled. Guys are signing for $2 million and you don't even know if they can play in the majors.

DM: Favorite bubble gum?

LG: Bazooka.

DM: When did you know the online auction of your gum was out of hand?

LG: When they started talking about DNA testing to prove it was mine.

DM: You've played in both leagues: Yea or nay to the DH?

LG: Later in my career, I will be happy to say I love the DH. But now, I prefer letting the pitchers hit. It speeds the game up, because most of them can't hit.

DM: How do you relax during the season?

LG: *The Jerry Springer Show*, 2 P.M. in Arizona. The guys always get on me.

DM: Favorite creature comfort?

LG: A massage chair. Those rollers are awesome.

DM: Chess or checkers?

LG: Checkers. I'm not smart enough to play chess.

DM: Favorite movie?

LG: *Mr. Baseball*. Don't laugh.

DM: Too late. All those epic baseball movies out there, and you choose *Mr. Baseball*?

LG: No lie. Hey, there was something about Tom Selleck playing in Japan that hooked me. The action, the dialogue....It was filmmaking at its finest.

DM: Most bizarre thing you've ever witnessed on a baseball field?

LG: I'm playing left field for the Astros in Wrigley, it's the seventh-inning stretch, and a guy dumps powder near me. It looked like flour. After the game, the reporters told me that a son was spreading his father's ashes on the field. It freaked me out.

DM: Is it really true your closer, Byung-Hyun Kim, sleeps all day?

LG: Pretty much. Never seen anything like it. Just as long as he's awake in the ninth, we leave him be.

DM: Favorite Randy Johnson story?

LG: Can't be told. Too funny.

DM: Favorite Curt Schilling story?

LG: Likewise. Every day is a story with those two.

DM: Smartest player you've ever been around?

LG: Still looking for him.

DM: Favorite snack food?

LG: Pizza. I'm always eating pizza. Thin crust, pepperoni and green olives.

DM: Favorite health food?

LG: Geez, uh, well.... I don't like health food. I like fried food.

DM: Advice to youngsters playing the game?

LG: Enjoy it and don't be afraid to dream big. At the same time, make sure you have something to fall back on, because the odds of making it up here are long.

DM: What is it like to be the father of triplets [Megan, Jacob, Alyssa]?

LG: We happen to have a three-car garage: My wife's and my cars are parked outside; all their toy cars are parked inside. That about sums it up.

DM: Favorite video games?

LG: Galaga, Centipede and Bass-Up. I love Bass-Up. Throw the line out, reel the fish in. I expect the fish to flop through the TV screen.

Cammi Granato, *hockey*
August 2005

Where women's amateur athletics are concerned, hockey player Cammi Granato's accomplishments rate with the elite.

Granato is a former superstar at Providence College and the only player to have represented the United States in every women's world championships since 1990. When women's ice hockey debuted as a medal sport at the Nagano, Japan, Olympics in 1998, captain Granato's team won gold. She and the U.S. won silver in 2002.

Leading scorer in the history of the women's national team, Granato is recognized worldwide as a face of women's hockey.

It all began as a youngster in Downers Grove, Ill., while growing up with five siblings. Older brothers Tony, Donny and Robby indoctrinated her about hockey. Tony went on to become a solid NHL player.

Granato, a forward, is one of forty invited to try out for the 2006 U.S. women's team, which will compete at the Winter Olympics in Turin, Italy.

DM: As the Mike Eruzione of the women's team, why do you even need to try out?

CG: Thanks for the kind words, but no spot is guaranteed. Never has been. I'm getting older, and I need to keep proving myself. Approaching it any other way would be foolish.

DM: Describe growing up in the Granato household.

CG: Chaos. Awesome. All hockey, all the time. I wouldn't have traded it for anything.

DM: How much of your success is attributable to your older brothers?

CG: A lot of it. They pushed me. I was the tag-along. In order for me to keep up, I was constantly being challenged. And I learned so much from just watching them.

DM: How did the challenge manifest itself?

CG: They would stick me in goal and fire pucks at me all day long. Then they'd tell me I wasn't allowed to inform mom and dad that I was injured. As a result, I'd never leave a game.

DM: Was it all in the name of brotherly love?

CG: They were allowed to beat up on me, but if anyone else touched me, they were first on the scene. I suppose it was the typical big brother/younger sister relationship. They were great about protecting me.

DM: What hockey-related injuries have you suffered?

CG: We wear full-faced masks, so we don't really get hit in the face like the guys do. But I have had a couple of concussions, a broken bone in my leg, torn ligaments in my knee, a couple of small fractures in my back. A bunch of minor stuff. Luckily, no post-concussion symptoms.

DM: Did you ever have NHL aspirations?

CG: My dream growing up was just like my brothers' — to play for the Blackhawks. I wanted so badly to take the ice at Chicago Stadium. Probably the most difficult stage of my life was when my brothers kept growing and I didn't, and I realized the dream was in trouble.

DM: Favorite sports movie?

CG: The TV version of the Miracle on Ice [1981's *Miracle on Ice*] with Karl Malden as Herb Brooks. My brothers and I wore that tape out. It was not particularly well done, but we loved it.

DM: What about the recent big-screen version, *Miracle*, starring Kurt Russell?

CG: Amazing. Kurt did a tremendous job. He was so good at portraying Herb, it was eerie.

DM: Worst hockey movie?

CG: *Youngblood*. Some really ridiculous scenes in there.

DM: Several years ago, you were diagnosed with Attention Deficit Hyperactivity Disorder. How did you take the news?

CG: Honestly, I was happy to finally have an explanation for certain struggles, especially school-related.

DM: How difficult has it been to play with ADHD, regardless of when you were diagnosed?

CG: From the athletic standpoint, it's helped me achieve because I have the energy, the drive, the complete restlessness where I have to be doing something. I can't sit still for very long. That's helped me train at a high-intensity level. I'm very fortunate that hockey is not a game in which you over-think. It's about reaction and quickness. It's perpetual movement.

DM: How does it affect you off the ice?

CG: I'm not good at finishing projects. I'm forgetful. I'm thankful I don't have a desk job, because I'm incredibly disorganized. I've had to learn to cope.

DM: What treatment have you received?

CG: First of all, if you have ADHD, talk to your doctor. Every case is different. Medication works for some but not for others. I use medication for restlessness, and I have mechanisms to help me cope with the other stuff.

DM: I read where one mechanism is your husband, former NHL player Ray "Razor" Ferraro.

CG: He's been invaluable. He's over-the-top organized. I have no problem using his strengths to help my weaknesses.

DM: Favorite hockey player of all time?

CG: Wayne Gretzky.

DM: What? Not your brother Tony?

CG: Well, you know, Tony's special to me. But Gretzky is Gretzky.

DM: So Tony's in the top five?

CG: No doubt. My husband, too. He makes the cut.

Tonya Harding, *figure skating*
June 2006

In 1991, Tonya Harding became the first American woman to land a triple axel in competition. It was the highlight of a productive skating career. But the events of January 6, 1994, overshadowed anything she accomplished on the ice.

During a practice session at the U.S. Figure Skating Championships in Detroit, competitor Nancy Kerrigan was attacked with a retractable metal baton. Harding went on to win the event; Kerrigan withdrew. In the Olympics that year, Kerrigan finished second; Harding eighth.

Authorities determined that the attack was orchestrated by Harding's ex-husband, Jeff Gillooly, and ultimately carried out by Shane Stant, who struck Kerrigan on the knee. Shawn Eckhardt and Derrick Smith also played roles. Harding denied any involvement in the execution of the plot, but did admit to taking part in a cover-up. She pleaded guilty to hindering the investigation and was sentenced to three years probation, 500 hours of community service and a fine.

Gillooly pleaded guilty to racketeering and was sentenced to two years in prison. He reportedly told investigators that Harding was involved in the planning of the attack.

The U.S. Figure Skating Association later stripped Harding of her 1994 national championship and banned her for life from competing in any of its sanctioned events.

Harding has lived a tumultuous existence since, including pleading guilty to disorderly conduct in 2000 for assaulting her boyfriend with a hubcap. She also has boxed professionally and dealt with health concerns related to asthma.

DM: What is your highest high and lowest low?

TH: Highest high: being the first American woman to land the triple axel. Lowest low: Losing my career because of bad judgment.

DM: Bad judgment, meaning what?

TH: Being young and naive. The bad judgment was listening to high-up officials telling me I would be better as a married woman because I'd be stable, that I wouldn't make it on the Olympic team if I weren't with [Gillooly].

DM: You always have maintained you had nothing to do with the attack on Kerrigan.

TH: Absolutely. I had nothing to do with it.

DM: What percentage of the public do you think believes you when you say that?

TH: Maybe 70-75 percent.

DM: Will the other 25-30 percent ever come around?

TH: I don't know and, honestly, I don't care. If you don't want to believe me, fine. I can't worry about trying to change people's opinions.

DM: What are your thoughts on Gillooly?

TH: He's not worth talking about.

DM: You insist the entire mess was his brainchild?

TH: Absolutely. His and his buddies'. But none of them has a brain. I mean, come on. It's probably one of the most stupid things I've seen or heard about except for *Funniest Home Videos*, or whatever you call it. They were complete idiots. How can they think they could ever pull off something like that? I mean, it's ridiculous, just ridiculous.

DM: Your bodyguard, Shane Eckhardt…

TH: He wasn't my bodyguard. He never was my bodyguard. He was just Jeff's friend.

DM: Do you think the motive for Gillooly and his crew was the cash that your Olympic triumph might bring?

TH: Yes. I know it was.

DM: How have you changed as a person since 1994?

TH: I don't let people take advantage of me. I make good decisions. If I have questions, I ask. I still have walls around me from not being able to trust people, but who can blame me?

DM: Do you perceive the memorabilia shows and the meet-and-greets as some sort of rehab for your image?

TH: It does help. I think people change their perception of me after they meet me. They see me for who I am, not just somebody in interviews talking about the past.

DM: Is there anything an interviewer cannot ask?

TH: I don't care what the questions are. I have nothing to hide.

DM: But there must be something that would set you off.

TH: Actually, yes, there is. I'm not going to tell you, though, because then you'll put it in the paper.

DM: When I told a colleague I was going to interview Tonya Harding, he said to make sure I ask her about hubcaps, an obvious reference …

TH: I know what it refers to. First of all, it wasn't a hubcap, it was a darned center cap. You tell him if he wants to criticize me, he needs to get it right. (*Laughs*)

DM: What's the most hurtful thing someone has said to you in public?

TH: I don't know anymore. It's not like I keep track, you know? I try to block out that stuff.

DM: What do you sign the most these days?

TH: Skating pictures.

DM: How many boxing gloves?

TH: I've signed probably fifteen.

DM: Has anyone ever put a hubcap—check that: center cap—in front of you?

TH: No, but people have asked about it. I'm like, Well, if you've got 10 grand, I'll sign... Hey, I'm kidding, OK? I'm kidding.

DM: Have you ever been asked to...

TH: I know where this one is headed, too. The answer is, I've only had two people the whole time—once at a show, once at an exhibition—put a piece of metal pipe in front of me.

DM: Your response?

TH: I said, "I'm really, really sorry, but I don't sign anything like that," and, "You should put it away because if security sees you, you're probably going to be asked to leave."

DM: So you remained calm?

TH: I was very polite about it. I found out later that, in one of the two cases, the person was going to win $100 from a radio station for standing in line and presenting it to me.

DM: Would you give up any fame you achieved if it allowed you to expunge the infamy?

TH: Yes. I'd like to be a normal person.

DM: But if you were "normal," the public would not be fascinated with you—agreed? Certain opportunities likely would not have come your way in the aftermath.

TH: I'm trying to make the best of a tough situation. It's not like I planned this life after competition. Put yourself in my shoes, go through what I've gone through, and believe me—you'll wish you were living a normal life.

DM: Is any more boxing in your future?

TH: I hope so. It all depends on how much better my breathing gets.

DM: If it were concocted, would you ever agree to a boxing match with Kerrigan?

TH: No. I would not disgrace her or the boxing community.

DM: Elaborate, please.

TH: If we were to meet in the ring because it's what we do, that's one thing. But never as some kind of exhibition. Boxing is not a joke to me.

DM: Best punch?

TH: Straight right or left hook.

UPDATE: Tonya Harding's career took various turns once she hung up her competitive skates. She became a boxer and tried singing. Harding, who became a villainess in the public square during the Olympic figure skating fiasco with Nancy Kerrigan in 1994, helped save a woman's life in a bar in suburban Portland in 1996.

Padraig Harrington, *golf*

September 2005

That Padraig Harrington shot an effortless 8-under 64 in his first look at Chardon's demanding Sand Ridge Golf Club did not necessarily amaze me. It was impressive, no doubt, especially because it could have been a 59 if not for four birdie putts and one eagle attempt missed by a combined five inches. But given Harrington's status as one of the world's best, expectations are always high. What truly wowed me about the 64 is that it came with me on the bag. Or, to be precise, guarding the bag.

Representatives of Harrington's club manufacturer, Wilson, had offered *The Plain Dealer* reporter the opportunity to caddie for the affable Irishman during a corporate outing August 15. I bartered two vacation days for the "assignment."

"I've never been a caddie," I warned Harrington in the clubhouse.

"I've never been a journalist," Harrington countered, "so we're even."

As it turned out, experience as a caddie was not required. I learned this immediately, when we climbed into a cart and Harrington drove to the first tee. Upon reaching the green, I asked him what he needed.

"Nothing," he said, politely. "Don't feel bad. The same goes for my real caddie. I only ask for his input if I'm desperate."

Made sense. Even if I had a Ph.D. in green reading, how could I enlighten a terrific professional player who is innately bright and whose strength is his short game?

Harrington did not need my input at the tee box or in the fairway, either. Any questions he might have had about yardage were answered by his beloved Bushnell PinSeeker 1500 range finder. "Can you believe the R&A is going to make these legal?" he said.

For the remainder of the round, I had a front-row seat basically to watch a master at his craft make matters look ridiculously easy. (He never got remotely close to a bogey.) Once in a while, I cleaned a club or fished a fruit from the cooler for him, but that was for show, and both of us knew it. My biggest contribution? Quickly finding a ball marker he dropped in the rough off the eighth green.

With Harrington's blessing, my job evolved into quietly absorbing as much information as possible, particularly when he talked shop with his tour caddie, Ronan Flood, and Wilson's director of tour promotions, Ron Graham. My head still spins from the knowledge imparted in the discussions between Harrington and Graham. I now have an acute sense of the completely different plane on which the accomplished professional operates.

After Harrington sank a right-to-left fifteen-footer for birdie at the last—I had misread the six-inch break by five inches—he thanked me.

"I'm not exactly sure for what," I said, "but you're welcome."

DM: What do you want/expect from your caddie?

PH: Getting the yardage, having all the clubs in the bag—those types of things are givens. On top of that, I look for somebody who knows when to talk and not to talk; will voice his opinion—right or wrong—and not just be a "yes" man; and has enthusiasm for the job and is enjoyable to be around. I want my caddie to want it as much as I do.

DM: Why do you putt cross-handed?

PH: I was struggling with left-to-right putts at European Tour School [mid-1990s], and it felt comfortable right away. The first year, I used it for left-to-right putts. Then I changed over completely because I didn't have enough time to practice both ways.

DM: You were a member of the European Team that upset the

United States on American soil at the Ryder Cup last September. How did your team do it?

PH: We raised our games, we really did. We had something to prove.

DM: Did the European players view the Americans as the enemy for one week?

PH: It wasn't like that at all. We have a tour [European Tour] that relies on us to get out there and win the Ryder Cup. If we don't win, we lose face and we're viewed as a secondary tour. There's more on the line for us.

DM: You and Colin Montgomery won the signature match, in Friday fourball, against heavyweights Tiger Woods and Phil Mickelson. Were you surprised U.S. captain Hal Sutton paired those two?

PH: No, but we didn't expect he would tell everybody he was doing it. We knew two days before the match, so we had time to sit down and go over what we wanted to do. If [Sutton] wanted to create some atmosphere, he could have kept it a secret until the pairings had to be announced.

DM: How did you and Monty get paired to play them?

PH: We asked for that match because we knew we would play our game and wouldn't be intimidated. In the public's eyes, Monty and I were decided underdogs, and the outcome was a foregone conclusion. But the reality was, because it's golf, we were only underdogs by a marginal bit. If we played well, we had a good chance to win.

DM: If you had to pick one with whom to play a round—Woods or Mickelson?

PH: Nothing against Phil, but I'd want it to be Tiger. I've played well when I'm paired with Tiger because he's an easy guy to play golf with, as good a guy as you could pick. He never, ever, gets in your way, he compliments you on a good shot, he shares a laugh and converses when appropriate. A perfect gentleman on the course.

DM: Are your clubs custom-made?

PH: No, they're off the rack. The shaft stiffness is a little different, and I twist the grips, but they're available to anyone. I get to help change a few things in the design, but that's usually cosmetic. I don't tell the shop what to do. I just tell them what I would like to see when I look down at the club and when the ball takes off. What makes Wilson so great is, the people there listen.

DM: You won the Barclays Classic this season with a spectacular eagle putt on the 72nd hole.

PH: It was 65 feet, 7 inches. The objective was just to get it close, obviously. I started it fifteen feet left of the flag, and it eventually broke eighteen inches back right. It was an unbelievably difficult putt. All things considered, it's the most exciting putt I've ever made.

DM: Condolences on the recent passing of your father, Patrick. How did he contribute to your development as a top-flight golfer?

PH: My father was a very successful sportsman, an accomplished footballer in Ireland, so he never tried to live his life through me. He taught me a lot about the game of golf, but it wasn't about technique as much as the mental side.

DM: You never seem to get angry. If that a reflection on your father?

PH: He was a very calm person. He was competitive, but never let his emotions get out of hand, and he installed that in his children. There's no point in behaving like a spoiled child. When I play with or against somebody who acts that way, I don't get mad. I actually find it funny. All they're doing is defeating themselves.

DM: Dream foursome: You and three legends.

PH: Ben Hogan, Bobby Jones, Jack Nicklaus.

DM: Dream foursome: You and three historical figures whom you would teach to play if needed.

PH: Cleopatra, Napoleon, Caesar. I want people who are going to be interesting.

DM: Worst rule in the rules of golf?

PH: During a tournament, if you were found to have made an honest mistake, such as inadvertently recording the wrong score because of an error, they should retrospectively penalize instead of retrospectively disqualify.

DM: Best course you've ever played?

PH: Royal Portrush in Northern Ireland. Tough, but you can score.

UPDATE: Padraig Harrington continues to play on the European Tour and the PGA Tour. He has won three major championships: The Open Championship (2007–2008) and PGA Championship (2008). In March 2015, Harrington won the Honda Classic—his first victory on the European or PGA Tour in seven years.

Franco Harris, *football*
October 2007

Franco Harris is one of the NFL's all-time great running backs. A first-round pick of the Steelers in 1972, Harris rushed for 12,120 yards and 91 touchdowns in 173 games. He also caught nine TD passes. Harris was an integral part of a Steelers dynasty that went 4-0 in Super Bowls. He achieved legendary status by making the "Immaculate Reception" to beat the Oakland Raiders in a 1972 AFC playoff game at Pittsburgh.

Harris, inducted into the Hall of Fame in 1990, stopped by *The Plain Dealer* last month to talk football—and donuts. Harris presides over Super Bakery, Inc., in Pittsburgh. He is working to get his "Super Donut" in stores nationwide.

DM: Talk about the Super Donut.

FH: We want to offer a healthier choice. We're still a donut—we still want the texture and flavor of a donut—but with some benefits.

DM: The Super Donut boasts of "MVP" nutrition. What is that?

FH: We added fourteen minerals, vitamins and proteins. We have no artificial colors, flavors or preservatives. The goal is the highest quality possible.

DM: Now on to football ....

FH: I haven't talked about the MVP program yet.

DM: OK.

FH: In each of the cities where the donuts are sold we feature a player on the box. Cleveland's is Andra Davis. We honor these players for what they do off the field to improve, change and make a difference in the community. We call it the Most Valuable Person. A card in the box shows their community work.

DM: Is it strange to come into Cleveland to promote your product?

FH: I tell people that, after Pittsburgh, I root for Cleveland teams. I'm not kidding. I don't say that in every city I go to. I like Cleveland and admire the passion of its fans. And I will say, it's amazing how many Pittsburgh fans live in Cleveland.

DM: Best player you ever played with?

FH: The best Steeler of all-time, no doubt in my mind, is Joe Greene. What he meant to that team is just incredible. He was the heart and soul. He set the standard, the attitude, and he hated to lose.

DM: Toughest team you ever played against?

FH: The Houston Oilers in the Bum Phillips years.

DM: The Steelers typically had their way with the Browns when you played. Did it take away any of the sizzle from the rivalry?

FH: No. We had physical battles with Cleveland. There is no love lost between the Steelers and Browns, regardless of who has the upper hand. When I broke in, I kept hearing about the Browns, how we had to beat the Browns. I quickly found out what everybody was talking about. Those games had a special feel to them.

DM: What were your goals as a player?

FH: The only thing I really focused on was getting to the Super Bowl. I didn't worry about individual stats.

DM: You never seemed to get the publicity you deserved for being a great player ....

FH: I never thought I was underrated at all. I got plenty of attention; sometimes, I thought I got too much. As I said, football is a team game.

DM: Fondest memory of the Immaculate Reception game?

FH: It would be that 1972 was the year everything changed for the

Pittsburgh Steelers. You had the Steelers before 1972 and after 1972. Fans look at the immaculate reception as a symbol of the start of something for the Steelers that continues to this day. I keep shaking my head at how big that play is. Here were are, thirty-five years later, and people continue to talk about it.

DM: Do you have a favorite Super Bowl title?

FH: The first one's always the favorite.

DM: Word association—Chuck Noll.

FH: Great leader, respected players. Gave players their own responsibility, yet he was in command.

DM: Rocky Bleier.

FH: Achieved so much more than people thought he would. He gave everything he had.

DM: Jack Lambert.

FH: Tough, mean, winner, leader.

DM: Jack Ham.

FH: One of the best. Always strategized to make sure he wasn't out-played.

DM: Mike Webster.

FH: Obsessed with football. Great player and wonderful person. I loved being around Mike.

DM: Do you own any memorabilia? If so, your favorites?

FH: I have two favorites: the football from my first pro touchdown and the piece of carpet from where I made the immaculate reception.

DM: How did you come upon the piece of carpet?

FH: They were tearing up the field, shredding the turf and tossing it. They were on lunch break one day and I went up to a guy and said, "Will you cut this part for me?" He said, "No problem." I don't know why it hit me, because we weren't big collectors of memorabilia back then.

DM: Toughest part of playing NFL football?

FH: Good question. Maybe I blocked it all out. It's a wonderful life, you're playing your passion, so I don't know .... Other than injuries, it's probably the training to get ready to play, the hours you put in that people don't see.

DM: On the field, of which Browns player were you most aware?

FH: I never concerned myself with an individual on the other side of the ball. And I didn't look at a player after he tackled me, because I didn't want anything like that in my head.

DM: But if you could have picked a Brown to watch as a fan, who would it be?

FH: The Pruitts. They made things happen that were pretty awesome.

DM: If you were commissioner for a day, what is one thing you would do?

FH: (*Laughs*) Give retired players more money.

Rickey Henderson, *baseball*

September 2002

Rickey Henderson has played in more than 3,000 major-league games and amassed more than 3,000 hits. He has appeared in 54 postseason games and owns two World Series rings.

He is the all-time leader in walks, stolen bases and runs.

Yet, Henderson's incredible career has been overshadowed by his image, that of a cocky, me-first player who always makes sure to look good in the mirror.

He is a reserve outfielder on the Boston Red Sox.

DM: How much longer will you go?

RH: I really have no timetable. The good Lord has blessed me with the health. I'm not going to give it up if I can still perform, compete and enjoy the game.

DM: What is left to do?

RH: Nothing I can think of.

DM: Any regrets?

RH: The only thing I wish I could figure out is how I got misunderstood regarding the type of person I really am and what I accomplished.

DM: You think people don't appreciate the scope of your performance?

RH: I don't think—I know. Each and every day I set a record, but we never talk about it. We'll talk about a home-run hitter 24/7. Well, they haven't broken any all-time records, but they hit homers, and that's what matters nowadays. You continue playing, you accomplish a lot, and you'd think people would look at it as a fantastic career. Instead, I think people want me to quit more than anything. (*Chuckle*)

DM: At least you find some humor.

RH: It is what it is. I'm not going to lose sleep over it, but at the same time, I'm human. It bothers me to some degree, sure.

DM: How did the misunderstanding become so pronounced?

RH: I don't know.

DM: Will history be kinder to you than the present?

RH: Oh, yeah. It's got to be. If you talk about baseball, you can't eliminate me, because I'm all over baseball.

DM: You don't sound cocky making the statement, but you know it will sound that way in print.

RH: Telling the truth isn't being cocky. What do you want me to say, that I didn't put up the numbers? That my teams didn't win a lot of games? ... People don't want to talk about me because of that thing I said back then.

DM: OK, take us back to when you said that you were the "greatest [base-stealer] of all time." It came moments after breaking Lou Brock's career record in 1991.

RH: Muhammad Ali was my idol. So I said, if I ever break the record, I just want to say, "I'm the greatest," out of respect for Muhammad Ali.... Lou Brock had no problem with it. In fact, he helped me write what I was going to say that day. He stayed with me for a week leading up to the record, and we went over everything.... The "greatest" line was at the end of my remarks. I talked about Lou, too, but that's all anybody remembers.... Those words haunt me to this day. They overshadow what I've accomplished in this game.

DM: Do you regret making that statement?

RH: No. I wouldn't take it back, because I know why I said it.

DM: Your critics use the infamous third-person references as proof of arrogance. Rickey's response?

RH: (*Laughs*) Good one, man, good one. Listen: People are always saying, "Rickey says Rickey." But it's been blown way out of proportion. People might catch me, when they know I'm ticked off, saying, "Rickey, what the heck are you doing, Rickey?" They say, "Darn, Rickey, what are you saying Rickey for?" Why don't you just say, "I?" But I never did. I always said, "Rickey," and it become something for people to joke about.

DM: Jimmy Rollins of the Phillies said you are his favorite player because you packaged the skills with the entertainment. Was that a conscious decision?

RH: Yes. People pay to see you play. If you're not entertaining to them, why should they watch?

DM: Hobbies?

RH: Fishing, working on the ranch.

DM: Rickey Henderson has a ranch?

RH: Close to Yosemite Park in California. Believe it or not, I'm a ranch-type guy. I like to get out and do the regular work, getting dirty with the dust and everything.... Cows, horses, pigs.

DM: Word association—Eric Plunk?

RH: Traded for me, twice. Took him deep twice, too.

DM: Toughest pitcher you ever faced?

RH: Goose Gossage. I think I faced him eight times, and he probably struck me out eight times. I told him, "When we meet in an old-timers' game, I'm going to get a hit off you, stop the game and retrieve the ball."

DM: Favorite player of all-time?

RH: Willie Mays, Reggie Jackson.

DM: How do you deal with heckling?

RH: I try to make it a positive—at least they're acknowledging you. They know who you are. I try to get them to laugh.

DM: Which stat do you most treasure?

RH: Scoring the most runs in major-league history. You have to score to win.

DM: Is cheating a problem in baseball?

RH: Everyday, somebody's doing something to try to get the advantage. But as long as it's not illegal, like steroids, it's not really a problem, just part of the game.

DM: What about former players making allegations of rampant steroid use throughout baseball?

RH: It ticks me off, because the innocent ones, the guys who do it the right way, are forced to defend themselves.

DM: How have you stayed chiseled over such a long career?

RH: It's all natural: push-ups, sit- ups, push-ups, sit-ups—and a lot of running. I barely lift weights.

DM: How do you want people to remember you?

RH: That I played hard, played to win and respected the game. I accomplished things that most players dream of doing. In order to do that, I had to play hard.

DM: Will we ever see 100 steals in a season again?

RH: It's a big business now, more than the love of the game. You're not trying to achieve what the greats did, you're thinking about how much money you can make. You're not going to make it stealing bases.

DM: If you played every day next year, how many bases could you steal?

RH: If the manager lets me go? Seventy-five to 100.

DM: You know you'll turn forty-four in December?

RH: All the better. Seventy-five to 100 bags, at forty-four. Sounds cocky, doesn't it? But I know I could do it.

UPDATE: Rickey played for nine MLB teams from 1979 to 2003. He amassed 3,055 hits, 2,295 runs and 1,406 steals. He was elected to the National Baseball Hall of Fame in 2009, his first year on the ballot (94.8%).

Torii Hunter, *baseball*

July 2002

Minnesota Twins center fielder Torii Hunter no longer is under wraps.

The national baseball community has discovered this year what American League Central Division fans have known for a while: Hunter, 27, is a special player. No snapshot captured it better than his spectacular catch to rob Barry Bonds of a home run in the All-Star Game.

"We're watching a future MVP blossom before our eyes," Twins teammate Doug Mientkiewicz said.

Hunter, batting .310 with 23 homers and 67 RBI and with countless great catches for the division-leading Twins, was fined and given a three-game suspension Friday for throwing a ball at Cleveland's Danys Baez.

DM: Welcome to stardom.

TH: I still don't see where I'm a star. If you want to make me one, that's cool. But I don't get caught up in that stuff.

DM: Were even you amazed by the catch in the All-Star Game?

TH: I was surprised how high I got. The adrenaline's flowing, and sometimes you don't realize what you can do. When I looked at the tape later, I was like, "Whoa. I can't believe I jumped like that." I felt like Michael Jordan for a second.

DM: Any congratulatory calls from Jordan?

TH: I wish. But I did get a care package from Joe Dumars, president of the Pistons. It had all kinds of good stuff.

DM: What is your first tiebreaker solution for when both managers run out of pitchers in the All-Star Game?

TH: (*Laughs*) You've got me there. I guess it would be each side picks one guy to take five swings. Most homers wins.

DM: How has life changed since the All-Star Game?

TH: I used to walk through the Mall of America and only the hard-core baseball fans noticed. Now they're calling out, "That's Torii Hunter!" It's neat.

DM: Favorite player on the Indians?

TH: Jim Thome. Thome's a soldier. He's a great player and great guy. He's always down-to-earth and humble, and I try to act that way.

DM: Favorite musician?

TH: Tupac Shakur. He rapped the truth. He's dead, but he's still my guy.

DM: What batter-pitcher matchup would you pay to see, mixing and matching all eras?

TH: Satchel Paige—the old, old, Satch—against Babe Ruth.

DM: Favorite reading material?

TH: The Bible.

DM: Professional goals?

TH: I want to be the best defensive center fielder to ever play. I won't forget where I came from, and that's defense. Hitting is a bonus, and right now, I'm raw at the plate.

DM: Is cheating a problem in baseball?

TH: Oh, yeah, definitely. It's right there, definitely. Wait—what kind of cheating?

DM: Scuffed baseballs, corked bats, steroids ...

TH: Oh ... I thought you were talking about girls. There's cheating within the game, sure, but it's not a problem because cheating's been going on since the Babe Ruth days.

DM: Do you resent it when former players talk of rampant steroid use in clubhouses?

TH: No, because I've got nothing to hide. The only way to really find out is to test. If you want to drug test, fine. But we don't have that in the agreement right now.

DM: Hobbies/interests outside of the game?

TH: Bowling and going to the movies.

DM: Bowling? A big-time athlete likes bowling?

TH: Yeah.

DM: What's your high game?

TH: Two-thirty-two. I'm happy with it, but I know I can do better.

DM: If you could be an athlete in any sport, who would you be?

TH: Free safety with the Dallas Cowboys, trying to knock somebody's head off.

Zydrunas Ilgauskas, *basketball*

The left foot of Cavaliers center Zydrunas Ilgauskas is a contraption of bones, muscles, ligaments and tendons more RoboCop or Steve Austin than standard issue homo sapiens.

"When you look at the foot, you definitely notice a difference," he says.

His left foot has seven screws holding it together, the necessary evil of a radical, reconstructive surgery in February 2001. When Ilgauskas speaks of a difference, his frame of reference is different than most: The left foot has the right foot beat by four screws, each foot having suffered multiple breaks over a six-year period, 1995 to 2000.

Anybody with ten screws to the pair necessitates maintenance beyond a few massages. Multiply exponentially for a 7-3 person playing NBA basketball, daily, for months.

Ilgauskas, while admitting that "ice is my best friend," downplays the extent of the treatment before and after games and practices, and the rehab-oriented work on off-days. It is no big deal, he says.

Don't buy it. The walls of the training and weight rooms inside The Q know differently. They recognize the affable Lithuanian's pain tolerance as off the charts.

Cavaliers trainer Max Benton and other members of the club's support staff have the unenviable task of making the pain go away, or at least mitigating the discomfort enough to enable Ilgauskas to take the court unencumbered.

Benton acknowledges Ilgauskas' feet require extra care, all the way down to the orthotics in his size seventeen Nike Air Force Operates. Then Benton leaves the rest to the imagination. On the matter of Ilgauskas behind the scenes, he plays the role of Colonel Sanders.

"We decided as a group not to disclose what we do, to keep it private," Benton says, politely. "I will tell you this, though: Z's work ethic is second to none."

Understand, too, that the Ilgauskas project begins, but by no means ends, with the feet. Strength and conditioning coach Stan Kellers oversees a rigorous stretching program, the primary focus being Ilgauskas' lower-lumbar region. It is part of a series of checks and balances covering eighty-seven inches and 260 pounds.

For this season, in particular, special attention also has been paid to his left knee sprained December 10; head concussed December 7; and his right finger dislocated February 2.

Whatever the support staff has concocted, it should be patented. Ilgauskas, 30, is in the midst of arguably the most proficient, comprehensive season of his NBA career. In forty-seven of a possible forty-eight games through Thursday, he is averaging 16.1 points, 7.4 rebounds and 1.8 blocks in 29.7 minutes. He is shooting

.514 from the field and .866 from the line.

Based on points per minute and points per field-goal attempt, Ilgauskas stands with the most efficient scorers in the league.

His free-throw accuracy is a story in itself. Ilgauskas entered this season with a .766 career success rate—good, especially for a center, but far from automatic. Now he ranks first in the league at his position and top twenty overall. The accuracy is magnified by his ability to draw fouls and get to the line in the first place.

Ilgauskas credits side sessions with former assistant coach Ron Ekker several years ago. Ekker tweaked his setup, grip and release. Ilgauskas began to implement the changes in earnest last season, when he made 79.9 percent.

Ilgauskas has become so dependable at the line, it is no secret whom coach Mike Brown wants with the ball when free throws absolutely need to be made.

The latest example came Wednesday in Minnesota. With the Cavaliers ahead, 93-91, and eight seconds left, they prepared to inbound at halfcourt. Fox Sports Net Ohio analyst Scott Williams predicted the play the Cavaliers would run to free Ilgauskas; it happened. After a Trenton Hassell foul, Ilgauskas calmly sank both free throws to help secure a 97-91 victory.

Defensively, Ilgauskas appears increasingly dialed into Brown's system, which calls for him to stay home and disrupt dribble penetration, block or alter shots and be ready to help. Ilgauskas never will be confused with a lockdown defender, but Brown's emphasis on patrolling the low block caters to his strengths (size, length) and minimizes the exploitation of his weaknesses (quickness, agility).

"I like not having to chase the little guys outside the three-point line," Ilgauskas said.

"I can't say enough about what "Z" has done, at both ends of the floor," says Brown, a first-year head coach. "I think there was a month when he led the team in charges and blocks. If someone were to tell you that your 7-3 guy would lead the team in blocks and charges, you'd pass out from disbelief."

It is not as if Ilgauskas got good overnight. He is a two-time All-Star (2003, 2005) and entered this season with career averages of 14.8 points and 7.7 rebounds in 413 games. He played superbly in the second half last season. But he has not had all phases dovetail quite so nicely as in this season. That he is an integral part of a playoff-caliber team with LeBron James at the controls adds significance.

"Z's having an All-Star season," James said.

Nonetheless, Ilgauskas will not be an All-Star for a third time, unless he replaces someone injured. He did not make the list of All-Star reserves announced Thursday.

"We're second in our division in wins and we have the third-best record in the Eastern Conference," said James, an All-Star starter for the second year in a row. "He should have been voted in."

No matter Ilgauskas' level of effectiveness, it might never be enough to satisfy the critics, who have made him a primary target over the years. Radio talk shows, readers' letters/emails and chat rooms pertaining to the Cavaliers make sport of picking apart Ilgauskas as any combination of immobile, slow, not agile enough, foul-prone, slow, predictable on offense, unable to pass out of the double-team and slow. Whenever the Cavaliers falter, the criticism intensifies.

Z's response? Guilty—to a degree.

"Look, I realize I'm not a complete player," he says. "I make mistakes. I have faults. I'm trying to improve stuff to become the best player I can possibly be. But I don't know too many guys in the league who do everything well. Perfect players are hard to find. It's not easy to come in every night and do what LeBron James does.

"People are entitled to their opinion, but no matter what they say, I know I play hard every night, and I bring more good to the table than bad. The criticism that matters to me is from my teammates and my coaches."

Ilgauskas grants that his injury-plagued pro career, which

lists 111 games played in his first five seasons, places him in the crosshairs. So do the Cavaliers' overall struggles since his arrival, and his eight-figure income during some of the down time.

"When you're injured and making a lot of money, you're an easy target," he says.

Cavaliers General Manager Danny Ferry, a friend and former teammate of Ilgauskas, shakes his head when he reads or hears of the nitpicking.

"I think, on the whole, he's very underappreciated here in Cleveland," Ferry says. "Ask around the NBA who the best centers are, and Z's name comes up regularly."

One on the outside who endorses Ilgauskas is Hall of Famer and television analyst Bill Walton. During a recent visit to The Q, he said, "I am so happy for him. He is one of the great stories in the NBA. I think he is playing as well as he's ever played. What he's doing is really inspirational. In fact, I think the NBA is missing out on one of its great stories."

From Walton's perspective, the most compelling aspect of the Ilgauskas tale is found in the agony of his feet. Walton, a center who played from 1974 to 1986, missed 516 of 984 games because of foot, ankle and leg injuries.

"I am the most injured player in the history of professional basketball," he said. "I had thirty-two foot and leg operations. I can appreciate what Zydrunas has gone through."

The tribulations of Ilgauskas almost sidelined him permanently at age twenty-five. He removed himself from a game at Miami on December 22, 2000, after experiencing sharp pain in his left foot. It turned out to be a fractured navicular bone, ending his season at twenty-four games. A similar injury decimated his previous two seasons: He played five games in 1998–99, none the next. The organization had signed him to a six-year, $71 million extension before the 1999–2000 season.

Ilgauskas was at a loss. The previous surgery, in January 2000, obviously had failed. What now?

"I'd reached a breaking point," he says. "Injuries and rehab take a toll, not only physically but mentally. It also takes a toll on the family and the people close to you. You're miserable mostly. It breaks you down after a while.

"I either needed to do something drastic with the foot ... or put my career to sleep."

Ilgauskas traversed the country seeking advice from specialists. He felt a kinship with Dr. Mark Myerson in Baltimore. Myerson had operated on Grant Hill's ankle and later put back together receiver Terrell Owens' ankle in advance of Super Bowl XXXIX.

Myerson made no promises to Ilgauskas when discussing a reconstruction of the left foot unlike anything his patient ever could have envisioned. Myerson warned him there always was the possibility that it could end badly, that he could be plagued with a limp and never play again. However, Myerson told Ilgauskas, if it went well there was no reason he could not return to the court at full capacity – and stay on it for years.

"If I hadn't given it one more shot, I would have regretted it for the rest of my life," Ilgauskas says.

Surgery took place February 7, 2001. It turned out to be the easy part.

"This rehab was especially tough," he says. "A lot of pain. I needed to get used to my foot being a different shape. Once I got back, it felt good."

Ilgauskas missed the first seventeen games of the 2001–2002 season while still in recovery mode. He has not missed a game because of the left foot since. The right foot has held up for 10 years.

Even though his birth certificate states he will turn thirty-one on June 5, Ilgauskas feels like a twentysomething in basketball years.

"My basketball skills were pretty much frozen for 3–4 years, from twenty-one to twenty-five, so my game is still developing," he says. "I'm getting a better feel each year. I've got a lot left."

Derek Jeter, *baseball*

July 2002

Derek Jeter is the ballplayer most would love to be:
Shortstop of the New York Yankees.

Owner of major-league-record 93 postseason hits, with five World Series appearances and four rings.

Matinee-idol looks, ultracool disposition, rich beyond measure. Turned 28 last month.

Jeter, who has more than 1,300 hits in less than seven full seasons, is part of a trio of American League shortstops with outstanding all-around games. But Alex Rodriguez of the Rangers and Nomar Garciaparra of the Red Sox, as good as they are, never have played in the World Series, let alone won one.

DM: Toughest part about being Derek Jeter?

DJ: I have no complaints.

DM: Toughest part of playing in New York?

DJ: Traffic.

DM: Strangest autograph request?

DJ: Someone's forehead.

DM: Is there a player you can't stand?

DJ: (*Laughs*) Yeah, but I'm not going to tell you who, of course.

DM: Key to producing in the clutch?

DJ: Not being afraid to fail.

DM: Highlight of amateur career?

DJ: Getting drafted [sixth overall, June 1992].

DM: Favorite TV show?

DJ: *SportsCenter*.

DM: What batter-pitcher would you pay to see, mixing and matching eras?

DJ: Ted Williams against Mariano Rivera.

DM: Hobbies/other interests?

DJ: Movies. I'm a big movie person.

DM: What do you do to relax?

DJ: Sleep, hang out, go to movies.

DM: Favorite baseball movie?

DJ: *61*, *Major League*.

DM: Do you have a mini-theater in your home?

DJ: No, I just watch them in my living room.

DM: Word association—Alex Rodriguez?

DJ: Complete.

DM: Nomar Garciaparra?

DJ: Red Sox.

DM: Omar Vizquel?

DJ: Defense.

DM: Jim Thome?

DJ: Strong.

DM: Favorite music/musician?

DJ: I like hip-hop, r&b. I like Jay-Z.

DM: Toughest pitcher you've faced?

DJ: Derek Lowe, Boston.

DM: If you could excel in another sport, which would it be?

DJ: Basketball.

DM: What position?

DJ: Two-guard. I'd like to score some points.

DM: Chess or checkers?

DJ: Checkers.

DM: Favorite board game?

DJ: Connect Four. I know it's technically not a board game, but I love it.

DM: Favorite food?

DJ: Chicken parmesan.

DM: Favorite junk food?

DJ: Chocolate-chip cookies.

DM: Person you most admire outside the game?

DJ: My parents.

DM: Ballplayer you most admired growing up?

DJ: Dave Winfield.

DM: Favorite vacation spot?

DJ: Puerto Rico.

DM: Most underrated player in the game?

DJ: Jose Vidro, Montreal.

DM: Favorite TV show?

DJ: You asked me that already. It's still *SportsCenter*.

DM: Is cheating a problem in baseball?

DJ: No.

DM: What would you like to do when your playing days are over?

DJ: Maybe be an owner.

DM: What motivates you?

DJ: A fifth ring.

DM: Do you feel for standout veteran players who haven't won a ring?

DJ: No, because I'm trying to win them.

DM: Which season would you take — .400 average but no World Series, or a fifth ring?

DJ: The ring.

DM: Really? You wouldn't want four titles and a .400 season by, say, age twenty-eight?

DJ: No. I play to win, that's it.

UPDATE: Derek Jeter played all twenty of his MLB seasons with the New York Yankees (1995–2004). He is a five-time World Series champion and is the Yankees' all-time career leader in hits (3,465), doubles (544), games played (2,747), stolen bases (358), times on base (4,716), plate appearances (12,602) and at bats (11,195). Before his season-long retirement tour in 2014, he achieved fourteen All-Star selections, five Gold Glove Awards, five Silver Slugger Awards, two Hank Aaron Awards, and a Roberto Clemente Award. He became the twenty-eighth player to reach 3,000 hits and finished his career sixth all-time in hits and first all-time in hits by a shortstop.

Chad Johnson, *football*

September 2006

The Bengals' Chad Johnson is a great receiver—just ask him.

But to dismiss Johnson as one more arrogant athlete in a culture of self-absorption would do No. 85 an injustice. Unlike the receiver who currently plays in Dallas and goes by T. O., Johnson is not about stirring the drink.

He is about having fun. Lots of it.

Unlike T.O., Johnson gets along with his teammates, and they get along with him. His teammates evidently love to watch him play, they love to watch him celebrate, and they (almost always) love to hear him talk.

Johnson has no problem talking, especially when he is driving around the Cincinnati area on an errand after practice and the person in the passenger's seat has a long list of questions.

DM: Why is the NFL so hell-bent on cracking down on end-zone celebrations?

CJ: I don't think it's as much ending the celebrations as it is trying to stop the taunting, the stuff that gives the NFL a bad name. When it's not done in a fun-loving way, that's when the problem comes in.

DM: But why would they throttle the guys enjoying themselves?

CJ: They can't say, "OK, this person can celebrate but this person can't." So everybody has to suffer for it. It doesn't bother me because I'm still going to do things this year, anyway. I have ways around it, regardless of what rules they make. That's the way it is going to be.

DM: Do the NFL bosses fail to grasp the entertainment aspect of pro football?

CJ: They understand. They know. They know it's a big reason half the people watch the game. People want to see touchdowns, and they want to see celebrations.

DM: Are you upset with yourself that you didn't think of the Sharpie in the sock before Terrell Owens?

CJ: Upset? Why would I be upset?

DM: Well …

CJ: I'm not upset. That's not my personality. That's his personality.

DM: Was the Sharpie fun-loving or taunting?

CJ: He wasn't taunting. He was just having fun. It was exciting. Whoever was fortunate enough to get that ball will remember that moment for a long time. It had nothing to do with the person covering T. O.

DM: How well do you know T. O.?

CJ: Very well.

DM: Is he misunderstood?

CJ: Yeah. It seems like they're always out to get him.

DM: He brings a lot on himself, though.

CJ: You said that, not me. To understand T. O., the player, you have to understand T. O., the person, understand where he came from, what he went through to get where he is.

DM: Was T. O. justified in demanding to renegotiate with the Eagles in 2005?

CJ: It's not my place to answer that, because it's his business. He had his reasons.

DM: Two years into your new deal, you have put up huge numbers. Would you want to renegotiate?

CJ: If I'm playing at a high level like I have been, then the deal is renegotiable, yeah. (*Pause*) You don't think so? Isn't that the way it works?

DM: I suppose.

CJ: I mean, when things aren't going well, they don't have a problem cutting you, do they? They don't have a problem making you take a pay cut in this league when you're not playing at the right level, so why, when you're playing at a high level, can't you ask for more?

DM: Because a deal is a deal?

CJ: I want to get paid what I'm worth, just like you want to get paid what you're worth. It shouldn't matter when that is.

DM: Can T. O. and Bill Parcells co-exist?

CJ: Sure. Bill's straight-up-front with you; T. O. will go out and perform. No reason to butt heads.

DM: Is it difficult as a receiver knowing that, no matter how good you are, you depend on the QB? The numbers might not be there even if you're getting open all the time.

CJ: The numbers will always be there.

DM: But what if the QB's not good?

CJ: If you're a good receiver, regardless of who's throwing the ball, the numbers will be there.

DM: Are you ever concerned that Chad Johnson, entertainer, will overshadow Chad Johnson, receiver?

CJ: In order to entertain, you have to put up the numbers. That's how it works. That's common sense. I'm not entertaining anybody if I'm dropping passes and not getting into the end zone.

DM: I read where you worked extra-hard in the offseason, even harder than normal, coming off a terrific year. Why?

CJ: I want to be great, plain and simple. Instead of being grouped with a bunch of good or really good receivers, I want to be known as the one who raised the bar, like Jerry Rice did. Jerry

Rice set the standard.

DM: Would you think about competing, as Rice did, in *Dancing With the Stars* after retirement?

CJ: I guess.

DM: Would you win?

CJ: You have seen me in the end zone, haven't you? With the right partner, of course I'd win.

DM: If you could be a top athlete in another sport, which would it be?

CJ: Soccer, soccer, soccer.

DM: Soccer? You're kidding. You don't look like a soccer fanatic.

CJ: Yes, soccer. In all sincerity. Soccer's my first love, then football. Because I'm flashy and flamboyant, I would have to play for Brazil.

DM: And you'd have to be a goal scorer?

CJ: Of course.

DM: Word association — your quarterback, Chad Palmer?

CJ: Best there is right cnow.

DM: Your agent, Drew Rosenhaus?

CJ: The Shark. Best agent out there.

DM: New NFL Commissioner Roger Goodell?

CJ: (*Chuckle*) I'm looking forward to meeting him. I'm going to send him a nice message.

DM: What will the message be?

CJ: I can't tell you. Stay tuned. All I'll say is, I'm sure he'll enjoy it. Gotta bring him in the right way.

DM: Greatest CB of all-time?

CJ: Deion [Sanders].

DM: What happens in one game, you vs. Deion, both in your prime?

CJ: He'd lose. And he knows it.

DM: How many balls would you catch?

CJ: How many balls would be thrown to me?

DM: How would you manage to beat Prime Time so soundly?

CJ: The key is, knowing what he's great at and what he's not great at. In any great player, there's always a weakness—I don't care what anybody says. I could attack that weakness because I've studied the heck out of him. I know what will work and what won't.

DM: What is your weakness?

CJ: You think I'm going to tell you? Come on.

DM: But I figured you would say Chad Johnson does not have a weakness.

CJ: Nobody's perfect. 85's not perfect.

DM: How much smack between you and Deion?

CJ: Oh, my goodness. The game wouldn't last long enough. And the smack between me and D. Hall [Falcons corner DeAngelo Hall] …

DM: What about it?

CJ: That smack is going to be better than Ali-Frazier. The matchup is going to be so good, they're going to need to change it to pay-per-view.

DM: You are a funny guy in person. And your smack, when you run it, is funny. But when you're on the field, you're not joking when you run the smack, are you?

CJ: No joke. I'm dead serious. You can look at me and laugh and think it's a joke, but when we touch the field …. You know what's funny? You really aren't going to stop me.

DM: OK.

CJ: No, I don't think you understand fully. You *really* aren't going to stop me. Because I have studied you to a T, your defense to a T, your schemes to a T. I'm like Peyton Manning at receiver.

DM: Or Carson Palmer.

CJ: Or Carson. There's nothing you're going to do that will fluster me. Nothing. I'm not, man ... it's ... I'm telling you ...

DM: You obviously get excited just discussing this.

CJ: The reason I can talk the way I do is because I'm in a freakin' comfort zone, because I've studied you from every angle. I know that, no matter what, I know exactly what's going on in front of me at all times. At all times. So it makes the game easy and puts me in a comfort zone to where I can talk the way I do. It's not because I'm a great talent—everybody's good up here—but it's my state of mind.

DM: Does your mental/physical preparation get overshadowed by the pomp and circumstance surrounding you?

CJ: All people hear is the talking, all they see is the celebrations. They don't see what goes on behind the scenes, all the work that goes into it. Only people on the inside, the people you're with every day, truly understand. That's fine. I want everybody to think I just roll out of bed and onto the field. There's a reason I'm able to talk the smack—because I put the work in.

DM: From where does your motivation come?

CJ: Growing up, man. Just wanting to be great at everything, wanting to be number one. There's something about growing up in Miami, where you're not satisfied unless you're like, that "Dude." No matter what you're doing, you want to be the best. It's the way everybody is down there. When I was growing up, that's the way many of us were—flashy, flamboyant. I've just been fortunate enough to take it to the NFL. I'm doing it, but I'm doing it in the right way.

DM: Elaborate.

CJ: I respect the game. I want my team to win. I do what I do to help me perform the best I can, so my team has a better chance to win.

DM: What would you say to the critics who grumble, "In a team game such as football, Chad Johnson needs to be a little less cocky and a little more humble."?

CJ: Are you one of the critics?

DM: Uh, no, as a matter of fact.

CJ: Are you just saying that because you're a passenger as I'm driving through the city?

DM: Honestly, no. I'm happy you brought me along, but no. I try to be as objective as possible; at the same time, I wouldn't have driven from Cleveland this morning to interview you if I weren't a Chad Johnson guy.

CJ: Well, good. The critics use the word cocky—that's why they're known as critics. But a player's word would be confident. It is the critics' job to criticize, no matter what. If I was quiet, the critics would have another criticizing word to use. They'd call me moody or something else negative. What I call confidence makes the people around me better. It doesn't hurt my game, and it doesn't hurt my team. If it hurt my team, I'd stop doing it.

DM: What bothers you most about the critics?

CJ: Funny how they usually are the ones who never played the game. I'm not saying you can't criticize a player if you never played, but make sure it's justified. Do your homework. A lot of critics don't realize how tough it is to perform at a high level in this league.

DM: Will you ever change?

CJ: No, I'm not going to change what makes Chad, Chad. It makes me who I am. Look, everybody's different. That's what makes the world interesting.

DM: Anybody in the NFL you absolutely cannot stand?

CJ: No. I love everybody, man.

DM: Anybody in the NFL who absolutely cannot stand you?

CJ: I don't know—that's a good question. We need to hold a survey. But how could you not like 85? If you don't like me, something's wrong .... You are really bitter.

DM: Do you prefer Chad or 85?

CJ: 7-11—always open—if need be. As long as I get into the end zone, call me whatever you want.

DM: Do you believe in going all-out in practice?

CJ: I try. You make your money in practice.

DM: Can the 2006 Bengals get to the Super Bowl?

CJ: Oh, yeah. Easy. Easy. Of course we can. We just need to be consistent all year. Execute on offense and defense.

DM: Can you imagine 85 during Super Bowl week(s)?

CJ: Oh, my goodness. That would be hi-larious. I'd have to get a writer from one of those TV shows to follow me, there would be so much material.

DM: If NFL commissioner for one day, what is one thing you would do?

CJ: I'd change the initials from NFL to FFA. Instead of No Fun League, it would be Fun For All. Let's go, do whatever you want.

DM: In regard to your celebrations, is there a disconnect with what the fans want from their stars and what the suits want?

CJ: The bigwigs want to see what I'm going to do, believe me. I don't care what they say. Everybody needs some sort of excitement. You can't be an oldwig all your life. you can't be serious 24/7. You'd die early.

DM: Are you controversial?

CJ: No. What, exactly, have I done wrong? I don't disrespect the game. I don't disrespect my opponent. I'm just having a good time, and the fans get into it.

DM: Is T.O. controversial?

CJ: Yes.

DM: What is the difference between you two in that regard?

CJ: I always want to please everybody. I don't want to tick off anybody. That's why I don't get in any scrapes.

DM: You have a book out now, *CHAD: I Can't Be Stopped*. Why a book?

CJ: They came to me. Then I thought, for all the people who don't understand me, this is important. This book will help you understand why 85 does what he does. You find out where I came from and what I've been through to get here.

DM: Why the subtitle, *I Can't Be Stopped*?

CJ: Because I can't be stopped. For real. I can't. I wouldn't let that be the title otherwise.

DM: Are you concerned it will add fuel to the opponents' fire?

CJ: Are you serious, man? If they need my book to get them worked up, they've got a problem.

DM: What about the cover photo: You look like The Thinker.

CJ: I like it. It's a different Chad—subdued, serious, poised, student of the game.

DM: What do you have in store for the NFL and the fans this season?

CJ: There will be different parts each week. You can't miss one week and understand the rest. It will keep you guessing.

DM: Are you worried about getting fined?

CJ: Heck, yeah. I work too hard to lose my money. I'm not going to get fined on purpose.

UPDATE: Chad Johnson, also known as Chad Ochocinco from 2008–2012 before he legally changed back to his birth name, is a wide receiver for the Montreal Alouettes of the Canadian Football League (CFL). He played most of his career with the Cincinnati Bengals and one season with the New England Patriots in 2011. That year, the Patriots played in Super Bowl XLVI. He was a six-time NFL Pro Bowler, named to three All-Pro Teams, and was voted as the No. 1 receiver on the Bengals fortieth Anniversary Team. He has competed on various reality shows and made it to the final four contestants before being voted off on *Dancing With the Stars* in a 2010 season. In 2011, CNBC listed Johnson as No. 1 "Most Influential Athletes in Social Media."

Randy Johnson and Curt Schilling, *baseball*
June 2002

Randy Johnson and Curt Schilling give it an honest effort.

They speak of twenty-five players trying to win a second consecutive championship for the Arizona Diamondbacks, saying none should be elevated over another. Each maintains that he constitutes a mere 20 percent of the team's rotation, thereby limiting impact.

Out of respect for both, knowing they mean well, nobody

laughs. Deep down, they must know that nobody's buying—most notably, their teammates.

"They want to be one of the guys, but you recognize they're special players," infielder Craig Counsell said. "How can you not?"

"It bothers Randy and Curt how people think the rest of the rotation doesn't really exist," said Brian Anderson, Arizona's fifth starter. "They know we're working our tails off. At the same time, you can't blame people for thinking the way they do about those guys, because they're so impressive. They absolutely deserve to be propped up."

Anderson knows the truth: He owns a World Series ring because of Johnson and Schilling. So do Mike Morgan, Greg Swindell, Jay Bell and Byung-Hyun Kim. And Luis Gonzalez.

Gonzalez, an All-Star left fielder, posted ridiculous numbers during the 2001 regular season and easily was Arizona's most valuable offensive player. Then he hit the flare heard 'round the world—an RBI single over shortstop, bottom of the ninth inning, Game 7—to beat the Yankees and win it all.

For all of his brilliance, however, Gonzo watches the Series from his den without Johnson and Schilling, who went a combined 43-12 with a 2.74 ERA in 506 innings during the regular season for a 92-70 club.

They were 9-1 with a 1.30 ERA in 89 postseason innings.

"Everybody contributes on this team, but we all benefit a ton from Curt and Randy," Gonzalez said. "We give them an awful lot of responsibility. They're a couple of thoroughbreds and we ride them as hard as possible."

Question is, which one would be Secretariat?

Johnson is 12-2 with a 2.38 ERA in 124 innings in seventeen starts this season. He has allowed 97 hits, walked 33, and struck out 155. Schilling, scheduled to start against the Indians today, is 12-3 with a 3.31 ERA in 122 innings in seventeen starts. He has allowed 99 hits, walked 12 and struck out 170.

They have accounted for more than half of the victories for

Arizona, which was 46-32 going into last night's game in Jacobs Field and in second place in the National League West, three-and-a-half games behind the Dodgers.

Since the beginning of last year, including postseason, Johnson is 38-9 with a 2.36 ERA and 574 strikeouts in 415 innings; Schilling is 38-9, with a 2.86 ERA and 519 strikeouts in 427 innings.

They have been teammates for the equivalent of just two full seasons, but their simultaneous displays of dominance have evoked comparisons to the greatest pitching duos ever. Two on everybody's list are Sandy Koufax/Don Drysdale and Greg Maddux/Tom Glavine.

When Arizona acquired Schilling from Philadelphia in July 2000, General Manager Joe Garagiola Jr. was asked to think of a comparable left-right power combination. He said Koufax/Drysdale and caught some grief.

No more.

"It's difficult to compare across eras," Arizona manager Bob Brenly said, "but it's also hard to imagine too many who were as good together as our guys have been."

Of course, Schilling and Johnson downplay their historical significance. Neither likes comparisons, which could foster a clubhouse caste system. Both, after all, are just a couple of guys trying to join with twenty-three others to win a title.

Johnson, in particular, seems to have grown weary of being hailed as the present-day Koufax.

"I know Sandy Koufax was a great pitcher, but I can't worry about how I stack up against him," Johnson said. "All I'm trying to do is maximize the ability I've been given and to win my next start. The Diamondbacks pay me to win my next start."

For years, getting the most out of his talents amounted to a futile exercise for Johnson. At the conclusion of the 1992 season, he was a twenty-nine-year-old with a 49-48 record in the majors. Being 6-10 and left-handed, with a blazing fastball and minimal control, made him more of a sideshow.

Then it happened, virtually without warning: Johnson got dialed in. He cut down the walks dramatically and went 19-8 with Seattle in 1993. The transformation bore striking resemblance to that of — surprise — Koufax from 1960 to 1961.

Since the beginning of 1993, Johnson is more than one hundred games above .500 (163-55) and has bagged four Cy Young awards. Asked during a trip to Pittsburgh to explain the turnaround, Johnson likened it to, of all things, a sportswriter's journey.

"It's like what's happened to you since you came out of college," Johnson said. "You were probably a pretty good sportswriter back then. But seven, eight years out of school, your vocabulary's better, you've read other people's articles, you've incorporated intangibles into your own way of writing. And it's all served to make you much better than you were before, right?"

Uh, yes, Unit. Yes, it has.

"Well, experience made me better, too," he said. "It took me a long time to harness my ability. Everything finally came together, that's all."

Fair enough.

Schilling hardly overwhelmed early, either. At the end of the 1996 season, he was a twenty-nine-year-old with a surgically repaired right shoulder and 52-52 record in the majors. He had been with four organizations and traded three times, including from Houston to Philadelphia in 1992 for Jason "Bat Burglar" Grimsley.

In 1997, Schilling went 17-11 with a 2.97 ERA for the Phillies. He is forty games over .500 since the outset of that season (92-52).

One obvious reason for the reversal is a significant increase in fastball velocity, from the low 90s to the mid to high 90s. Schilling cannot identify exactly how it happened. Most important, though, he figured out what to do with it.

"I learned how to pitch," said Schilling, who also added a slider and curve to his fastball-splitter mix. "I'm smarter about pitching than I once was. You can have all the stuff in the world, but if you don't learn what to do with it, if you don't have a plan, you're not going anywhere."

The means to the end for Schilling are well-documented. He has become a hero to the computer geeks, the Christy Mathewson of the gigabyte generation.

Between starts, Schilling spends hours staring at a laptop computer screen, critiquing freeze frames of his mechanics and studying hitters. He can access a player's career at-bats against him with the click of a mouse. He prepares his own scouting reports and pitches games in his head.

"In the four or five steps I might take between pitches, I've seen the at-bats I went over for five days," said Schilling, who will make notes to himself in a journal between innings. "The information appears like flashcards, and I know exactly how I want to pitch a guy."

Schilling's goal is to know the hitter better than the hitter himself. Evidently, he must come close.

"I've had hitters tell me that their teammates go to the plate psyched out because they know I've already been watching them," he said. "I'd like to think it gives me an edge."

Conversely, the Big Unit simply rolls off the couch, strolls out to the bump and deals. Fastball, fastball, slider, sit. Nothing to it.

Or so it appears.

Want to rile the Big Unit? Tell him it comes easy. Tell him others automatically would dominate if they possessed his repertoire. Cast him as the anti- Schilling in terms of preparation.

"There's a misconception that because I throw 95 to 100, I've got it made," Johnson said. "I've been blessed with a fastball, but I can't just go out and blow the ball by everybody. I've got to hit my spots, I've got to execute. I need to mix in other pitches. There are days when my fastball is maybe 91–95, and I have the same pitches as everybody else, so I have to go out and pitch."

Johnson spurns a laptop or notebook to construct a game plan, but that hardly means he goes out there naked.

"I work very hard at this game," he said, "whether it's physically, in the weight room, or mentally, knowing who I am going to face and their strengths and weaknesses. How much time you put in is what you'll get back in return."

One element of Johnson's game that is not labor-intensive is the scowl. Already a formidable mound presence because of his height, the Big Unit glares over his glove before pitching from the windup. He growls at hitters and himself, especially later in tight games. Even a hint of a smile is rare between the lines.

On those occasions when Brenly finally decides to remove him, sustained eye contact is out of the question.

The hard-boiled persona extends into the clubhouse. Teammates swear by Johnson, but even they proceed with caution around the Big Unit.

"I can be funny when I want to be, but a lot of those days are behind me now," Johnson said. "For the most part, I let the other people on this team have all the fun. I'll laugh, but I'm not going to initiate."

Reporters, a link to the outside world, tend to experience anxiety around Johnson. It can lead to faulty characterizations—although, if caught at the right moments, he has been known to give insightful interviews.

"People think Randy's this big, mean, unapproachable guy," Anderson said. "He's just quiet, introverted, reflective. When you're quiet and keep to yourself, you get those kinds of labels."

Whereas Johnson does not exactly project warmth at the ballpark, Schilling is vivacious and talkative, one of the most accessible big-name players in the game. But don't mistake the amiability for anything that remotely resembles gentle or tame.

The closer it gets to the first pitch, Schilling is as unapproachable as Johnson. On the mound, Schilling wants nothing more than to erase a batter on strikes.

"As competitive as they come," Gonzalez said of Schilling. "No matter what the game is, Curt wants to beat you, and to make you remember it."

Schilling has found his best competition in Johnson, he of the Cy Young standard. It is no accident that the best statistical year of Schilling's career came in 2001, his first full season alongside Johnson.

"Curt loves the fact that he and Randy are on the same staff," Anderson said. "He's always harping on Randy, 'You better put up some big numbers, because if not, I'm going to take that Cy Young from you.' And I think it makes Randy a better pitcher knowing Curt is breathing down his neck."

Perhaps, although Johnson already owned three of the Cy Young awards before Schilling was on the scene full time. If Schilling hasn't forced Johnson to ratchet matters up a notch, at least he has kept him sharp.

How long they will continue to feed off each other remains to be seen. Age would appear to be an obstacle: Johnson turns 39 on September 10; Schilling will be 36 on Nov. 14. Yet, both have shown little sign of slowdown, as if making up for lost time.

"There's no reason it can't continue for a while," Brenly said, "because of the effort these guys put into their craft. But what matters now is they want to get back to the World Series and win it again."

As two of twenty-five guys.

UPDATE: Randy Johnson's final MLB season was in 2009, with the San Francisco Giants—his sixth team. In his twenty-two year career, he went 303-166 with a 3.29 ERA and 4,875 strike-outs in 4,135-$1/3$ innings. He won five Cy Young Awards. He pitched a no-hitter and perfect game. In January 2015, he was elected to the National Baseball Hall of Fame after being named on 97.3 percent of the ballots in his first year of eligibility. (an update on Curt Schilling follows his Q&A)

Shawn Johnson, *gymnastics*

February 2009

And Shawn Johnson thought she was busy before the Beijing Olympic Games.

Johnson's four-medal haul and amiability have made it easy for her to fill up the weekends with appearances across the nation. Fans, especially young girls, cannot get enough of the Iowa dynamo who won gold on the balance beam and silvers in team, all-around and floor.

DM: How is post-Beijing life treating you?

SJ: It's been amazing. It's been very crazy and hectic but I love it. It's all been worth it.

DM: How much are you in the gym these days?

SJ: I'm not doing gymnastics right now. I'm taking a little break. But I still work out every day. I'm still in shape, running a lot. I'm hoping to run a marathon later this year.

DM: Sum up the Beijing experience.

SJ: It was the hardest and most rewarding experience of my life. It's what made me who I am today, and I worked sixteen years to get there.

DM: Do you have unfinished business, though, for 2012?

SJ: I don't feel like I do. I exceeded any expectation and goal that I ever had at the Olympics. 2012 would be a whole new set of goals.

DM: When do you think you'll make that decision?

SJ: I don't know. It's a really hard decision to make in a day. Once the traveling starts to slow down, I'll get back in the gym and see how things go.

Shawn Johnson
photo by Dennis Manoloff

DM: The Chinese team was accused of using at least one under-age gymnast. Nothing came of it on the scoreboard ex post facto. Deep down, did you want the Chinese team to be ruled ineligible so your team could win?

SJ: No. I never wanted that. They did their job, they competed like they wanted to, and it wasn't the girls' fault.

DM: Do you believe the Chinese played by the rules?

SJ: I feel like (*pause*) the girls (*pause*) did. The girls went out and competed. That's what they worked for. They worked their whole lives to get there.

DM: Rank the following in order of how much you cherish them: individual gold, all-around silver, team silver.

SJ: 1) All-around; 2) Team; 3) Individual gold.

DM: Most enjoyable time away from the competition at the Games?

SJ: I went to see the men's basketball gold-medal game. And I went to see the Great Wall. I did a handstand on the Great Wall.

DM: Smartest person you've ever met?

SJ: My parents.

DM: Toughest part of being an elite gymnast?

SJ: I feel like it's the hardest sport there is. You're trained so young, and you're doing some of the hardest stuff. You're being challenged physically and mentally. That takes a toll on everybody.

DM: Most enjoyable part?

SJ: It's what I love. I'm living the life that I dreamed of, and I'm doing it in the sport I've had a passion for since I was born.

DM: Any drawbacks to being a high-profile athlete?

SJ: Not at all. Everything has been a reward.

DM: You always seem to be smiling. Do you ever get mad?

SJ: Of course. Everybody gets mad, everybody gets frustrated. You have to work through it and be happy again.

DM: Compare fan-mail volume pre- and post-Olympics.

SJ: Before I'd probably get 100 every two weeks. Now I've got stacks of thousands. I do what I can to reply to everyone, but it takes time.

DM: What is your estimated career-high for autographs in a day?

SJ: Probably 3,000.

DM: Do you have a stamp for your signature in case of writer's cramp?

SJ: No.

DM: Hobbies/interests?

SJ: I scrapbook, horseback ride, started skiing, hang out with parents and friends.

DM: Favorite meal?

SJ: Sushi.

DM: Junk food?

SJ: Ice cream.

DM: Is the notion of gymnasts needing to starve themselves largely mythological?

SJ: I think there are a lot of rumors and myths out there. It's definitely changed through the years. I eat very healthy, but I've never been told what I should and shouldn't eat. It's always been what I think can help me. Of course, an elite athlete doesn't live off candy. Everything in moderation.

DM: Favorite TV show?

SJ: *Dancing With The Stars*.

DM: Book?

SJ: The *Twilight* series. I just finished it.

DM: Gymnast of all-time?

SJ: Kim Zmeskal. She was so powerful. She's the sweetest person I've ever met.

DM: How does the body recover from so many falls / mishaps during the course of training?

SJ: You build up your strength to the point where any little fall doesn't hinder or hurt you. When your body's so used to it, you don't notice it.

DM: Advice to youngsters who want to be you?

SJ: Have fun and dream big.

DM: As good as the Games were for you, are there any thoughts of what might have been?

SJ: Never. I don't have a single regret from Beijing. I gave 150 percent and did exactly what I was supposed to do.

UPDATE: Shawn Johnson is a retired gymnast. In June 2012, she ended her comeback for the 2012 Olympic team and retired because of continuing problems with her left knee from a skiing accident in 2010. In May 2009, she was the winner of *Dancing with the Stars* (season eight). In November 2012, she earned second place among *DWTS* All-Stars.

Duane Kuiper & Rick Manning, *baseball*
July 2008

Duane Kuiper and Rick Manning are members of the Top 100 Greatest Indians roster, which was unveiled in 2001 as part of the 100th anniversary season celebration.

They also are close friends. Kuiper played for the Tribe from 1974 to 1981, Manning from 1975 to 1983.

Both have remained in the game as TV analysts; Kuiper for the San Francisco Giants and Manning for the Tribe.

DM: How long were you together in the minors?

DK: Two-and-a-half years.

DM: Favorite minor-league story from your days together?

RM: Can't be printed.

DK: Phil Seghi called me after Arch [Manning] got drafted in June. We'd already had an apartment, some others guys and I.

RM:: Four guys.

DK: Four guys, yeah. Seghi calls and says, "You've got another roommate. You're going to show Rick Manning the ropes." We were like, whatever. So Archie shows up. Well, I'm from a dairy farm in Wisconsin, he's from Buffalo. Even though there's four years' difference in age, who's going to show the ropes to whom? Just because I was older didn't mean I knew a whole lot of what was going on.

RM: Kuip was my first roommate, so you can blame him for anything that happened to me in pro baseball after that point.

DM: Word association, to Duane—Rick Manning?

DK: Go get 'em.

DM: To Rick—Duane Kuiper?

RM: You need a lot of words.

DK: Don't say tight pants.

RM: Let's say ... gamer. No, wait—dead-ender.

DM: Dead-ender?

RM: It's a group of players we had here in 1975, our rookie year with Dave Garcia, the third base coach. Duane, Buddy Bell, Frank Duffy, Ray Fosse and me. We played the game the way Dave Garcia liked it to be played—hard. We were dead-enders.

DK: Dave had a certain definition of a dead-ender from the movies. A dead-ender to him meant they were guys who played like it was their last game.

DM: Word association—Rico Carty?

RM: Big Mon.

DK: Big Mon, indeed.

RM: And you know how he got that name? He gave it to himself.

DM: George Hendrick?

DK: Silk. That was his nickname. That's how he played, silky smooth.

DM: Dennis Eckersley?

DK: Cocky. Maybe the cockiest guy I've ever seen, for a guy who was so insecure. He was like, "Because I'm insecure, I'm going to be cocky."

DM: Andre Thornton?

DK: Class.

DM: Mike Hargrove?

RM: Maximized his skills.

DM: What did you think of the fire-engine-red uniforms?

RM: We didn't mind them—because we were skinny. Boog Powell and the big guys, the older guys, they were the ones who had trouble with them. They looked like tomatoes, Bloody Marys.

DM: Best part of playing for the Tribe when you did?

DK: The group of guys we got to know. We didn't win a lot of games, but gosh darn it, we thought we were going to win that day.

RM: We had great guys on that team—just not enough of them. We weren't quite good enough to win.

DK: When I think of Arch, I think of the corner we had in the clubhouse where we laughed our butts off twenty times, at least, before games. We were going to laugh, belly-laugh, slap-your-thighs laugh, at least twenty times.

DM: Who was in the corner?

DK: The two of us, Buddy Bell, Ron Hassey, Tom Veryzer, Mike Hargrove. Frank Duffy was there, too.

RM: That was the corner you had to be in.

DM: So you had fun despite mediocre and bad teams?

DK: We were going to have fun, no matter what.

DM: Worst part about being an Indian back then?

RM: We didn't have a good organization. It was a bad organization.

DK: Listen: When you have to sell a player to meet payroll, it's a problem.

RM: Cleveland was lucky to keep the team.

DM: What was it like to witness the feud between Gaylord Perry and Frank Robinson?

DK: There was certainly a lot of friction when you had Hall of Famers butting heads. We're in our first year, 1975, thinking, "Is it like this all the time?"

RM: "Get me a Coke, kid."

DM: What?

RM: Gaylord would tell you, "Go get me a Coke." We'd have to do whatever he asked. You didn't dare say no.

DK: I had Gaylord in '74 because I got called up for a month. It was a revelation, let me tell you. You're standing at second base knowing that if you screwed up when he was on the mound, he would let everybody know. It scared me. Having said that, I loved playing behind the guy because he would do anything he could to win, and that says something.

DM: You both started on May 15, 1981 — Len Barker's perfect game. Fondest memory?

DK: When Ernie Whitt hit the ball in the air. (Manning caught it for the final out.) I'm not saying it because Archie is sitting here, but if somebody would have said beforehand, "You get to pick where you want the ball to go to make certain it's going to be an out," centerfield was it.

RM: Being in center, I got a good look at how awesome Lenny's breaking stuff was. That's what I remember most.

DM: Duane, I read where you smoked a lot as a player.

DK: Yes. I stopped two years after I retired.

DM: How much did you smoke?

DK: If I was in the lineup — nine. If I was riding the pine — eighteen.

RM: A lot of guys smoked. You didn't have the six-course meals like they do today. You'd go in after a game and say to the clubbie, "Get me a carton of heaters and make sure the beer's cold."

DK: A good clubbie always had your brand.

RM: It would be sitting in your locker. We didn't give a crap about the food.

DK: I got sick in spring training once. [Clubhouse manager] Cy [Buynak] was buying the cigarettes in Mexico.

RM: (*Laughs*)

DK: (*Choking noise*)

RM: The bootlegged ones.

DK: I'm thinking, "Why am I feeling really bad all of a sudden?"

RM: Cy: "I'm saving six bucks."

DK: You'd open up the pack, turn the cigarette over and all the tobacco would fall on the floor. We'd be like, "Cy, come on."

Chuck Kyle, *football*

January 2009

Chuck Kyle's nickname, "Chico"—after boyhood hero and White Sox shortstop Chico Carrasquel—has a nice ring to it. "The Closer" sounds good, too. When Kyle reaches state championship football games, he finishes the job.

Kyle has guided St. Ignatius to eleven title games in twenty-six years as head coach. His Wildcats have won ten of them, a success rate worthy of Otto Graham. Kyle is responsible for all of his alma mater's big-school crowns.

Kyle's tenth title came last year, meaning there is no better time for him to receive the Greater Cleveland Sports Commission's Lifetime Achievement Award. He will be honored as part of the GCSC's annual Greater Cleveland Sports Awards tonight at the Renaissance Cleveland Hotel.

Kyle is a longtime English teacher and track coach at St. Ignatius High School.

DM: Sum up your coaching philosophy.

CK: The mission statement would be: To teach kids how to prepare mentally, physically and spiritually for any challenge.

DM: Favorite elements of coaching football?

CK: First and foremost, the educational aspects. They come in as boys and leave as men four years later. Somewhere along the way, you helped them become men. I also enjoy the strategy.

DM: What does the Lifetime Achievement Award mean to you?

CK: At first, I was shocked. I said, "Are you sure you've got the right guy?" As people have offered congratulations, I've become more and more aware of the magnitude of it, and I'm truly humbled. There's a lot of amazing people involved in athletics in this community. I get a little frightened, though, when they say, "lifetime achievement." Because I'm hoping to still go along.

DM: How have you been able to put up such staggering W-L and title numbers at St. Ignatius?

CK: Oh, I don't know—luck. I'm uncomfortable with that question.

DM: If you had to pick something, what would it be?

CK: Work ethic, I suppose, helps. I don't take too many vacations. I like to study and prepare. I always hope the kids see that I'm making a commitment to them.

DM: What do you do to relax away from the field?

CK: Run.

DM: Favorite TV show?

CK: I don't watch much. When you're an English teacher, there are always some papers to check or books to read. But I suppose it would be Channel 3 news.

DM: Your daughter Maureen is a reporter for WKYC Channel 3.

CK: I've started introducing myself as Maureen Kyle's dad. How about that?

DM: How often do you catch yourself drawing up a play while you're teaching?

CK: I can honestly say I've never done that. You can ask any of my students: I go out of my way not to mix football with class time.

DM: Do you ever feel pressure to continue delivering state titles?

CK: As the years have gone by, it's become less and less of a big deal. The only stress I really feel now comes in making sure that what we're doing gives the kids a chance to win on any given week. Winning a state title is not easy. A lot has to go right.

DM: Do you have any pregame rituals?

CK: The only one I can think of involves little gold footballs. My grandfather won a state championship in Birmingham, Alabama, in 1918. My father won a state championship in Hammond, Indiana, in 1937. I have the little gold footballs from each of those teams and put them in my pocket for our first state title game in 1988.

　　When we won, I got a little gold football. The only time I put the three of them in my pocket is for state championship games. So it's been a good charm.

DM: Do you have a favorite of the ten?

CK: I always explain it this way: If you have ten children, you love them all. They're all unique. Sometimes I wonder, if we didn't get the first one, would the rest have followed? But I love them all.

DM: Do you remember the one —

CK: I surely do. It was 1996, against Lima Senior. I remember it vividly because it's the one we lost, and because my mother [Dorothy] died in Florida about 45 minutes after the game ended. To this day, I am convinced that she refused to die until the game was over because she didn't want to be a distraction. No one can convince me it didn't happen that way.

DM: Anything you wish you could change about your coaching career to this point?

CK: No. I deeply appreciate what has happened. Out of respect for that, I don't dwell on it. I don't want the past to have an effect on what I'm doing at the moment. Let's go to the next challenge.

DM: Do you have any vices?

CK: Well, uh, I don't know. Wow. That's a tough one. I try not to do anything obnoxious. My wife [Patricia] will probably tell you that, during football season, I'm not the most entertaining guy.

DM: Do you ever swear?

CK: Once in a while, but I try to be discreet about it.

DM: Wisest person you've ever met?

CK: I'd say my father-in-law, Paul Cassidy. He's a decorated World War II veteran and was mayor of Parma Heights for forty-something years. I've learned a lot from him, especially about leadership.

DM: If you were Browns coach Eric Mangini, what would you be thinking?

CK: That there isn't that big of a difference in pro football between the best teams and the teams at the bottom. Look at the Ravens, Falcons, Cardinals, Dolphins.

DM: Why have you opted not to coach college football?

CK: Never intended to. I never wanted to be talked into something I didn't want to do. Besides, I don't know if I'd be that effective on that level.

DM: How much longer will you go?

CK: I don't have any year in mind whatsoever. The 100 percent truth to this will be, I'll know when it's time to stop. It's going to revolve around energy. I pray for energy. When I don't have the energy to do things the way I need to do them, I'll stop. I don't want to take any shortcuts.

Cliff Lee, *baseball*
August 2009

It is good to be Cliff Lee.

The reigning American League Cy Young Award winner is 5-0 with a 0.68 ERA in five starts with the Phillies since being acquired from the Indians on July 29. He has given up twenty-four hits in 40 innings, walked six and struck out 39.

Lee is continuing a groove that began in early July. In his final five starts with the Tribe, Lee allowed ten runs in 38 innings. He has won eight consecutive decisions since July 16 to improve to 12-9.

Lee's 2.63 ERA in twenty-seven starts overall is approaching that of 2008, when he was 22-3 with a 2.54 ERA in thirty-one starts and became the Indians' second straight Cy Young winner (CC Sabathia).

DM: So what's it like to be Cliff Lee these days?

CL: Just like every other day, preparing for my next outing.

DM: Have you needed to make any specific adjustments from American League to National?

CL: Not really. Other than having to hit, and pitching to the opposing pitcher, it's basically the same deal. You're facing major-league hitters. You've got to make pitches. You miss over the plate, you're going to get hurt.

DM: You don't seem to be missing your personal catcher in Cleveland, Kelly Shoppach.

CL: Honestly, [Phillies catcher] Paul Bako reminds me a lot of Shoppach. He's a pretty savvy catcher. It didn't take long for him to understand the way I like to pitch. Bako and Shoppach are pretty crafty. They both call unbelievable games.

DM: What percentage of your success with the Phillies would you attribute to Bako/studying scouting reports/relying on your ability?

CL: I'm relying on Paul Bako, what he throws down, and a feel for the game. Obviously, scouting reports are important, but it's mostly working with my strengths.

DM: Last year, you rode your fastball to the Cy Young. This year, it's still the dominant pitch, but you appear to be mixing in more curves and changeups.

CL: I still feel like I'm commanding the fastball, but yeah, you've got to use all your pitches. It helps to be unpredictable.

DM: In your first two starts this season, you gave up eleven runs in ten innings and lost twice. Most of the twenty-five starts since have been quality. Are you pitching as well as you did in 2008?

CL: Similar. Every year's different. I'm giving the team a chance to win. I'm getting deep into games, throwing strikes, not walking many guys. I keep it simple — you know that. I just try to put up as many zeros as I can.

DM: Did any of the trades the Indians made as part of the summer sell-off surprise you?

CL: My getting traded surprised me.

DM: Seriously?

CL: Yeah. For sure. I really was expecting to stay. I figured that, I was pitching well and I potentially could have been back if they picked up the option. Victor [Martinez], the same thing. They had Grady [Sizemore]. They had some pieces there that you could build around to make a pretty good team. They viewed it differently. I'm not a GM, I'm not a coach. I don't make any of those decisions. I play the game. I was an Indian until I was told I was a Phillie, and now I'm here and I've got to help this team win.

DM: After the trades, Indians President Paul Dolan said you were not going to re-sign with the Indians after 2010. Did Dolan present it accurately?

CL: They told my agent that when we got to spring training this year, we'll talk about an extension. We get there, the first half of spring goes by ... nothing. We get down toward the end, they call me in the office and tell me, "Never mind. We've changed our minds." At that point, I told them: "For me, now's the time. After this year, I'm going to be one year from free agency, and you're going to have to pick up my option if I'm pitching well. Otherwise, I'm a free agent. It doesn't make sense to do it one year out when I just watched what CC did."

DM: Sabathia, of course, was traded to Milwaukee in 2008 and signed with the Yankees over the winter.

CL: Free agency is where you want to get as a player. That's where you get strength and have control of a situation. Obviously, the closer you get to that, the less likely an extension would be. That's kind of what I told them.

DM: What was their reply?

CL: They said, "We respect your stance on that, and if anything changes, let us know." And they said, "If the economy turns around, if things change, if we start winning, maybe we'll change our opinion, too." I said, "OK, fine." That was kind of the end of it.

DM: Do you feel sad about the sell-off in Cleveland?

CL: Yeah. You get comfortable with a city, teammates, coaches, staff, guys in the training room. Those things make it tough to leave. They run a really good program. They basically helped mold my program and what I do. I was wondering how I was going to be able to translate all those things over here, but it's worked out pretty smoothly for the most part.

DM: Do you feel bad for the fans who see the core of their team traded, fans who wonder, "Why can't Cliff Lee and Victor Martinez still be around in 2010, to try to make another run at it?"

CL: Uh, it would help if the fans showed up and came to the games. That's why the team didn't make money, because the fans weren't there, supporting the team. That's what happens when the fans don't support—

DM: But you guys weren't winning.

CL: Right. It goes hand-in-hand, though. It definitely goes hand-in-hand. Yeah, I feel sorry for them. I wish we were all still there, that we had won the World Series in '07, come back and won it again last year and were going to win it this year. That's not reality. That's not … It's a business. It's a total business.

DM: Many Tribe fans, and other observers, think you began to grind an ax on management when you were sent down to Class AAA Buffalo in 2007—two years removed from an 18-win season—and that that was the beginning of the end. True?

CL: No. Not at all. I wasn't upset at anyone. They were in position to go to the postseason and potentially win a World Series and were arguably one game away from doing that. Their concern was not whether they're making me happy, it was trying to get to the postseason and winning a World Series, as it should be. I was not getting the results I expected out of myself. You can look at the stats. They were black and white. Obviously, I didn't want to go to Triple-A. But you have to make the best of the situation.

I didn't want to be a major leaguer sent to Triple-A who's bitter and mad at the world. I've seen that before, and I didn't want to be that guy. I tried to do everything they asked me to do, and I expected to get back to pitching well, to get back to Cleveland and help the team get in position to win the World Series. It didn't work out that way.

DM: You pitched out of the bullpen four times in September and were not on any postseason roster. Still not bitter?

CL: No. In the long run, I think [what happened in 2007] motivated me to push that much harder in the offseason and prove everybody wrong. I wasn't mad at anybody or anything. I felt like they had kind of changed their views on me as a pitcher, and I wanted to prove that that wasn't right, that it wasn't the real me.

DM: So when you say they changed their view of you, and that you wanted to prove people wrong—that's not indicative of grinding an ax?

CL: No. That was the Indians doing a business move. They were trying to win a World Series. That's what it's all about. They viewed me going to Triple-A and replacing me with someone else as making the team better. That's their prerogative.

DM: As objectively as you could view it, did you think the Cleveland team that broke camp this spring would contend?

CL: I thought our ballclub was a lot better than it turned out to be.

DM: What went wrong?

CL: We figured out how to lose every way possible, it seemed like. What made it the toughest is, it wasn't one thing. It wasn't something you could put your finger on and say, "This is what you need to get better at." It was one thing one day, something else the next. For whatever reason, we weren't playing complete baseball.

Tara Lipinski, *figure skating*
April 2006

Tara Lipinski always has been a favorite because of her remarkable skills on the ice. Headlining her long list of accomplishments are youngest U.S. figure skating national champion (age fourteen in 1997), world champion (age fourteen in 1997) and Olympic gold medalist (age fifteen in 1998). She also proved dominant in professional competitions.

But Lipinski, a U.S. Figure Skating Hall of Famer, did not achieve icon status in DMan's World until she landed a guest spot on one of TV's greatest comedies in the past twenty years, *Malcolm in the Middle*. For the episode that aired April 16, Lipinski played a quirky vegetarian who tried to convert hard-core carnivore Reese (Justin Berfield).

The spot on Malcolm, whose run ends after this season, is the continuation of a challenging career shift for Lipinski. She retired from skating several years ago and could have played it safe for years to come as a commentator or ice-show queen. Instead, she climbed into the briar patch that is Hollywood and dedicated herself to becoming the best actress she can be.

DM: When did you truly get interested in acting?

TL: Not long after the Nagano Olympics, I was asked to do a guest spot on *The Young and The Restless*, which turned into a recurring role. As soon as I got on the set, I said, "I love this."

DM: When did you make a full-time commitment to the craft?

TL: About three and a half years ago. I went to Paris to do an independent film for three months. I had a lot of time to think. I decided that when I got home, I was going to tell everyone I'm moving to L.A. That's what I did.

DM: Your growing list of TV credits does not include *Skating with*

Celebrities. Assuming you were approached, why pass?

TL: Yes, I was approached. Skating is a part of me, and I never want to forget that. I did skating parts early on, but at this point in my career, I'm really trying to separate myself from the skater when I'm acting.

DM: With all due respect, Tara, there has to be more to it than that. This was, after all, *Skating with Celebrities*, whose "celebrity" list included the legendary Todd Bridges.

TL: (*Pause*) *Skating with Celebrities* just wasn't the type of thing I wanted to do. Even if I were skating full time, I wouldn't have wanted to do it.

DM: Much better. And congrats on your discretion.

TL: Well, I'm sure the show turned out great, and that the people who were on the show did a great job and had a lot of fun.

DM: Favorite athlete?

TL: Tiger Woods.

DM: I read somewhere that you were engaged.

TL: Really? You heard that? Interesting. I love being informed I'm engaged. It's so funny.

DM: I take it the answer is, no.

TL: I'm not engaged.

DM: Are you aware of how many people are into Tara Lipinski? The more research I did for the interview, the more I unearthed. Do such things as "websites devoted to Tara" make the spine tingle a bit?

TL: I try not to get involved in it. I don't go on the Internet. I'm not good with computers.

DM: Well, provided you are being straight-up with me, here's one thing you are missing: You love rock stars.

TL: Stuff like that is so bizarre. Sometimes my friends will tell me something that's out there, and I'll be like, Are you crazy? I was in the spotlight at an early age, so I grew up in a different world. The attention is normal to me. I love my fans, and I accept everything that comes with them as part of the job.

DM: You don't necessarily love the freaks, though.

TL: Not the freaks.

DM: If forced to have only one—gold medal or Emmy/Oscar?

TL: I can't give up the gold. How about gold medal and Oscar nominee?

DM: Do you miss skating at all?

TL: I watch it, and I get a rush of relief because I know I was able to accomplish a lot before retiring. But I don't miss it.

DM: Favorite movie?

TL: *Gone with the Wind.*

DM: TV show?

TL: You're going to laugh at me. It's *America's Next Top Model.*

DM: What about *Malcolm*?

TL: Oh, yeah, it's definitely up there.

DM: You have been able to secure guest spots pretty much since you arrived in Hollywood. How do you respond to the critics who say you have not paid your dues like other table-waiting actors, and that perhaps you get the roles because of your name?

TL: I feel like I am paying my dues. I've never set out to use my skating celebrity to get a part, or to be considered for one. Having said that, I know my skating has opened some doors. It's up to me, though, to take advantage of those opportunities. I work hard at acting. I try out like everybody else, and I've earned what I've gotten out here. This is serious stuff to me. It's not a joke.

DM: How do you deal with rejection?

TL: My skating experience helps here. There are always going to be setbacks when you're competing at the highest levels. Skating taught me to keep getting up and coming back better the next time.

DM: Is there a big role for which you tried out, only to barely miss landing?

TL: I've gotten close on a few big ones.

DM: So you were a silver or bronze medalist.

TL: Yes, I guess you could say that. But all I got was a handshake.

Nastia Liukin, *gymnastics*

January 2009

Nastia Liukin won the all-around gold medal at the Beijing Games last August and was part of the United States team that won silver. She finished with five medals around her neck, joining Mary Lou Retton and Shannon Miller as the only American gymnasts to win five in one Games.

Liukin owns nine World Championship medals, tied with Miller for most among American gymnasts.

Liukin was born in Moscow. When she was two and a half years old, her parents moved the family to the United States.

After fulfilling numerous post-Olympic obligations, Liukin has remained busy with myriad projects. She is part of the Progressive *Skating & Gymnastics Spectacular* to be aired by NBC Sports. On the show, she will do a duet performance with Ashley Tisdale to Tisdale's hit song, "What If?"

DM: Toughest apparatus?

NL: Vault.

DM: Favorite apparatus?

NL: Beam.

DM: Smartest person you've ever met?

NL: My grandpa.

DM: You have an eye on the 2012 London Games, correct?

NL: I'm taking it one step at a time, one year at a time, but right now that's the plan.

DM: Why not go out on top after Beijing?

NL: Gymnastics is always something I've had a passion for, something I love to do. Yes, I definitely did achieve my biggest goals and dreams in gymnastics, but I feel like I can keep going. I'm still learning. I think I can get better. If my body feels good, and I'm still having fun, why not?

DM: Best fitness tip for any age?

NL: Running. I run about three miles a day. It's also a great way to relax and clear your head.

DM: Best eating/dieting tip for any age?

NL: Don't deprive yourself. If you really want something like a cookie, then eat it. And: everything in moderation, as they say.

DM: So you've never needed to starve yourself as a competitive gymnast?

NL: Not at all. That's a personal decision, not something tied to being a gymnast. There is a variety of choices—fruits, vegetables, salads, proteins, chicken, fish—to make sure you don't need to starve yourself to lose weight or maintain your shape. I pretty much eat organic whole foods and stuff.

DM: Favorite things to do away from the gym?

NL: Reading, spending time with family and shopping are three that come to mind. Reading helps when I travel.

DM: Favorite book?

NL: The *Twilight* series.

DM: Favorite TV show?

NL: *Gossip Girl*. It's well-written with great characters.

DM: Advice to youngsters who want to be an Olympic all-around champion?

NL: You've got to put the time in. There are no shortcuts. For me, it wasn't just the months leading up to the Olympics when I got my strongest. It took all the way from when I started competing at age six, and it just kind of built up from there. The days that are hard, you have to push yourself even harder. Those are the days you're going to get stronger mentally and physically.

DM: Any regrets about Beijing?

NL: None.

DM: Are you 100 percent certain the Chinese girls deserved the team gold?

NL: Yes.

DM: But did they play by the rules re: age requirements?

NL: I want to believe they did because nothing could be proven otherwise. No matter what, they were phenomenal athletes and gymnasts. They had tremendous skill level and technique, and they dealt with the pressure of performing in their home country. They were amazing. They're great gymnasts and I have nothing against them.

DM: Word association—your father and coach, Valeri?

NL: Second to God for me. He's an awesome father, and he definitely got me to where I needed to be as a gymnast. If not for him, I would not have become an Olympic champion.

DM: Marta Karolyi?

NL: She always had trust and faith in me. She believed I could be all-around champion. I owe her a lot.

DM: Shawn Johnson?

NL: She's an incredible athlete, gymnast, dancer. Her skill level and concentration always amazed me.

DM: Was there a rivalry between you two leading up to the Games?

NL: Not at all. We're both competitors, we both want to win, but it wasn't a rivalry the way people use the word. We were happy for each other and supported each other.

DM: You have received a good deal of attention after winning the all-around and the other Olympic medals. But Johnson, silver medalist in the all-around, seemed to be everywhere, especially after signing with *Dancing With the Stars*. Any resentment?

NL: None. Shawn's a great person with a dynamic personality. She deserves everything she's gotten. I've been very busy. I didn't get into gymnastics for attention, but I've gotten a lot of it. My life's been a whirlwind. I've got no complaints, other than there's not enough time to do everything.

DM: One aspect of Nastia Liukin that people don't know?

NL: That's a hard one, because I feel like everyone knows everything about me now. I guess it would be that I'm a different person outside the gym. I'm very serious when I compete, but I have a very outgoing personality. I laugh a lot.

UPDATE: Nastia Liukin's career as a gymnast came to an end after the 2012 Olympic Trials. Her non-gymnastic career continues to thrive. She has made various appearances in movies and TV, has modeled, and is one of the celebrities who competed on the twentieth season of *Dancing with the Stars*. She has her own line of gymnastics equipment, which includes mats and balance beams.

Kenny Lofton, *baseball*
August 2010

Of all the electrifying moments on the Kenny Lofton highlight reel, none captures the essence of the player any better than his 180-foot dash to glory on October 17, 1995.

It happened in the eighth inning of Game 6 of the American League Championship Series between the Indians and Seattle Mariners at the Kingdome. With the Indians leading, 1-0, and Ruben Amaro on third, Lofton beat out a bunt against Randy Johnson. Lofton stole second. Moments later, Big Unit's pitch got away from catcher Dan Wilson and rolled toward the Tribe dugout on the first-base side.

Amaro, as expected, scored easily on the passed ball. The shocker—to everyone except the man himself—was that Lofton hit third base and kept on running. In a blur, Lofton slid in safely, catching Wilson and Johnson sulking/napping. The Indians went on to win the game, 4-0, and the series, 4-2, to advance to their first World Series in forty-one years.

"My instincts made that play happen," Lofton told DMan's World. "Once I took off, I knew I had the speed to take me where I needed to go."

Lofton will be inducted into the Indians Hall of Fame on Saturday in part because of his ability to impact games with such speed and daring. He also knew how to swing the bat and catch the ball. Everything was on display against the Baltimore Orioles on Sept. 3, 2000, when Lofton went 4-for-7 with a homer, walk, four runs and five steals in a 12-11 victory in thirteen innings at Jacobs Field.

Lofton played for eleven teams in a major-league career that spanned from 1991 through 2007, but he always will be known as an Indian. He had three stints with Cleveland (1992-1996; 1998-2001; 2007) and remains the franchise leader with 452 steals and

Kenny Lofton
photo by Marvin Fong/*The Plain Dealer*

ranks third with 975 runs. Five of his six All-Star selections and all four of his Gold Gloves came with the Indians.

Lofton retired as a .299 hitter in 2,103 regular-season games overall. He had 2,428 hits, 1,528 runs and 622 steals. He played in 95 postseason games, including fifty with the Tribe, and scored 65 runs.

DM: When you think of yourself as a Cleveland Indian, what is the first thing that comes to mind?

KL: Stolen bases. In Cleveland, I think people look at me as the guy who stole bases.

DM: Highlight of your career?

KL: Having been able to play on a lot of teams that made the playoffs. Having had a lot of opportunities to win a ring.

DM: You played in twenty postseason series in eleven years. Does one postseason stand out above the rest?

KL: The first one, with the Indians in 1995. That will stick out forever, because we were able to go to the World Series in Cleveland for the first time since 1954.

DM: Should the Indians have won the 1995 World Series against the Braves, or did they simply get beat by a better, more seasoned team?

KL: Honestly, I believe we played well enough to win. We put our hearts out there. But to be honest, with the teams and the situations what they were, I don't think we got a fair shot.

DM: Explain.

KL: In my opinion, we didn't get a fair shot from the umpires. The [Tom] Glavine and [Greg] Maddux strike zones were not right. They were getting the calls off the plate and our pitchers weren't. I'm not the only one who says that. You had to deal with it, though. You had no other choice.

DM: Your favorite Indians club?

KL: The '95 team, because of the personalities we had. We did a lot of freelancing. It was awesome.

DM: And you set the tone.

KL: The guys called me the igniter. Once I ignited the flames, everything took off. It was an exciting time.

DM: Which postseason ending in your career stings the most?

KL: The toughest to take is '95 because, as I said, I don't think the umpires were fair. Second is the Giants in 2002 because we were up, 3-2, in the World Series and had a five-run lead in Game 6 but lost to the Angels. We just lost.

DM: You also were on the Cubs when they fell to the Marlins in the infamous 2003 NLCS, during which fan Steve Bartman reached out and seemingly denied Moises Alou a catch late in Game 6.

KL: I've never viewed the Bartman situation as more than what it was—a fan reached out and didn't get the ball. Those things happen. But the play soon after that, when Alex Gonzalez booted the double-play ball … that was the deciding factor. Everyone put it on Bartman, but I saw the double-play ball that didn't happen. Regardless, we still had Game 7. We didn't get it done.

DM: Do you believe in the Curse of Colavito (Indians) or Curse of the Billy Goat (Cubs)?

KL: No. If you put the right team on the field and play the way you should play, there's no curse. Look at Boston in 2004. Everybody said there was a curse, but they had the right team to win it all that year—and they did. Bottom line: It's what you do on the field.

DM: You were a teammate of Barry Bonds in 2002. How do you view him? Is he a Hall of Famer?

KL: (*Long pause*) I'll say it this way: With Barry Bonds, for me, you have to be innocent until proven guilty in the Hall of Fame situation. So that's a tough one, because you have to show me some type of proof. I know there are allegations, but there's no proof. So, if the allegations had not come up—for sure, he's a Hall of Famer. But because the allegations came up, and there's a lot of doubt, it makes it very tricky to say he's a Hall of Famer.

DM: Do you believe Barry Bonds used PEDs [performance-enhancing drugs]?

KL: That's not for me to say. I won't say I believe anything about that, because it's my own personal answer or thought in my head.

DM: Is Alex Rodriguez a Hall of Famer?

KL: I would not vote for him for the Hall of Fame. He cheated the game, he admitted it, and the game acts like nothing happened. It's as if he got a slap on the wrist. There's something wrong with that.

DM: How much baseball do you watch these days?

KL: Not a lot, but more this year than at any point since I retired. I love the game, but I'll be honest with you: I'm upset with the game. I'm upset because I was put out of the game because I wasn't cheating the game, if that makes sense.

DM: It does.

KL: I could have cheated and put up better numbers. Then I could have cheated to stay in the game. But I didn't. I was clean and played by the rules. And I know there are people who cheated, cheated to extend their careers, and it's not right.

DM: So it's safe to say that you, as a clean player, are upset you were forced to compete periodically on an uneven playing field?

KL: Do I have a problem with it? Without a doubt. I have a huge problem with it. It sticks with me to this day, knowing that people were cheating and knowing I was playing against them, with them, whatever. What really ticks me off is that baseball could have done something about it but didn't.

DM: Please elaborate.

KL: It comes back to the emphasis on home runs, when they came out with the commercial campaign of "Chicks Dig the Long Ball." Baseball wanted guys to hit homers because it was good for business. Why do you think certain guys started hitting so many home runs?

DM: As a result, your contributions get overshadowed.

KL: When everybody started talking about the long ball, they forgot about the speed, which was my game. It took my impact from close to the top to middle/bottom. Once they emphasized the long ball, I was looked at as a totally different player.

DM: Word association—'95 Indians?

KL: Outstanding.

DM: Albert Belle?

KL: Intense.

DM: Joel Skinner?

KL: Very technical.

DM: I thought you would say of Skins: "Never should have held me at third in Game 7 of 2007 ALCS."

KL: (*Chuckle*) I can't hold that against him. He was the one who held me up, but I can't blame him, per se. He needed to make a decision; he just made the wrong decision. It's like when a pitcher should have thrown the fastball but throws a curve and the guy hits a homer. It's not about blame.

DM: How did Pat Listach beat you out for AL Rookie of the Year in 1992?

KL: To this day, I don't know how. I'm still trying to figure that out. But it worked out in the end for me. No disrespect to Pat Listach, but if you would have told me that I'd get Rookie of the Year and have my career end like his, I would have said, "I don't want Rookie of the Year. You can have it."

DM: On August 4, 1996, you made what many consider the greatest catch in Jacobs/Progressive Field history, scaling an eight-foot wall in center to bring back a potential two-run homer by B.J. Surhoff of the Orioles. Did you amaze even yourself on that one?

KL: I don't know how I did it, but it happened. I don't think people understand the difficulty involved. It was one of the best catches I made and one of the best I've seen on film.

DM: Any regrets about your career?

KL: Not winning the World Series. I wanted it badly, but it didn't happen. My career still was a lot of fun.

DM: Best player you ever played with?

KL: That's where it gets tough. Performance enhancing is what makes it tough for me to make that call.

DM: What made you the player you were?

KL: Focus, determination, love of the game.

DM: You seemed to play with a chip on your shoulder, as if you had something to prove. Is that accurate?

KL: I'm not sure I wanted to prove the doubters wrong as much as I wanted to let people know that, "Hey, I'm an athlete, I can play this game."

DM: How do you want to be remembered as a player?

KL: As a guy who played the game right, played it fair. As a guy who loved the game and respected it.

Charlie Manuel, *baseball*

September 2009

Many on the outside thought Charlie Manuel's managerial career—the major-league one, at least—was over when he and the Indians parted ways in July 2002.

In 2000, the Indians had given baseball lifer Manuel his first opportunity to manage in the majors. He was fifty-six. Less than three years later, Manuel was out after a heated meeting with General Manager Mark Shapiro over the All-Star break.

Manuel wanted to know his status beyond the season, and Shapiro was not willing to commit. Manuel refused to take "wait" for an answer.

End of tenure in Cleveland.

. Manuel has spent his life proving people wrong, so it's no surprise he resurfaced. And not only did he manage again, he won a World Series. Three years after replacing Larry Bowa in Philadelphia, The Good Ol' Boy was on top of the baseball world, the Phillies having defeated Tampa Bay last October.

Manuel's Phillies are in first place in the NL East this season.

DM: It looks like you've lost a lot of weight since last year. Is everything OK?

CM: Everything's great. I have lost a lot. In spring training, I weighed 284. I told [finacée] Missy, "Damn, I've got to lose some pounds." She suggested NutriSystem. I weighed myself the other day—230. How about that?

DM: Impressive. You should be in one of the commercials.

CM: That would be neat, wouldn't it?

DM: What was life like in the days after the World Series last year?

CM: I stayed in town for about ten days, then went back to my home in Winter Haven [Florida]. I sat down, and for about four or five days, I didn't do anything. I just sat there. That's when it really hit me. I thought, "Man, we won the World Series. Does it get any better than this?" Then I replayed the season, start to finish, what we did right and wrong. I kept thinking how we played so well when it mattered most.

DM: Did you need a World Series title to validate your standing as a manager, to gain respect?

CM: No. I know where you're going with that, and the answer is, "No." I can't worry what other people think about me. Besides, it's not about me, it's about the players and the team.

DM: Still, you must feel good about being able to flash a World Series ring in the face of your critics.

CM: You're always going to have critics. You could win ten World Series and still have critics. Everybody's got an opinion.

DM: In mid-July 2002, you were in the third year of your first stint as a major-league manager. The Indians had made the playoffs in 2001. Suddenly, you and the Indians parted ways after a meeting with General Manager Mark Shapiro. What happened?

CM: Mark told me things he wanted to get done and gave me plans about development of our players. What stood out to me was, he said I'd be re-evaluated at the end of the year based on how we developed our players. But I felt like I'd been doing that for fifteen years with the Indians organization, in the minors and the majors. I thought to myself, "How many times does someone have to evaluate you?" Those kinds of things upset me.

DM: Then what?

CM: He said to me, "You're my manager until the end of the year, but at the end of the year, I'd like to talk to some people, to interview some people." I said, "Mark, I look at that as, either I'm in or I'm out." It sounded like I was out.

DM: Did you end the meeting by saying, "I'm out of here," or words to that effect?

CM: No. I didn't say I was done. At the end of the meeting, Mark said something like, "Go home and think about it." I said, "I don't have to think about it."

DM: Doesn't that mean, though, that you effectively resigned on the spot?

CM: No, that's not what it means. Since then, I've heard I more or less fired myself. I didn't look at it that way then, and I don't look at it that way today.

DM: So you didn't quit?

CM: I didn't quit. Hell no, I didn't quit.

DM: It wasn't a case where you demanded a contract extension and didn't get it?

CM: I never demanded a contract. I have never demanded a contract. The contract never came up.

DM: What happened after the meeting concluded?

CM: Mark had asked me to come back the next day. I came in early. I went up to talk to him, and Mr. Dolan [Indians owner Larry Dolan] was there. He talked to me a little while. And that was it.

DM: Any regrets about how it all went down?

CM: No. Did I react a little quick? Maybe. I can be stubborn, but I have principles. I was very upset at the start, upset with myself. I wanted to do a good job with the Cleveland Indians, I loved that team, and I wanted them to want me. I enjoyed every minute of my time in the organization. I felt like I definitely deserved to be there. I didn't think I'd done anything to have to leave.

DM: What do you think of Mark Shapiro?

CM: Very dedicated in the minor leagues when I worked with him. When he became a GM, he had his own ideas. Mark and I definitely were going in different directions, but at the same time, I have a lot of respect for him and I think he's a good person.

DM: Has your view of him changed since 2002?

CM: At the time, I didn't realize what changes were all about. Now that I look back, Mark was doing his job. I have a better understanding of his position and his thinking. I realize there is a professional part to baseball and a business part, too.

DM: Were you worried that you might not get another opportunity to manage?

CM: I always felt like I'd get another chance. I'd been in the game a long time, and enough people knew me. I've never tried to promote myself. I felt like, if I worked hard enough, and the players were good enough, we could get the job done. That's what's happened in Philadelphia.

DM: What was your reaction to the Indians' sell-off this summer?

CM: What I got out of it was, they wanted younger players and wanted to improve their system. From the outside, it looks like they did a good job of getting players with major-league potential.

DM: And you get Cliff Lee.

CM: We got Cliff. And Ben Francisco.

DM: Do you feel bad for Indians fans who are forced to endure another rebuild?

CM: A couple of years ago, when we were in for an interleague series, the games drew 20,000, 25,000 people [June 18-20, 2007: 18,710; 17,371; 24,278]. It was a different feel. It was quiet. I remember when there was a lot of electricity and a lot of noise, and they were selling out every night. I'd like to see them get back to those days.

DM: Difference between Indians fans and Phillies fans?

CM: Phillies fans are more vocal. (*Chuckle*) They swear more.

DM: Do you get nervous before games?

CM: No. I do get mad when we lose, though.

DM: What is your managerial philosophy?

CM: I believe in honesty, attitude, chemistry and makeup. I believe you play the game day-to-day. I believe in even-keel, not getting too high or too low. I want the players to come to the ballpark relaxed and to come because they want to, not because they have to.

DM: Word association—Mike Hargrove?

CM: He had a good run. He did a tremendous job. It was just unfortunate he couldn't win a World Series.

DM: Albert Belle?

CM: I miss him. I miss watching him hit. I miss being around him. I wish him all the luck in the world.

DM: Jim Thome?

CM: I talk to Thome a lot. When I look at him, the career he's had, it's so impressive. I'm pulling for him to hit 600 homers. I feel kind of like he's my son.

DM: How does it feel when Thome credits you as much as anyone in the game for his success?

CM: It's a great compliment, but remember: I never got a hit for Thome. Thome did all the hitting.

DM: Manny Ramirez, another 500-homer guy, also was one of your pupils with the Tribe in the 1990s. Your reaction to the performance-enhancing-drugs cloud over him?

CM: I don't know everything that goes into that, but I want the best for Manny. I know this: Manny was a great hitter when he was young. Still is. But I do want baseball to clean up. I want baseball to enforce the drug policies. I want baseball to be clean, and it doesn't matter who's involved. At the same time, when I look at Manny's career, I can't help but remember all the good things. I know what kind of person he is.

DM: If you had a vote, would you vote Manny for the Hall of Fame?

CM: That's something I haven't really sat down and thought about because I'm not in a position to do that, anyway. But he's a great, great hitter.

DM: You've been through a lot in your life, including a heart attack. You wore a colostomy bag in the dugout for a while in Cleveland. Yet here you are, still plugging along, managing the defending world champions. How have you persevered?

CM: I enjoy life. I like to live. And I'm determined. Baseball's helped me survive.

DM: Thanks for the time.

CM: No problem. ... Hey, one more thing ...

DM: What?

CM: I didn't quit.

Tim McCarver, *baseball*

October 2007

Long before becoming a baseball analyst for Fox Sports, Tim McCarver enjoyed a productive career as a catcher. He batted .271 in 1,909 games of twenty-one seasons and won world championships with the St. Louis Cardinals in 1964 and 1967.

McCarver's biggest claim to fame is that he caught two of baseball's all-time great pitchers: Bob Gibson and Steve Carlton.

DM: Your most enjoyable moment as a ballplayer?

TM: I don't like to talk about what I did as a player, to be honest. But I would have to say Game 5 of the 1964 World Series. Gibson pitched ten innings and we beat the Yankees. I had a three-run homer in the tenth. I can't tell you how exciting that was, particularly being so young [22]. Young and innocent and stupid.

DM: What is it like to hit a game-deciding homer in the World Series?

TM: It's numbing more than anything else. You're almost aesthetically going around the bases.

DM: Talk about Gibson.

TM: He was one of the hardest friendships I ever had to make and now he's one of my closest friends. He was a ruthless competitor, and I mean that in the most optimistic way. He took no prisoners. You combine the athletic talent with the competitive drive, the drive to be above the rest, and you've got a man of gladiator status. I've never seen someone in sports combine them like Gibson did. Jack Buck said Bob Gibson was head-and-shoulders the best athlete he ever saw in any sport. Very few times does a pitcher lead a baseball team, but Bob was—in more ways than what he did between the white lines—our leader.

DM: What was it like to catch Gibson?

TM: It wasn't easy because of the movement of his pitches. Usually, if a guy's tough to hit, he's tough to catch. His ball had the latest movement of any pitcher I ever caught.

DM: What is one snapshot that captures the essence of Gibson?

TM: The night before Steve Carlton was inducted into the Hall of Fame they had a party. Hall of Famers and special guests were there. I was asked to say something but I didn't want to, because this was Steve's night. I finally agreed and said, "If Carl Hubbell had the greatest screwball in the history of the game, Sandy Koufax the greatest curve and Nolan Ryan arguably the greatest fastball, well, Steve Carlton would go down as having the greatest slider in the history of baseball." We hugged. Then, as everybody's breaking up, I see this figure swimming through the crowd toward me. It's Gibson, and he comes up and gets in my face and says, "The best left-handed slider in the history of the game." Classic Gibson.

DM: How cool is it that you caught Gibson, then Carlton?

TM: I was fortunate. I learned a lot from both of them. And Steve learned a lot from Bob.

DM: What is one thing Carlton learned from Gibson?

TM: That the mound was his office. Pete Rose, as an example, used to intimidate young pitchers by running back over the mound after he made an out. Rose never crossed over the mound when Gibson pitched. Never. Nobody did.

DM: For or against instant replay in baseball?

TM: I was adamantly opposed until about three years ago. That's not to say I'm leaning toward it, but I'm much more willing to listen.

DM: What is your opinion of Barry Bonds? Do you see him as innocent until proven guilty?

TM: Well, number one, he's not innocent. I mean who's kidding whom? Really. He hasn't been proven guilty, but the court of public opinion, in my view, is strong enough to conclude that Barry Bonds took steroids. Don't you believe that? Doesn't everybody believe that?

DM: I'm afraid of his lawyers.

TM: Well, why isn't everybody talking about Barry Bonds right now?

DM: Is it a shame, then, that the supposed all-time home run king ...?

TM: I can't give you anything new that hasn't been already said about Barry Bonds. This is not going to be any kind of revelation of any kind. I would be on the side of, and am part of, the court of public opinion. It's my business to be as fair as I can, and I think I'm being very fair along those lines.

Alyssa Milano, *acting/baseball*
October 2007

Alyssa Milano is more than an actress. She is an actress who loves baseball, making October her favorite month.

Milano serves as an online personality for TBS' new baseball broadband channel, TBS Hot Corner on *mlb.com*. She was in Boston Wednesday to write about the American League Division Series between the Red Sox and Los Angeles Angels. She also writes the Touch 'Em All blog on mlb.com *(http://alyssa.mlblogs.com)*.

Milano, whose TV credits include *Charmed*, *Melrose Place* and *Who's the Boss?* recently landed a recurring role on *My Name Is Earl*.

DM: I'm a big fan of *Who's the Boss?* Congrats on the successful run.

AM: Thanks.

DM: When did you become a baseball fan?

AM: I don't remember a time when baseball wasn't part of the family.

DM: When did you become a Dodgers fan?

AM: My dad was a huge Brooklyn Dodgers fan. He grew up in Flatbush [Brooklyn] and was heartbroken when they left. I was raised around those stories. And I grew up watching the Yankees on his lap. When we moved to L.A., I was eleven, and he slowly became a Dodgers fan again. As much flak as L.A. fans get, it's hard not to be a Dodgers fan when you live in Los Angeles.

DM: Without the Dodgers in the playoffs, which team will you root for to win it all?

AM: I'm rooting for Lou Piniella and the Cubbies. If you're a baseball fan with no loyalties to the teams remaining, the Cubbies are as good a choice as any given their history.

DM: What is your prediction for how the postseason will play out?

AM: Honestly, I can't even fathom giving one because anything can happen. Part of what makes the postseason so great is how unpredictable it is.

DM: Anyone in your Hollywood inner circle with whom you talk baseball?

AM: (*Laughs*) Not really. People tend to think I'm nuts because of my obsession with it.

DM: Following baseball doesn't seem to be the sexy thing to do in Hollywood.

AM: True, true. It's too bad. I think about what my contemporaries are doing, as far as the club-hopping and all that. I'd rather be at Dodger Stadium than at any club or film premiere. And I don't decide to be fashionably late to a game.

DM: Which do you read first—sports page or entertainment news?

AM: The sports page, of course. Box scores. I told you: I'm obsessed. I probably log onto mlb.com at least a dozen times a day.

DM: You must be thrilled that the interest in your writings for mlb.com has been through the roof.

AM: I'm very excited, sure. I'm definitely outside my comfort zone, so it was scary at first, mainly because of perceptions and how it would be accepted. Female fans have been really supportive. I suppose they're just happy that someone with an intelligent mind-set can represent what they're all about regarding baseball.

DM: Favorite piece of baseball memorabilia that you own?

AM: Two signed photos of Sandy Koufax.

DM: Favorite player of all-time?

AM: Roberto Clemente. He represented everything a ballplayer should be. He used his voice to effect positive change in the world. He helped set the stage for a lot of players to reach out to the community.

DM: Your greatest moment as a fan?

AM: This year, at the All-Star Game, I was able to bring my dad and my brother on the field for batting practice. I had this moment when I looked around and saw all of our heroes, all of the greats in the game today, and they were so close. I looked at my dad and my brother and felt so good that I was able to share the experience and access with them.

DM: Favorite food at Dodger Stadium?

AM: Nachos with cheese, guacamole and jalapeno peppers.

DM: Are you serious?

AM: Yes. Delicious.

DM: What about the legendary Dodger Dog?

AM: No. But they do make a great tofu dog.

DM: What are similarities between acting and baseball?

AM: You can't do it alone; it takes a team. Perseverance. Long hours behind the scenes.

DM: How cool was it to work with Tony Danza on *Who's the Boss?*

AM: A lot of fun. Hey … wasn't Tony's character on the show a former pitcher for the Indians?

DM: I don't know.

AM: I thought you said you were a big fan of the show.

DM: Uh, well, you got me there. Sorry about that.

AM: (*Laughs*) That's OK. I don't remember—and I lived it for eight years. [Tony was a former St. Louis Cardinal.]

DM: What is your take on Barry Bonds?

AM: I think it's sad that the greatness he already had within him is overshadowed by this crazy controversy. And I don't particularly like him as a person, so it's hard to root for him and want him to come out of this on the other side. I don't think he's gracious with the media or the community. If he were someone more accessible and more likable, it wouldn't be as much of an issue. Look at Jason Giambi. I respect Giambi because he's actually honest.

DM: Any tweaks to the game itself?

AM: I love the game as it is.

DM: What about instant replay to mitigate human error?

AM: Definitely not. I'm a traditionalist.

Kevin Millar, *baseball*
June 2005

Kevin Millar is far from the most talented player for the Boston Red Sox, but he plays a crucial role in their success. Millar, aside from being dangerous in the clutch, is responsible for keeping the highly scrutinized clubhouse loose.

Since arriving from the Marlins in 2003, Millar has helped eradicate a 25-cabs-for-25-guys mentality and turn the Red Sox into a jocular, if slightly dysfunctional, family. The ultimate payoff came last season, when the loosey-goosey Sox rallied from an 0-3 deficit to shock the Yankees in the ALCS, then swept the Cardinals for their first World Series title since 1918.

DM: Describe the Red Sox clubhouse.

KM: Crazy. Fun. Goofy. But I'll tell you what—it competes. We don't worry about anything until 7:05, or 1:05, or whenever they throw the first pitch. Once the game starts, we all pull the same rope.

DM: What kind of pranks do you guys pull on each other?

KM: It's not so much pranks; that doesn't happen much in baseball these days. But you're going to rip on each other constantly. Nobody's exempt. And you're not going to be allowed to take your shirt off.

DM: Why?

KM: Have you seen the bodies we have around here? If somebody takes his shirt off, too many people are going to throw up.

DM: The matinee idol, Johnny Damon, would take issue.

KM: Damon and [Jason] Varitek. That's about it.

DM: Describe [Curt] Schilling in twenty words or fewer.

KM: Great competitor, probably the best big-game pitcher of our generation. Bad body. White like Casper—and he lives in Arizona, where the sun shines.

DM: Manny Ramirez?

KM: Greatest right-handed run producer in this game for the past ten years. Amazing hitter. Hilarious.

DM: Funniest thing you've ever seen Manny do?

KM: You have to ask? Funniest I've seen—and the greatest highlight of all, Manny or otherwise, came last year at Fenway Park when he came over from left to cut off Johnny's throw from center. He didn't just cut it off, he laid out for it. He played it into a web gem. Greatest catch he's ever made in his career. Everybody was in awe. To this day, we don't know what Manny was doing. If he knows, he's not telling.

DM: How often does Manny get razzed?

KM: Twenty-four/seven. Nonstop. But Manny gives it to himself, too. He's very smart. He plays dumb, plays stupid, but he knows what's going on.

DM: What were you doing as Edgar Renteria chopped to Keith Foulke to end Game 4 and win clinch the Series?

KM: I was grabbing Schilling's love-handle. He went to hop the dugout fence and almost fell. I was hoping he would, because it would have been the funniest highlight you've ever seen.

DM: First baseman Doug Mientkiewicz, defensive replacement for David Ortiz, caught the ball from Foulke, then claimed ownership of it. Agree or disagree with him?

KM: I wouldn't have kept the ball because I always hand it to the pitcher. I'm not going to say I disagree with Doug. Obviously, there was a thought process involved. Whose ball is it? Tough call. It's not Boston's. It might be St. Louis'. Who knows?

DM: In the postgame celebration, actors Drew Barrymore and Jimmy Fallon slipped onto the field and took part in the celebration for a scene in the movie, *Fever Pitch*. Did that annoy you?

KM: No. I give them credit for having the guts to sneak out there. They weren't the only ones who did it, either.

DM: Jack Daniel's or Crown Royal?

KM: Good one, man.... Both.

DM: Your Series afterglow was adversely affected by comments you made on national TV that Red Sox players consumed whiskey during the postseason, particularly the World Series. Please explain.

KM: Before Game 6 of the ALCS, I poured Jack Daniel's in a small cup, and we all did a symbolic toast. I took a sip, and that was it. If we won, of course we would do it again. We'd keep doing it until we lost, because superstitions are part of baseball.

DM: That's all there was to it?

KM: Yeah. All of a sudden, the story takes on a life of its own. Two weeks later, we're all hammered playing in the biggest games of our lives. I said, "Timeout, timeout." Have you ever hit a 95 mph pitch sober? You're not going to hit one drunk, I promise you.

DM: So the Boston Red Sox were not imbibing during postseason games?

KM: Correct. Nobody drank alcohol, other than beer, before or during games.

DM: You and your teammates seem to have recovered from the PR hit.

KM: My only regret is, mothers were calling me two days after the World Series saying I was a bad role model, that I was teaching their sons to drink. I'm truly sorry about that.

DM: You originally were signed by Florida out of the independent leagues in 1993. After the Series, did you pause to reflect how far you had come?

KM: Absolutely. The road I've taken is laughable, really. I was never drafted--high school, junior college or college. I played one year for the St. Paul Saints of the Northern League and made $600 a month. Eleven years later, I was on the team that gave Boston its first World Series title in 86 years. You couldn't sell that script.

DM: Greatest promotion you witnessed in St. Paul?

KM: It came in three parts. On one dugout, we had a nun—a real nun—giving massages. If we score six, seven runs, you wind up getting about a half-hour massage. On the other dugout, a barber was cutting hair. And a trained pig was taking balls out to the umpire. All at the same time.

DM: I read where the independent leagues remain close to your heart.

KM: Every chance I get, I take in a game. Last year, we had an off day in Pittsburgh, and I found one nearby. I went into the clubhouses and said, "Guys, I'm telling you, people can say whatever they want, but [expletive] them. Don't let anybody tell you that you can't do it, because I was in your exact spot."

DM: Best part of being a Red Sox?

KM: Being part of the passion of Sox Nation, West Coast to East Coast.

DM: Regardless of the negativity that comes with it?

KM: I enjoy it, but, hey, it's not for everybody. It's cold and miserable and rainy in April and May. You'll get blasted in the media from time to time. Anything you say or do will get magnified and maybe blown out of proportion. But if you like baseball, why wouldn't you want to play for the Red Sox?

DM: Is it true you've played five years of winter ball?

KM: Yes. It's a great experience, and I like relating with the Latin guys. Not a whole lot of white guys go down and play winter ball regularly, so they don't understand what the Latin guys go through over here.

DM: If MLB commissioner for a day, what is one change you would make?

KM: Put the designated hitter in the National League. I like the NL game. It's baseball. You bunt, hit-and-run. As a fan, though, you want to see the ball hit around. Besides, I've seen Schilling hit, and it's a pathetic sight, believe me.

DM: Do you believe in the curse of the Bambino?

KM: Look into my eyes. Does it look like I do?

DM: Uh, no.

KM: There was no such thing.

Dominique Moceanu, *gymnastics*
July 2006

They arrived at the 1996 Atlanta Games as seven girls with high expectations. They departed as the "Magnificent Seven," the first U.S. women's gymnastics team to secure Olympic gold.

The Magnificent Seven's most recognizable component was its youngest and smallest Member, fourteen-year-old Dominique Moceanu, who was listed at 4 foot 5 but says she was closer to 4 foot 4. Her charisma and "It" factor were immeasurable. Lingering effects from a stress fracture in her right tibia left Moceanu at less than 100 percent for the Games. Nonetheless, she made significant contributions in the team event, whose finals unfolded ten years ago Sunday in the Georgia Dome.

Dominique Moceanu
photo by Dave Black

The lasting memory of Moceanu from that magical night, however, comes from her consecutive falls on the vault with the opportunity to clinch gold. Moceanu's mistakes put the spotlight on Kerri Strug, who fell on her first attempt and severely injured her left ankle. On the second attempt, a grimacing Strug managed to stay upright and deliver the gold.

As it turned out, Moceanu's lowest vault score would have sufficed, regardless of what Strug did. But to reflect on that fact is to tamper with arguably the Games' most enduring snapshot and the legend that grew from it.

In the years post-Atlanta, Moceanu has done just fine. She gravitated to Northeast Ohio, where she is a student at John Carroll University and resides on the East Side. She coaches at Gymnastics World in Broadview Heights and is in the midst of a comeback attempt, with eyes on the U.S. National Team.

Moceanu's coach, Ohio State product Mike Canales, also is her fiancé. They will marry later this year.

DM: How wild was it to be Dominique Moceanu at the Atlanta Games?

DM: They had extra security for me, because you couldn't see me through a crowd and there was a fear I would get snatched up.

DM: Fondest recollections of the night you and your team won gold?

DM: Entering the Georgia Dome with a crowd of 32,000; helping Kerri get onto the podium after she had been injured; thousands of flashbulbs staring us in the face while we were on the podium; the intense emotional rush when the national anthem was played.

DM: You realize that your misfortune on the vault helped make Strug a household name and, for that matter, a millionaire.

DM: Of course. I'm happy she was able to enjoy that moment. I'm happy people remember her because of it, given that it really helped our sport. It was a great moment in gymnastics history. People always remember the girl who landed on one leg.

DM: But the fact remains, she owes you.

DM: Even though we still would have won with my score, the story happening the way it did was fantastic. Kerri doing the vault the way she did was an exclamation point. It added drama, anticipation and all sorts of emotions.

DM: I read where Kerri is your closest friend from the Magnificent Seven.

DM: That's true. We were never that close through the Olympics because of our age difference, but we've gotten really close the last several years.

DM: No wonder you are her best friend.

DM: (*Laughs*) She is my good friend, so we help each other out. I always wish Kerri well.

DM: You were ultra-tiny in 1996. Did it ever annoy you when coaches, teammates and others kept patting you on the head, as if you were some teddy bear, even if their relative height made it the most convenient thing to do?

DM: (*Laughs*) I hadn't thought of it that way. Looking back, I can't say that it bothered me. I was always appreciative of any support, and let's face it—I was small. It would have been hard for me to keep looking up at them.

DM: You never let on that the leg was hurting during the Games, but it must have hampered you. [She finished ninth in the all-around].

DM: You don't show signs of weakness in competition. You are trained to be tough like a warrior. I didn't want to show that, at the Olympics, the biggest competition of my life, the injury was a factor. I wasn't able to do landings on my vaults and barely got any work in before the Olympic Games, but I wasn't going to use the injury as an excuse.

DM: How much fan mail did you receive in the summer of '96?

DM: More than 1,000 pieces per week. It came in U.S. Postal Service boxes. We had to crawl through the boxes in the living room to get to the couch.

DM: What were some of the more notable gifts you received?

DM: Lots of stuffed animals, earrings, necklaces, photos of me and my sister, drawings of me off the TV, plastic engagement rings …

DM: Whoa … engagement rings?

DM: Engagement rings. You know, the ones you get out of the quarter machines.

DM: Do I have to ask to what those pertained?

DM: Well, they were from people asking me to marry them.

DM: Estimated number of plastic engagement rings and other proposals you received?

DM: It was in the hundreds—at least.

DM: That's incredible. You were fourteen years old, for crying out loud.

DM: I know, I know. It was unbelievable. I couldn't even drive, yet people were asking me to marry them. I couldn't fathom it. If I hadn't actually seen the stuff in front of me, I wouldn't have believed it.

DM: Did some dude honestly think you were going to open up a piece of mail, look at a plastic engagement sign and 10 lines of cheesy prose and say, "Yep, that's my future husband?"

DM: (*Chuckle*) Some thought it was worth a try, I guess.

DM: Any other oddities?

DM: Letters from inmates.... I got them quite often, actually. I still get them to this day.

DM: Do you open them?

DM: Not really. I used to, just to see what they wanted, but I don't anymore. I don't want to put myself in a predicament, you know?

DM: What do they want?

DM: They ask for an autographed picture, or they write, "Don't judge me because I am in here, I am trying to change my life around, I turned my life over to God, and I'd just like an autographed picture."

DM: Did you ever get a marriage proposal from an inmate?

DM: I probably did, but it so happened that I didn't open the letter.

DM: Beyond the wackos, the fan support must have been gratifying.

DM: Absolutely. You realize something motivated them to write. A lot of people said I was a motivation for them, or that I got them interested in the sport. That's humbling.

DM: What advice would you give to young gymnasts?

DM: A very wise friend of mine passed this on to me: Remember, gymnastics is what you do, not who you are. Gymnastics can be very rewarding but also very challenging. It's a tough road, but if you can see the big picture and use the sport to refine life skills such as time management, discipline, constructively dealing with disappointment and humbly accepting success, you'll be fine.

DM: When you reflect on the '96 Games, what amazes you most?

DM: Some of the routines we were able to do. And, how I survived the system to get to that point in the first place. We were put through rigorous training and made a lot of sacrifices at a very young age, so I look back at that time with a lot of pride for what we accomplished.

DM: The demands of the Bela Karolyi camp in preparation for Atlanta are well-documented. Do you think we'll ever see that again?

DM: Not quite, no. It was more accepted back then, and the girls were younger. Their bodies could handle more.

DM: Do you ever miss the rush of being one of the biggest names at a Games?

DM: The Olympics were a great chapter in my life, but I am level-headed. I knew it wouldn't be like that forever, and I was prepared to move on once it died down. I made the most of it at the time, and I am very happy now.

Joe Montana, *football*
May 2005

Joe Montana is an American sports icon. During a sixteen-year NFL career, he threw for 40,551 yards and 273 touchdowns and made the Pro Bowl eight times. He led the San Francisco 49ers to four Super Bowls—and won them all.

Retired since 1994, Montana has had no problem staying busy raising a family and working on various projects. He was in town last month to promote hypertension awareness. Montana suffers from high blood pressure, and has teamed with cardiologist Dr. James Rippe to educate people on the condition.

DM: How long have you been on the high blood pressure / hypertension awareness campaign?

JM: A little more than two years.

DM: What is your history with high blood pressure?

JM: I found out I had it during an annual physical. I was as surprised as anyone. The first medication to treat it didn't work. Fortunately, my doctor stayed on top of the situation, and now I'm on two medications to control it.

DM: What is the crux of your hypertension message?

JM: Hypertension is a major risk factor for heart disease and stroke, and we want people to start a dialogue with their doctor to find out what their blood pressure is. Also, the message to those who have it and know they have it is make sure to stay on the prescribed program and monitor the b.p. success zone. Of the 65 million who have high blood pressure, seventy percent don't have it under the control they think they do.

DM: Have you spoken with Alex Smith, the number one overall pick of the 49ers? If not, what advice would you give him?

JM: I have not spoken with him. My advice would be to stay patient. Everybody wants to play, but sometimes it's just not the right thing to get in there and play right away. College to the NFL is a huge jump, obviously. And the reality is, his college team [Utah] had a lot of success and the 49ers haven't recently, which makes the adjustment that much more difficult.

DM: Toughest part of playing quarterback in the NFL?

JM: Recognizing defenses. Around the time I was ready to retire, they'd leave people open and focus on getting to the quarterback. It didn't matter if the lineman was covering the running back, you weren't going to have enough time to find him. They do so much stuff now that in college you'd never see or wouldn't anticipate.

DM: What is your advice to [Eagles wide receiver] Terrell Owens?

JM: He's such a good player, but I'm not sure he thinks about a lot of things he does. Unfortunately, it's not just his problem. I think you see that problem throughout the United States these days, where people feel It's OK to do or say anything. That's not the way it should be. Terrell is such a talented player, he doesn't need to do the other stuff.

DM: You have been nicknamed "Joe Cool" for good reason. You never seemed to get upset. Did you ever lose your composure during a game?

JM: I don't remember really losing it, although I'm sure I did. Everybody does at some point.

DM: What do you consider the greatest game you ever played as a pro, a game after which you felt the best coming off the field?

JM: We played the Eagles in Philadelphia in 1989 [September 24]. I came out and threw a touchdown to Jerry Rice and thought it would be an easy game. The next thing I knew, I spent three quarters picking myself up off the turf. We were behind in the fourth quarter, 21-10, and we came back to win it, 38-28. You start out on a high, then feel as low as you can during a game, then battle back and win. There was a great feeling in the locker room. [Montana threw for 428 yards and five touchdowns, including 227 and four in the fourth; he needed 5:32 for the four fourth-quarter TDs, using 18 plays to cover 252 yards].

DM: How have you compensated for the NFL adrenaline / competition rush?

JM: I don't think you can. Right now, cutting horses is about as much of an adrenaline rush as I've found.

DM: When you hear of quarterbacks such as Tom Brady compared to you, what is your reaction?

JM: I feel good, I guess, but I don't like comparisons. People tried to compare me to certain quarterbacks in my career. It's too hard to do that. Just enjoy the guy, enjoy him for what he's doing. Let him be his own person.

DM: Which would you take—5,000 yards passing, NFL MVP but no Super Bowl; or, decent season, no MVP, Super Bowl only to lose, 55-10?

JM: (*Chuckle*) Wow. Hmm…. To be honest, even though the Super Bowl speaks for itself, I wouldn't want to go to a Super Bowl and lose. Thankfully, I don't know that feeling. I can't imagine it feels very good.

DM: What, if anything, did you tell John Elway after your 49ers drubbed the Broncos, 55-10, in Super Bowl XXIV?

JM: It was a game where everything went our way. When you run into a team that's playing like we were at that time, it's difficult to handle, no matter what type of season you've had or how confident you are before the game.

DM: Why can't more than a handful of NFL players get guaranteed contracts beyond one year?

JM: The owners…. They have the tightest monopoly going. They don't have a lot of people who try to buck the system. They look around at the two, three other major sports and say, "We're doing the right thing." Above all else, what they have going for them is unity.

DM: Were steroids visible in the locker room in your day?

JM: No. I never saw anyone take them. I hear stories where guys out of the game say they saw players injecting other players. Well, they must have been in the wrong place at the wrong time.

DM: You seem perfectly suited to be a general manager. Have you considered it?

JM: Not yet. I've got boys growing up who are playing sports. That's what I've been concentrating on.

DM: How do you handle the father/coach role with your sons, Nathaniel and Nicholas?

JM: As far as giving advice, what I've told the boys is, "Look, if you want to play the game for fun, that's OK. Just tell me. But if you want to get better, and you don't like being the second-team guy, just tell me and I'll help you any way I can." I leave it at that.

DM: Have they opted for the former?

JM: Yes.

DM: Who joins you at your dream quarterbacks roundtable?

JM: Johnny Unitas, Bart Starr, Sammy Baugh, Dan Marino.

DM: Any regrets in your NFL career?

JM: I loved Kansas City, but I wish I could have stayed in San Francisco for the duration. Other than that, none.

DM: Your coach in Kansas City was Marty Schottenheimer, who remains sans Super Bowl appearance. Is he snakebit?

JM: I don't know—but it sure seems like it.

(For more information on hypertension, Montana and Dr. Rippe recommend the Web site *www.healthybp.com*).

Danica Patrick, *auto racing*
June 2004

The young adult male nervously makes small talk with race-car driver Danica Patrick, who is signing autographs and posing for pictures at the Galleria downtown. Patrick, her eyebrows pitched, cuts through the muck.

"Are you asking me out?" she says.

In a convoluted way, he was.

"Come to the race," she says, "and we'll see what happens."

Nonplussed, he procures the autograph and quietly shuffles away.

Another man critiques the publicity photo she is signing as

Danica Patrick
photo by Mike Levy/*The Plain Dealer*

entirely too blasé. Patrick wonders what kind of photo he would suggest as an alternative.

"You don't want to know," his buddy says, laughing.

Several other older adult males linger away from the table. Patrick asks one if he would like a signature.

"We're just here to stare at you," he says.

Such is five minutes off the track in the life of Patrick, 22, a budding open-wheel talent who happens to bring a striking physical presence to the proceedings. The 5 foot 1 and 3/4-inch dynamo is as comfortable crammed into a cockpit as she is posing outside of it for a sexy photo shoot.

Patrick, who began her racing career thirteen years ago in Go Karts, ranks second in Atlantic series points through three events. The Atlantic cars are a cut below Champ Car, the featured attraction at Burke Lakefront Airport, July 1–3.

DM: Does anything give you the creeps at autograph signings?

DP: The people who don't come up to you and instead just stand back and watch. They fake like they're not listening, but you know they are. You feel them around you, and it's kind of strange. I mean, say something to me, please. I promise I'll be nice to you.

It's also weird when someone has a big pile of pictures, candid shots when I was caught off-guard. I try to be as polite as possible when looking at those, but I'm saying to myself, "Why do you want me when I'm caught off-guard? And, why the pile? Did you really need eight photos instead of one or two?"

DM: Why did you put yourself in the crosshairs of fellow drivers and critics by agreeing to the FHM publication shoot [April 2003]?

DP: The exposure, when tastefully done, is good for the sport and good for me. I don't feel any extra pressure to win because I posed for FHM. I know I can drive. All the other stuff means is, more people are watching. The right people know I can drive the car, that my intentions are good.

DM: What is the biggest misconception about you?

DP: That I think about being a "chick" in racing. Until people started talking about it and writing about it, I never thought in those terms. I didn't race Go Karts with the idea of one day being recognized as a female racer.

DM: But can you blame those who—at least initially—cast you in that light, given your off-course appeal?

DP: No, I can't. I understand why it happens and what comes with the territory. I choose to put myself out there. Out of the car, I surely am a "chick." I'm a girl. I like to get done-up. I like to look pretty. What's wrong with that?

DM: Nothing, I suppose.

DP: If it helps me to keep sponsorships and raise levels of awareness, so be it. I'm not going to apologize for that.

DM: In your second year of Atlantics, are you confident your competitors take you seriously?

DP: Yes. There's got to be a certain level of respect for anybody at this stage. Once you've reached Atlantics, within reason you can drive.

DM: Who makes up the Danica demographic?

DP: It seems to be divided in two: families with little girls, who look to me as a role model; or, older men, hard-core race fans, in their thirties and forties. I find that a bit bizarre, because the eighteen to twenty-five-year-old male, the group that would make the most sense … I don't see too many of them. I don't know if they're scared to approach me, or what.

DM: At 5 foot 1 and 3/4 inches and 105 pounds, you are one of the smallest racers in the game. Has the frame been something to overcome?

The Plain Dealer | Thursday, June 10, 2004

Wayne Gretzky of the Los Angeles Kings is named the NHL's MVP, winning the Hart Trophy for a record ninth time.

DMAN'S WORLD

AROUND THE HORN

Ice Cube chooses to play it cool

From wire reports

Talk about being put on the spot.

Los Angeles Lakers fan O'Shea Jackson, better known in the rap music world as Ice Cube, was sitting on the Staples Center court Sunday night as a guest of Ahmad Rashad on NBA TV's "Live at the Finals" pregame show.

About 45 minutes before the start of Game 1, the Detroit Pistons' Rasheed Wallace, on the court warming up, walked over to Ice Cube and, while the cameras were rolling, asked, "Who you picking?"

Said Ice Cube, "I was just saying, if you were not on the Pistons, they would have never made it to the Finals."

Wallace replied, "That isn't what I asked."

Candid answer: Athletes usually shy away from ranking former teammates. Not Shannon Sharpe.

According to the Baltimore Sun, he was asked during his Las Vegas retirement party who was the better player, Baltimore linebacker Ray Lewis or Denver quarterback John Elway.

"I'll put it to you like this," the newspaper quoted him as saying. "I would take my 1997 [Bronco] team over that 2000 Raven team. . . . I'm going to have to take my homeboy, No. 7."

Lewis wears No. 52.

No doubt about it: Former New York Giants quarterback Phil Simms was asked by James Brown on his Sporting News Radio show if Eli Manning would be the Giants' starter in Week 1.

"To think a rookie quarterback will be ready to start Week 1, it's

SPECIAL TO THE PLAIN DEALER

Race car driver Danica Patrick has used her looks off the track to help bring more attention to the track. Patrick was in town to promote the upcoming Atlantic car race in Cleveland from July 1 to 3.

HEARTS RACING

Patrick uses looks outside track and tough grit on it

Danica Patrick

clipping from *The Plain Dealer*

DP: The only real hindrance is, I'm just boney enough that my collarbone gets bruised from the HANS device and my hip bones get bruised from the lap belt.

DM: Boney or not, it certainly appears you take your fitness seriously.

DP: I work out all the time. I guarantee I'm more fit than a lot of guys out there. It's important for my racing and my marketability. I couldn't do a photo shoot or be on TV if I didn't look good.

DM: What comprises the fitness regimen?

DP: Being outside, running, yoga, Pilates, mountain climbing, lifting weights.

DM: Car of choice as a civilian?

DP: Mercedes.

DM: Lifetime speeding tickets?

DP: I'm not sure. I've been pulled over about a dozen times, but I don't have any tickets on my record that I'm aware of. I'll do whatever I can to get out of a ticket, short of, "Do you know who I am?" I'll never pull that. If they figure it out, fine. But I'm not going to act all high and mighty.

DM: What is the most angry you have gotten with another driver?

DP: In Go Karts, I would occasionally try to pull guys out of their seats by the helmet. I was really mean. A lot of people were scared of me in go-karting. I'm much nicer now.

UPDATE: Danica graduated to the IndyCar Series in 2005. She moved on to NASCAR full time in 2012. As of April 2015, she had 1.18 million Twitter followers.

Johnny Pesky, *baseball*
March 2004

Johnny Pesky today is in some respects the Red Sox version of Bob Feller, a former player still active in his 80s as an ambassador for the club and the game. Pesky was nowhere near the talent of Feller, but did bat .307 in 1,270 games over ten seasons as an infielder for the Red Sox, Tigers and Senators.

Born John Michael Paveskovich on September 27, 1919, he made his major-league debut on April 14, 1942. Pesky scored at least 100 runs in each of his first six seasons, including a career-high 124 in 1948. He ranked in the top ten in batting five times and lived up to his name at the plate, finishing with 662 walks and just 218 strikeouts.

Pesky, who remains a special instructor, also is one of the "Three Kings of Fungo," alongside Frank Howard and the late Jimmie Reese.

DM: How many fungoes have you hit?

JP: At least a million. And I mean, literally, a million.

DM: Does it ever get old?

JP: No, but I do. I don't have as much pop as I used to. I've got to choke up too much. I used to be able to hit balls straight up in the air consistently. People say, "Johnny, you've got an excuse." But I don't see it that way.

DM: Talk about October 4, 1948 — the one-game playoff for the pennant at Fenway Park won by the Indians, 8-3.

JP: You had to bring that up, didn't you? Of course — didn't you say you're from Cleveland?

DM: Yes.

JP: Well, I remember Lou Boudreau killed us. He was MVP that

year, and he showed why that day. What a ballplayer. And the
kid Cleveland sent out there, Gene Bearden, give him credit. He
kept us off-balance, and when he didn't, we hit balls hard right at
people.

DM: Were you overconfident against Bearden, given that he was a
rookie pitching on the road on short rest?

JP: No. You respect everybody, and Bearden was a nineteen-
game winner to that point. I do remember Ted Williams saying
afterwards, "You watch: Bearden won't win twenty games for
the rest of his career." Ted was pretty much right [Bearden won
twenty-five more], but Bearden beat us that day, which is all that
matters.

DM: What were your impressions of Bob Feller?

JP: Awesome. In my mind, he's probably a top-five pitcher of
all-time, definitely top ten. Great fastball, outstanding curve and
wasn't afraid of anybody. And, he left to fight in the war [World
War II] in his prime.

DM: How did you fare against him?

JP: You're not going to believe this, but I actually hit a homer off
him. One of my seventeen career homers is off Bob Feller.

DM: Was it majestic?

JP: No, if I recall it barely went 300 around the pole in right at
Fenway. What's funny is, Feller used to call me a pissant. He
walked me a few times because I wouldn't swing at some close
pitches, so he'd yell, "That [expletive] Pesky's always taking. He
never swings the bat." But he hung a curve one day and I got
enough wood on it.

DM: The right-field pole at Fenway is known as "The Pesky Pole"
or "Pesky's Pole." How did that happen?

JP: When Mel Parnell was broadcasting, somebody hit one
around the pole late in the game. Parnell said, "Pesky won a

ballgame for me around that pole in '48. We called it Pesky's pole." Then [broadcasters] Ken Coleman and Ned Martin kind of picked it up and ran with it.

DM: How many homers did you hit around the pole?

JP: For the longest time, I told people it was eight. But the guys at SABR said I only hit six. So I lied.

DM: What is ...

JP: Excuse me for a second. I know Ken Coleman is a familiar name in Cleveland, and I just want to say what a class guy he was. A very good announcer and a very good man.

DM: What is the biggest change in the game from when you played?

JP: Money, for sure. My gosh, there's so much money available now. What does a rookie make — $270,000 or something? I didn't make that in my entire career. We were Depression people.

DM: Do you begrudge it to the players today?

JP: Absolutely not. I'm happy for them. I wish I were a twenty-two-year-old right now, because even the little guys get paid. I'd settle for $270,000.

DM: What was the dollar value of your first Red Sox contract?

JP: Four thousand. I sent the original proposal back because I wanted five. Our GM replied within a week. He wrote: "Please sign the enclosed contract, because we don't know if you can play in the big leagues." My older brother was a worry wart; he was afraid they'd release me, so he made certain I signed it.

DM: It must have felt good coming up with the season you did in '42. (Pesky batted .331 with 205 hits and struck out thirty-six times in 620 at-bats.)

JP: Yes, and I got a $5,000 bonus from Mr. Yawkey, our owner, in part because I was going into the service for the next three years.

I sent the money home to my family.

DM: What are your thoughts about the state of the game today?

JP: The game is still great. In a lot of ways, I think it's better. Fans are more interested, for one thing. I'm not one of those guys who says, "It was so much better back in the day." There were great players then just like there are great players now. And today's players are bigger, stronger, faster.

DM: What is the most significant improvement in the game from when you broke in?

JP: Integration. I am happy to see black players getting the attention they deserve. Boy, did they take a lot of abuse back then. When you consider what Jackie Robinson and Larry Doby went through, it makes you sick. Black players were stereotyped, and it was totally unfair.

DM: What advice would you give today's player?

JP: Appreciate what you have. Try to remember the contributions and the sacrifices made by the people who came before you.

Phil Pfister, *strongman*
March 2004

Being one of the world's strongest humans has its drawbacks. For Phil Pfister, it means the tire he needs to transport for training sessions weighs merely 500 pounds instead of 800 or 900.

"It can't be too heavy, because I have to load the tire onto the truck by myself," he said. "I can't exactly get people to help me."

Pfister drives the tire to the firehouse in Charleston, West Virginia, where he will flip it during down time at work. He also will spin a 300-pound log or harness up to a fire truck and pull it across the parking lot—just for grins.

Pfister did not lift weights with a purpose until twenty-one and did not commence his strongman career until 1998. He has made up for lost time. Five months after being introduced to the sport, he placed fourth in the world's strongest man tournament. It was the first of three top-five world finishes to date.

Last season, he won four events in the X-Treme Strongman Series. He has placed first and second in two events this season.

DM: Which do you prefer—firefighter or strongman?

PP: Each has its moments and pays about half the bills. If I could make my living solely as a strongman, I probably would choose that.

DM: You have a reputation as a gentle giant. How did it come about?

PP: You can't afford to walk around being loud and overbearing at 6 foot 6, 325 pounds. The physical presence alone can be intimidating. If you don't downplay yourself, you become a complete oddity or complete spectacle or complete ass. You really can't raise your voice. You can't do a lot of things—unless you're around your family and friends, because they know you're not some super-mutant from hell.

DM: How big were you upon graduation from high school?

PP: 6 foot 3, 225 pounds.

DM: What is your greatest Herculean feat?

PP: I don't think of them in that context, but there are two [feats] people talk about. The morning of a competition in New Orleans a couple of years ago, I harnessed up to a riverboat, the Cajun Queen, and pulled it fifty feet. I did that four more times over the course of the morning.

DM: How much did the riverboat weigh?

PP: About 600,000 pounds. But I've had tougher pulls.

DM: What is the other extraordinary feat?

PP: At an exhibition, in what's called a farmer's walk, I carried 345-pound solid-steel suitcases in each hand 200 feet, 3 inches, without setting them down. My goal was 200 feet.

DM: Greatest show of strength as a firefighter?

PP: A woman who was every bit of 400 pounds—probably closer to 450—needed to be lifted from a seated position on the floor into a cot about two feet off the ground. I had her shoulders and two guys had a leg each. But they couldn't lift their end. After about thirty seconds of that, I moved my arms to her back and lifted her whole body onto the cot. I didn't think too much about it at the time, but the guys told people it was something to see.

DM: What advice would you give those interested in being a strongman?

PP: Keep things fun. Try not to look at this as work. Don't get too carried away, or you'll make yourself miserable. And don't use drugs. They will be all around you, but don't give in.

DM: To the last point, you unabashedly proclaim yourself a drug-free strongman. How big of an issue are drugs in your sport?

PP: Unfortunately, it's no secret that a number of my fellow competitors are loaded to the gills.

DM: That's a pretty powerful statement.

PP: Well, what do you think? You think it's true? I'm not going to lie: It's a tragedy. And I'm tired of the clean guys having to proclaim their innocence. I think it's so much more impressive when you can accomplish great things without drugs. There's a tremendous number of guys using drugs who aren't champions, which shows there's a lot more to winning than using.

DM: Why are drugs so prevalent?

PP: I wish I knew. It's not just in sports, either. Take something to look great, lose weight. We have pills for anything and everything. Everybody wants the magic little product to gain an edge. The problem is, perspective gets lost. People forget about good, old-fashioned hard work and the results it brings.

DM: Do you have a pre-competition routine?

PP: I pray. I ask God to keep me safe and keep me strong. I ask to be an instrument of God's will and power. I take the prayers seriously, because when you're looking at some of the platform lifts we do, there's a real injury possibility.

DM: What is a classic platform lift?

PP: Sometimes we'll lift one with seven or eight spokesmodels on it. The weight is about 1,100, 1,200, 1,300 pounds.

DM: Aren't you the least bit distracted?

PP: Not at all. Can't afford to be.

DM: What is your greatest eating performance?

PP: At a Super Bowl party, there was an all-you-can-eat sushi bar. I basically ate five hours straight, stopping only for a couple of five- or ten-minute breaks.

DM: What did you consume?

PP: Probably ten different sushi rolls plus tuna, salmon, octopus, squid, yellow tail, shrimp, soft-shell crab, sea urchin. I also had green-tea ice cream, red-bean ice cream, mayo ice cream, plum ice cream—six or seven bowls in all. I drank four or five pots of green tea.

DM: Sounds yummy. How did you sleep that night?

PP: I was a little scared when I left, to be honest. I was afraid my stomach would break apart. But everything turned out all right.

DM: Your son, Wyatt, just turned three. Is he a strong-man-in-training?

PP: He'll do what he wants to do in life, but there's no question he's very strong. He's three and a half feet tall and about forty-four pounds. He's been flipping tires since he was thirteen months old.

DM: What is your longest car lift?

PP: Ninety seconds.

DM: Have you ever been challenged mano-a-mano in public, joking or otherwise?

PP: You get a lot of looks, and there's plenty of stupid people out there, people who act like they've got something to prove. But nobody's approached me that way.

DM: What would you do if someone did?

PP: I'd say, "I'm not going to fight you. But if you insist, I'll break your spine." That will get the message across pretty quickly. You don't know about people these days. You don't know if they'll cut your throat or shoot you.

DM: Most impressive dinner you consumed at a restaurant?

PP: At a competition in Canada a few years ago, I ate six 1.5-pound T-bone steaks. My competitor had seven.

DM: How much food do you eat each day?

PP: I don't eat particularly large meals. Instead, I eat four, five, six times per day. I ate more of everything in my twenties.

DM: Explain.

PP: My metabolic rate was so high, I had to eat until it hurt, literally, because an hour later, I'd be starving.

DM: What constituted a snack back then?

PP: When I first started strongman and was trying to put on weight, I'd take half-gallons of Breyer's ice cream and two liters of Sprite and make floats. Or, I'd wash down 1- or 2-pound chocolate bars with quarts of half-and-half a couple of times a day.

DM: How much longer will you go?

PP: I have room to grow in gym strength. I'm 32 and still have a young body, so I'm not close to my peak. If I can stay motivated and keep progressing and continue to enjoy it, I'll do this for a long time.

Mary Lou Retton, *gymnastics*
February 2007

The lasting image of Mary Lou Retton is of a teen-aged dynamo vaulting into the air and onto the cover of a cereal box, arms raised, flashing a gold- medal smile.

It is not of a woman in her thirties hobbling from the bed to the kitchen to fix breakfast for the kids.

For years Retton navigated a painful existence, the result of an ailing left hip. Now she is back to her former high-on-life self thanks to hip replacement surgery performed June 24, 2005.

No lie: Mary Lou Retton, the little Olympic gymnast who could, has an artificial left hip.

As word has gotten out in recent weeks through a national-advertisement campaign, reaction from her legions of fans has ranged from flabbergasted to stunned.

"People keep saying, 'You had a hip replacement? No way,'" Retton said in a phone interview Thursday near her home in Houston, Texas. "Well, I did—and I'm feeling fantastic. I'm young and fresh and new."

Retton delivers more startling news in the ad for Biomet, the company that supplied her with its M2a-Magnum Large Metal Articulation System and Taperloc Hip Stem.

It is only a matter of time before she will own a matched set.

Retton, the women's all-around champion at the 1984 Olympic Games in Los Angeles, has hip dysplasia, a hereditary abnormal formation of the hip joint.

While its effects likely were accelerated by a physically demanding career as an elite gymnast, Retton refuses to point a finger at the sport she holds dear.

"Gymnastics is not the reason I had hip replacement," she said. "I don't blame gymnastics at all. I was born with this condition; I just had my problems in my thirties instead of later in life. I absolutely would do everything from my career all over again."

Retton's surgeon, Dr. Brian Parsley, told her gymnastics actually was among the best sports she could have chosen given the circumstances.

"I had more mobility and rotation in my hips than most," she said.

In the wake of the revelation, countless parents of gymnasts have contacted Retton to extend well-wishes. None has expressed concern that his or her child might be a hip replacement waiting to happen if gymnastics remains a passion.

"There's no reason to be concerned," Retton said. "Everybody's case is different. And the pounding of gymnastics doesn't truly take place until you get to the elite level, when you're training for nationals, worlds, Olympics. That's a finite number of gymnasts."

Retton also speaks of advances in awareness that make the 1980s, when she trained, seem like the Stone Age.

"In my day, we taped ankles ourselves," she said. "We didn't have trainers in our gym, or massage therapists. Coaches and trainers today are so much more educated in preventative measures and treatment."

That Retton's gymnastics experience would be tied in any way to hip replacement is ironic. She suffered a variety of injuries on her road to glory, some of which required surgery. But she never felt so much as a twinge in her hips. She never fell on a hip or pulled a muscle in the area.

Doctors who examined her in the early 1990s evidently let the lack of hip history fool them. They kept insisting her agony, which she likened to a "massive toothache that won't go away," stemmed from the back. Not until Dr. Parsley entered the picture did the dysplasia come to light.

When Parsley presented his diagnosis, Retton stared past him in disbelief.

"I was floored," she said. "I'm thinking, I'm too young. I'm an active mother of four. I can't have a metal hip!"

Retton, fearing the unknown, delayed the inevitable for a year. The pain refused to yield. She had gotten tired of taking medication, and injections to ease the discomfort stopped working. She could not sleep.

"I reached the point of desperation," she said.

The surgery lasted about four hours. It took longer than normal because of Retton's 4 foot 9 inch, 95-pound frame.

"The doctor did not anticipate my little bones," she said. "It took him a while to make sure he got the implant into the femur just right."

Retton maintains she was pain-free almost immediately. She reports no setbacks. She said the main reason she is doing the advertisements and telling her story is out of gratitude.

"Three years ago, I was dying—dying inside, dying from pain," she said. "I was just existing. I'm back living again."

Dave Roberts, *baseball*
June 2005

One reason for the success of the Padres, against whom the Indians conclude a three-game series today in San Diego, is center fielder Dave Roberts. The former Indian is batting .288 with 22 RBI, 24 runs and 10 steals for a first-place club.

A major-leaguer since 1999, Roberts had been relatively anonymous in baseball circles until October 17, 2004. In Game 4 of the American League Championship Series, Roberts' Red Sox trailed the Yankees, 4-3, entering the bottom of the ninth inning. They were three outs from being swept and extending the misery of Red Sox Nation another year beyond 1918.

Leadoff batter Kevin Millar walked against Mariano Rivera. Pinch-runner Roberts then stole the most significant base in franchise history, for it triggered a positively stunning turn of events that eventually brought Boston the elusive world championship. Roberts scored from second on Bill Mueller's single to tie the score; Boston won it in 12, 6-4.

The Red Sox prevailed in the next three games to erase the Yankees before sweeping the Cardinals in the World Series.

Because of the Red Sox's place in MLB lore, Roberts stole one of the most significant bases in *baseball* history.

DM: Where were you during the late innings of Game 4?

DR: I was in the clubhouse watching video, getting stretched out, waiting for the one moment when I might get the call. I studied tape on Rivera and a couple of their other relievers.

DM: What happened after Millar walked?

DR: Before the inning started, [manager] Terry Francona told me, "First guy who gets on base, you're going to run for him. Go do what you do." I was at the other end of the dugout when Millar got on. Francona looked over at me and winked—he didn't say anything—and I went out to first.

DM: What was going through your mind at that moment?

DR: A bunch of things, in a blur.

DM: Were two of them that the Red Sox were three outs from being swept by the Yankees, and that you likely represented any glimmer of hope remaining?

DR: Oh, yeah. No question. But I remembered what Maury Wills told me when I was with the Dodgers. He said there would come a moment in my career when I would be asked to steal an important base, when everybody knew it was coming. He told me, "When that opportunity comes, don't let it pass. Find a way to steal the base."

DM: Were you nervous?

DR: Sure. To be honest, I had some fear of failure, too, because I hadn't played in a while and didn't feel fresh. It went away as soon as I touched the bag.

DM: As Mueller came to the plate, how did the check-in go at first with coach Lynn Jones?

DR: [Third base coach] Dale Sveum initially flashed the bunt sign for Bill, assuming we'd sacrifice. Terry hadn't sent it. I told coach Jones, "No, no, no, I'm going to steal." [Jones] got the bunt sign taken off and said, "OK, you're on your own."

DM: What was your plan against Rivera?

DR: The only other opportunity I had to steal against him was in September, at Yankee Stadium, in a similar situation. I stole second and scored. They held the ball on me, trying to catch me jumping, so I made sure not to be too eager. I had made up my mind that, the first time he went to the plate, I was going.

DM: Rivera evidently was thinking along with you, given that he threw over several times before making a pitch. The second one almost got you.

DR: I was safe, but it was a bang-bang play. I don't know what I would have done if I'd been picked. All I could think about was Bill Buckner.

DM: Did the pickoff attempts help you get settled?

DR: Absolutely. If he had gone to the plate right away, and I had stuck with my plan, I don't think I would have made it because my legs weren't under me yet. After the second throw, I got into the flow. After the third one, I felt like I hadn't missed an inning in a month.

DM: Rivera finally throws a pitch, and you're off ...

DR: I had seen something on the tapes that made me certain he was going home, and he did it. I got a good jump and felt fast. I thought I beat the throw fairly easily.

DM: As you know now, though, you barely beat it. Rivera was cat-quick to the plate, Jorge Posada made a terrific throw, and Derek Jeter applied the slap-tag a fraction of a second after your hand touched the bag.

DR: I didn't realize how close it was until I watched the video. Their time from pitcher to catcher to second was as fast as we had seen them for any pitch all year.

DM: Eight months later, has the historical significance of the steal, which teammates have cited as the key to the title run, sunk in?

DR: It's only begun to hit me. There are so many Red Sox fans all over, and they recognize me and offer congratulations. For us to rewrite history the way we did, and for me to contribute to the team that finally won another championship for the Red Sox, is awesome. I wish everyone who put on a uniform could play for the Red Sox at some point, because the fans are so passionate.

DM: Yet the Red Sox traded you to the Padres in the off-season. Why?

DR: I wanted the chance to play every day, and I wasn't going to get it with the Red Sox. I'm grateful to [General Manager] Theo Epstein for finding a place where I could.

Alex Rodriguez, *baseball*
May 2002

Texas Rangers shortstop Alex Rodriguez signed a ten-year, $252 million contract in December 2000. He has done nothing but validate it since, adding to an already stellar resume. Last Tuesday, A-Rod became the second-youngest player in major-league history to hit 250 homers, reaching the milestone at twenty-six years, 277 days. He lost out to Jimmie Foxx by eight days.

Rodriguez already has more than 1,200 hits and 760 RBI, as well. Factor in outstanding defensive skills, and the result is one of the most complete players in the game, a lock for the Hall of Fame.

DM: What motivates you?

AR: Competition.

DM: Toughest part about being a major-leaguer?

AR: In the big picture, there is none.

DM: What makes you so good?

AR: I don't like to talk about myself, but I think God has given me a unique talent, size and the ability to maneuver and have some grace. And I feel I work extremely hard. I don't know if I'm the best, that's not for me to determine, but I consider myself one of the hardest workers in the league.

DM: Who helped you learn the professional work ethic?

AR: Joey Cora, while we were in Seattle.

DM: Joey Cora? Are you kidding?

AR: No. Why would I be kidding?

DM: No reason. Sorry. Cora's just an interesting choice, I guess.

AR: Well, he's the hardest-working guy I've ever been around. He maximized his talent to the utmost. I used to say, "If I can work as hard as he does, and prepare myself like he does, I can be a good player."

DM: How important is baseball to you?

AR: After God and family, I love this game more than anything in the world. I try to treat baseball as if I'm working on my masters and Ph.D. I really study it.

DM: You have quite a grasp of baseball history. What is its primary lesson?

AR: History tends to repeat itself, so respect for the game is very, very important. People paved a beautiful road for us to be here today, and it's important to realize what they've done.

DM: How did you avoid cracking under the pressure of the contract?

AR: My expectations are so much higher and larger than those of the media, the fans and others. I've just tried to live up to my expectations and not worry about anything else.

DM: Has the money changed you as a player?

AR: No. If you look at my career, I've never had the peaks and valleys. Whether I'm making $1 million, $2 [million], $3 [million], $4 million — or what I'm making this year, I always love the game. If your love for the game is first and foremost, then what you're getting paid has to be secondary.

DM: Toughest pitcher you've ever faced?

AR: Pedro Martinez.

DM: Chess or checkers?

AR: Chess. I'm a huge chess player. I love chess. It's my favorite board game ever. I've been playing since I was six.

DM: Are you the grand master of this clubhouse?

AR: Can't tell, because a lot of guys don't play. I wish they did.

Then we'd find out who's the best.

DM: Favorite player growing up?

AR: Cal Ripken Jr. He had incredible respect for the game.

DM: Favorite player outside of your clubhouse?

AR: Roberto Alomar.

DM: What is one thing you wish fans better understood about ballplayers and the game?

AR: That it's not as easy as it looks. Everybody in the stands at some point has played baseball, so everybody feels like they can hit a baseball, throw strikes, make a play. … They can't say the same thing about the NBA, for example, because they're not seven feet tall and they can't dunk. Major leaguers make it look easy, too easy at times. I would hope people would have some compassion for guys who are struggling. I'm not talking about sympathy—none of us expects sympathy—just a recognition that baseball is a difficult game to play well.

DM: Favorite baseball movie?

AR: *Major League.*

DM: That will score points for you in Cleveland.

AR: (*Chuckle*)

DM: Least-favorite baseball movie?

AR: *Field of Dreams.* I realize a lot of people love it, but it didn't do anything for me. I'll take *Major League* any day over *Field of Dreams.*

DM: Favorite movie, in general?

AR: *Air Force One.*

DM: Any particular reason?

AR: My dream is to get a tour of Air Force One. That would be something else.

DM: Advice to youngsters playing baseball?

AR: Stay in school.

DM: Favorite subject in school?

AR: Government. I really enjoyed studying how our system works—checks and balances between the braches, veto power, things like that. I had a great teacher.

DM: Is Omar Vizquel a potential Hall of Famer?

AR: Sure. He's a phenomenal fielder with a lot of Gold Gloves, and he's a very respectable offensive player who can maneuver the ball. He's an asset to every lineup. Most important, he has a special gift for baseball. He's got an instinct for the game that you can't teach. You never see Omar out of position.

DM: Have you and the other offensive forces at short these days ruined it for the defensive-minded Vizquel?

AR: Not at all. Omar's been a fantastic player for a long time. He stands out, no matter the era. I think he's the best I've ever seen play the position.

DM: What defines greatness in baseball?

AR: In a nutshell, it's executing fundamentals in the high-pressure situations.

DM: Plans after baseball?

AR: I've always thought about owning a small part of a ballclub. I'd also like to get into the business world a little bit.

DM: Favorite visiting ballpark?

AR: Yankee Stadium. I'm from New York. I've always loved that place.

DM: Would you like to be a Yankee someday?

AR: Who wouldn't? But I'm happy in Texas, as a Ranger.

UPDATE: In February 2004, Alex Rodriguez was traded to the Yankees. He entered the 2015 season with 654 homers, 1,969 RBI and 2,939 hits in a twenty-year career. Rodriguez's numbers are tainted, however, because he admitted to using PEDs from 2001 to 2003. In August 2013, MLB suspended him for his involvement in the Biogenesis scandal; the suspension sidelined him for the entire 2014 season.

Curt Schilling, *baseball*
August 2002

Arizona Diamondbacks right-hander Curt Schilling is 47-10 since the beginning of 2001, including playoffs and World Series. No one in the majors has won as many games in that span.

Through twenty-eight starts and 208 innings this season, Schilling owns more victories (21) than walks (20), as well as 259 strikeouts. His winning percentage is .840.

All of which gives him a platform. Schilling, 35, can speak on a variety of subjects, and people will listen. It helps that he is one of the more intelligent, articulate players in any clubhouse.

DM: What makes you tick?

CS: Fear of failure.

DM: You realize that you broke Indians' fans hearts several times in recent years by not coming to Cleveland, via free agency or trade?

CS: Sorry about that. I recognize how passionate Cleveland fans are about their team. I will say, the whole 1997 All-Star Game experience was one of the most unbelievable of my life. From the moment I arrived, people were incredibly nice. They did everything they could to convince me to come. It just wasn't meant to be.

DM: Who would join you at your dream pitching roundtable?

CS: Greg Maddux, Johnny Podres, Jim Palmer and Don Sutton. There wouldn't be any idle chatter, I guarantee you.

DM: What is your dream World Series matchup, mixing/matching all eras?

CS: The 2001 Diamondbacks against the 2001 Yankees.

DM: Dream batter-pitcher matchup, mixing/matching all eras?

CS: Babe Ruth against Randy Johnson.

DM: The outcome?

CS: Three pitches and sit your fat butt down, Bambino.

DM: Are you serious?

CS: Yes. I've held one of Babe Ruth's bats, and let me tell you: He could choke up to the label and not get around on R.J.

DM: What would Johnson throw him?

CS: Three fastballs—and he'd tell Ruth before each pitch.

DM: How would you deal with him?

CS: Same way. All fastballs—and I'd tell him, too.

DM: You wouldn't even mix in a split or hook?

CS: No need. He's not going to get a 48-, 50-ounce bat around on the hard stuff. If he does, I better quit.

DM: Wouldn't he adjust accordingly?

CS: If you assume that, though, then you have to ask how he was able to be so successful in the first place using the bat he did.

DM: Where would you locate the fastballs to Ruth?

CS: I'd keep them up and in. But if it's a day game, location wouldn't matter. He'd go down, regardless, and I don't have to tell you why.

DM: How would Ruth fare today?

CS: He wouldn't hit 714 homers. He'd have to go with a lighter bat and go on a diet.

DM: Do you think the majority of players today could have played in Ruth's era?

CS: No question—and not only played, but thrived. There's nothing wrong with cherishing the history of this game, but it shouldn't come at the expense of the guys who play now. Funny how this is the only sport where the players have gotten worse over the years. Nobody talks about how football or basketball players are worse than they were forty, fifty years ago. They're bigger, faster, with more skills. But we couldn't play back in the day? Come on. It's especially true of pitchers. All we ever hear about is how amazing Cy Young and the boys were. I'm all for giving them their due, but how do you think R.J., Pedro Martinez—or the seventh, eighth, ninth man on a staff today—would have looked back then? I like their chances.

DM: Are you a "throwback?"

CS: I'm built like a throwback. What's a throwback? Ten years ago, I thought that was one of the highest compliments you could receive. The more I play, though, I wonder if the reverse is not true.

DM: Explain.

CS: I mean, could some of the guys from the past play now? You had guys as recently as fifteen, twenty years ago who were barely .200 hitters but played great defense, and they were considered good. They wouldn't make a big-league roster today. Those players don't exist anymore.

DM: What is your best pitch?

CS: Strike three.

DM: Describe the Big Unit in thirty words or less.

CS: I can do it in one: introvert.

DM: Is he a mystery?

CS: To me, no; to 99.9 percent of the public, sure. And that's how he wants it.

DM: Is he misunderstood?

CS: There are some aspects of him that are grossly misunderstood, mainly that he's mean. Just because you're introverted, doesn't mean you're mean.

DM: What do fans most misunderstand about players?

CS: That we're greedy. Tell me, how on God's green earth did we get the word greedy attached to us, especially when it comes to negotiations between owners and players?

DM: Because of all the money you make, obviously.

CS: But we're not asking for anything; we've asked for the status quo. Nobody's forcing the owners to pay us. The bottom line is, I can't give you $10 if I only have $5 in my pocket. The owners have been asking us to stop them from spending money on ... us. You apply that to any other industry, and people would be like, "What?" But because it's baseball, it's different.

DM: Why do you suppose that is?

CS: The difference between baseball and the other three major sports—basketball, football, hockey—is that 99 percent of the male population has played this one, and they feel they can relate to what we do. Well, I can grab someone out of the stands anywhere in the ballpark and there's a legitimate chance that he can't play catch with me from sixty feet. Yet he's the same guy who's up in arms screaming about somebody booting a line-drive one-hopper. They understand what it's like to lose their high-school championship game, the biggest event in their athletic life. Come on, dude, are you kidding me? You can't compare one to the other.

DM: True, but it's going to happen. It's what fans do.

CS: One word you can never, ever use in anything, and it has to do with everything, is jealousy. The problem is, people are jealous of what we make playing a kid's game. If you say that, though, you offend everybody.

DM: You just did.

CS: I'm not trying to offend anybody. I appreciate how important the fans are to this game. I'm a fan. But other than jealousy, why wouldn't you like us? You can not like us because we commit crimes, do stupid things—the same as every other walk of life. But our income makes us targets.

DM: Will you ever quit dipping [using smokeless tobacco]?

CS: Yes, as soon as I can. I've been cutting down. I've got four kids and a wife and a responsibility to them.

DM: You have a reputation as a serious student of military history. How did that come about?

CS: I was an Army brat…. My dad was in the service for twenty-two years.

DM: Which general most fascinates you?

CS: Patton, hands-down. From a military standpoint, he was brilliant. It was so simple that it was brilliant. The Second World War was the first mechanized war, and he adapted to it like he had been brought up in the environment. If you understand how he fit into the context of the times, you appreciate his genius.

DM: Given that you have a residence in Pennsylvania, you probably visited the Gettysburg battlefield, correct?

CS: Yes. Gettysburg is awesome. When you walk the grounds, it's chilling. You think about the way they fought—line-to-line, charges. It's scary stuff. Scary, but fascinating.

DM: What is your favorite battle to study?

CS: I don't like to use that word, favorite, because of the grave nature of warfare. If you're asking which one interests me the most, I'd say the Second World War. It's the last conventional world war of our time.

DM: Why?

CS: With the advent of the jet, conventional warfare changed drastically. The next global war will be, well, just read the Bible. That will tell you what the next one will be. Clubhouse observers will note that you recently finished a novel that is eschatological in nature. Do you think we're living in the end times, as described in the Bible? I think we'll see it in our lifetime.

DM: Are you worried about the state of humankind?

CS: Read the paper any day of the week, and you have to be concerned about what we've become.

DM: On a lighter note, what is your favorite food?

CS: Macaroni and cheese.

DM: Favorite junk food?

CS: Macaroni and cheese.

DM: Word association — Bud Selig?

CS: Fantastic guy, bad for the game. He's trying to appease 30 people at once, which is an impossible task.

DM: Barry Bonds?

CS: A tremendous hitter.

DM: Is there an ongoing feud between you and Bonds?

CS: A feud? No. I think he's a great ballplayer. We were friends a long time ago, but we're certainly not as close now. We had a falling out. When I became a Christian back in 1997, I lost the ability to hate anybody.

DM: Is cheating a problem in baseball?

CS: I'm sure some guys cheat, but no, it's not a problem.

DM: Do you cheat?

CS: Honestly, I haven't had to.

DM: Will you, eventually?

CS: I don't know. I don't think so.

DM: If you could be a chess piece, which would you be?

CS: Depends on the day of the week. On the days I pitch, I'd be the king. Any other day, I'd probably be a pawn.

DM: Merely a pawn?

CS: Yeah, because I'm white, I have no vertical and I'm slow.

DM: You turned down numerous book deals after last season. Why?

CS: I didn't have the time to do one the way I wanted. If I write a book someday, I want it to be about the science of pitching. I think some people were figuring I would write a tell-all autobiography. That's not me. I'm not Jim Bouton.

DM: Notwithstanding, are you controversial?

CS: I don't ever set out to be. I say what's on my mind. That shouldn't automatically mean I'm controversial.

DM: What bothers you the most about the industry of sports, in general, and baseball, in particular?

CS: The media. I think people are oversaturated with information, stuff they don't need to know about.

DM: Such as personal stuff away from the game?

CS: This is no news flash: Sex sells, controversy sells. And in baseball, when you have so many people covering thirty teams, you've got to find a story every day, even if it isn't there. That's when the trouble starts. A lot of people will use the platform they've been given to try to advance their careers, and it will come at the expense of invading private lives.

DM: You seem to have an ax to grind with the media, yet you are a reporter's dream. How so?

CS: I try my best to accommodate you guys, because I understand you've got a job to do. Then one of the writers in Arizona wrote that I'm a media whore. And I said, "I stand at my locker after I pitch, win or lose, and answer all the questions you ask me. I respond to interview requests if I have time. And that makes me a media whore?" I guess I'm a media whore because I don't answer questions with a simple yes or no. I answer how I feel, so that makes me talkative and chatty and hard to shut up. Well, I've been playing this game since I was four. I don't have a yes or no answer to any of those questions. Outside of God and my family, it's all I do. The problem, I realized too late in my career, is that I'll never win against the media. If the media doesn't like you, they can make people not like you. You'll always have the last word.

DM: You get it this time.

CS: Thanks.

Curt Schilling, *part II*

August 2006

The Plain Dealer this week asked baseball fans to ponder two questions: Are pitchers deliberately hitting batters too often? Or, have batters (and umpires) become too touchy about a staple of baseball?

With the Red Sox in town Tuesday through Thursday, DMan's World thought it wise to elicit Curt Schilling's response. Schilling is a huge baseball fan who happens to own a 196-131 major-league record in the regular season, 8-2 in the postseason (with two World Series rings). He debuted with the Orioles in 1988.

DM: Are pitchers deliberately hitting batters too often?

CS: Not at all. I don't know how many guys I've hit in my career [48 through Tuesday], but I can assure you only five have been on purpose. I'll bet the percentage is a little higher for other guys, but nowhere close to what people think it is. When hitters get hit, I'll bet they think it was intentional 75 percent of the time, when it's probably no more than ten percent.

DM: So batters are too sensitive?

CS: Absolutely. Having said that, I'm not the guy getting hit in the ribs with a 95 mph fastball.

DM: If, as you say, the batters are too sensitive—why is that?

CS: It's a combination of factors, beginning with comfort level. Hitters are very comfortable in the box because of the rules that are in place today, where an umpire can throw out a pitcher without warning the second he believes he did something intentionally. Hitters know the pitchers don't want to get warned, which can affect how you pitch them, much less get ejected, so they dig in without fear. When you do invade the space they think belongs to them, they're bound to get ticked off and overreact.

DM: Logic holds that the more comfortable the batter, the more productive he will be.

CS: It's no secret we're in an offensive age, and hitters obviously want it to continue. They don't want to have to worry about the inner half [of the plate]. Pedro Martinez hits guys, and hitters and fans automatically assume it's intentional. But that's Pedro's game. He's got a fastball with a lot of movement that runs hard inside. He needs to be allowed to make that pitch.

DM: What are the sure-fire signs of a pitcher hitting a batter intentionally?

CS: The easy one is if the pitch goes behind the guy, because nobody misses behind at this level. And if the guy gets hit in the back or backside, it's probably for a reason.

DM: Are the umpires too eager to make their presence felt when a batter gets hit?

CS: Of course you're going to have umpires who jump the gun, just like you have pitchers and hitters who jump the gun. But in fairness to the umpires, they've been put in a tough spot trying to determine intent—when to warn or eject. I've talked with a number of umpires about it, and from what I gather, they hate that they've been handed all the responsibility to make those judgment calls. It's a hot potato they don't want to juggle.

DM: So the umpires' boss, the MLB office, should take a certain amount of responsibility?

CS: The league needs to examine why we've gotten to the point where it's almost as if you want to be the first to strike, to get your shot in. If not, you're going to get thrown out or suspended.

DM: Should the MLB office and the umpires simply allow the players to police themselves, as seemingly happened in the old days?

CS: Ideally, yes. The problem is, we're not doing a particularly good job of: you hit my guy, I hit your guy, it's settled—like it used to be. We're charging the mound, which leads to bench-clearing brawls and injuries and bad PR [public relations]. We've kind of taken it out of our own hands.

DM: What is one change you would make to improve how the matter is handled?

CS: There should be some type of prohibitive penalty for charging the mound, such as: If you leave the batter's box and charge, you're automatically suspended fifteen days. That would put a stop to the extracurricular stuff.

DM: But wouldn't it give pitchers free shots at batters?

CS: No, because if I'm taking free shots at your hitters, then your pitchers are going to take free shots at mine. And my hitters aren't going to stand for that. They're going to be ticked at me if I'm getting them hit for my own reasons, and they're going to let me know it.

DM: Which might be happening in Colorado, where Rockies batters must be wondering about their reliever, José Mesa, who is feuding with San Francisco's Omar Vizquel. Mesa basically has vowed to plunk Vizquel every time he faces him because Vizquel called him out in his autobiography for gagging in the 1997 World Series. Your thoughts?

CS: I would never carry a feud around like Mesa is, regardless of how upset I might be. He's putting his personal agenda ahead of his team's, and you can't do that. It could affect the outcome of games. Look what happened the day after the most recent time he hit him [five ejections].

DM: What is your reaction to pitchers who drill a batter just because the guy might have homered in the previous two at-bats, or the two batters before him homered?

CS: It's a stupid, stupid, stupid reason to hit somebody. It should never happen that way, but it does.

DM: If your teammate were blatantly drilled in the bottom of the eighth inning, would you hit someone as payback to lead off the top of the ninth even if it meant ruining a perfect game?

CS: Absolutely.

DM: What if the batter you hit represented the tying run?

CS: Doesn't matter in this case. Of course you don't want to jeopardize your team's chances of winning, but you never, ever, want a teammate to wonder if you're protecting him. You do whatever you need to do to make sure your teammates understand that you have their backs at all times.

UPDATE: Curt Schilling retired from MLB after the 2007 season, He went 216-146 with a 3.46 ERA. He was a six-time All Star, three-time World Series champion, World Series MVP (2001), NLCS MVP (1993) and recipient of the Roberto Clemente Award in 2001. Post-playing career, he battled oral cancer (in remission) and is an ESPN baseball analyst.

Don Shula, *football*

September 2007

Don Shula, whose 347 total victories as an NFL head coach are unmatched, will be in Cleveland on Tuesday for a blood-pressure screening event.

Shula will be at The Atrium of University Hospitals, 11100 Euclid Ave., from 8 to 10 A.M. He is a spokesman for the BP COACH Approach, a national campaign to raise awareness about managing high blood pressure.

Shula suffers from hypertension.

Shula, 77, a native of Grand River, excelled at Harvey High School in Painesville and John Carroll. He went 347-173-6 in 33 seasons as head coach of the Colts (7) and Dolphins (26). He was inducted into the Pro Football Hall of Fame in 1997.

Don Shula
photo by William S. Nehez/*Cleveland News*

DM: Fondest memory of your childhood?

DS: My dad was a commercial fisherman. I remember going out on Lake Erie and bringing in fish and getting seasick every day.

DM: Fondest memory of days at John Carroll?

DS: My senior year, we played powerful Syracuse at Cleveland Stadium and beat them. Paul Brown and his staff were there scouting Syracuse. Carl Taseff and I had big nights, and we ended up getting drafted by the Browns in 1951. No question, that day factored heavily in our being drafted by Cleveland.

DM: You played for Brown in 1951 and 1952. How much did he influence you down the road?

DS: Well, the basis of my coaching philosophy came from Paul Brown's school of coaching. It centered on incorporating the classroom into coaching. He approached everything from a teaching point of view. I learned from Paul and, later, Blanton Collier.

DM: If you could change one thing about your career, what would it be?

DS: Not losing Super Bowl III to the Jets as coach of the Colts. It was the most disappointing loss I ever had. We were heavily favored, as you know. Joe Namath brashly predicted they'd win and they did. My relationship with owner Carroll Rosenbloom, who was from New York, was never quite the same after that.

DM: Does the loss still gnaw at you?

DS: I wouldn't put it that way, but I'm certainly not happy to have been the losing coach in Super Bowl III. Whenever the talk turns to Super Bowls, that game is brought up. We got outplayed and outcoached.

DM: It's not as if you never recovered, though.

DS: As it turned out, it helped me. I used it as a stepping stone, a learning experience for the rest of my career. I went on to Miami and we had success.

DM: You coached in a record six Super Bowls, winning two. A close friend of yours, Marty Schottenheimer, never has gotten there. Does Schottenheimer get a bad rap because of the void?

DS: I've followed his career closely, and I know what he's accomplished. But the bottom line is, when people talk about his career, they're always going to end with … "he couldn't win the big one." It's always going to end with a negative unless he wins one.

DM: Do you think Schottenheimer sees it as such?

DS: I'm sure he understands. I'm sure he wishes he could have won that big game somewhere down the line.

DM: What do you miss most about coaching?

DS: The competitive nature of the profession, getting ready to play against the best teams and the best coaches.

DM: What do you miss the least?

DS: Cutting players would have to be right up there. It was always tough, especially the last cuts. You think about how it's going to affect a player, how it's going to change his life.

DM: Best player in the NFL?

DS: Peyton Manning, hands-down.

Robert Smith, *football*

January 2007

In two seasons as an ESPN college football analyst, Robert Smith has demonstrated to the nation's viewers what Northeast Ohio fans have known for years: He has a sharp eye for the game and routinely makes salient points. Smith never hesitates to peel away one more layer to offer a fresh perspective rather than regurgitate standard assessments.

Smith is a former standout running back at Euclid, Ohio State and with the Minnesota Vikings.

DM: What is your solution to the so-called BCS mess, or do you think it is a mess?

RS: I don't think it's necessarily a mess. Everybody makes the comparison with Division I-AA, Division II and III and how they have playoffs. No knock on those guys, but there's a reason they play in those divisions, they're not the same physically as the top-level Division I players. People make the argument that, well, they do it in high school and in the pros. But you have to think about the level of competition. When you're dealing with guys sometimes eighteen, nineteen, and in their early twenties, they're just not ready physically to go through a full playoff system at a high level. It's hard enough making the jump to the NFL; guys really hit the wall after a preseason, regular season and playoffs. I think, on the whole, the system is fine the way it is. There are going to be problems with any system, and any time subjectivity is involved, somebody's going to be left out or feel left out. What's important to remember is, the point of the NCAA and college football is not to make sure everybody gets treated fairly where a national championship is concerned. It's to allow these guys to play football, to enjoy the experience, to get an education, to improve their lives.

DM: Boise State shocked the world by beating Oklahoma in overtime last week to remain undefeated, but the Broncos have no chance for a national title. Doesn't Boise State's triumph in the Fiesta Bowl validate the cries for a playoff system in Division I?

RS: A team like Boise State obviously showed they can play with the big boys, but the very reason [Boise State coach] Chris Petersen went for two at the end of overtime is because he saw the way [Oklahoma running back] Adrian Peterson was able to run through his team. I think Boise State can hold up for one game, but if they were faced with a playoff system where they had to come back, say, this weekend and play another game against an Ohio State or USC or Florida, they wouldn't be able to hold up physically. If teams like Boise State have a strong out-of-conference schedule, roll through their conference and end up undefeated, they should still be considered for a national-title shot. But a playoff system wouldn't help those guys; it would probably hurt them.

DM: Why has Notre Dame lost nine straight bowl games?

RS: They're generally overrated. When other people see them perform well, they think it's the Notre Dame of the glory days. They automatically assume it is one of the upper-tier teams in the country. And the bowls want to sell tickets, they want the fanfare around their game, so they're going to look to a Notre Dame. That means Notre Dame ends up being in a game against a team much better than they are.

DM: Which do you prefer: college game or pro game?

RS: I like college because it's so pure: The players are playing for their teammates, their school and tradition, their coach. That excitement is hard to match. In the pros, it's much more of a business. At the same time, I love the precision of NFL football. You're talking about the very best of the best.

DM: What is one change you would try to implement in college football?

RS: Given all the big contracts these coaches are getting, and all the money the schools are getting from BCS bowl games, the NCAA really needs to look into some sort of system analogous to workers' compensation for the players. If they have an acute injury, that's going to be taken care of. But if a player needs a knee replacement fifteen, twenty years down the road, and it's directly related to his playing days, something like that should be covered. Some of the NCAA's money should be put toward the long-term quality of health of its players.

DM: Biggest misconception fans have about NFL players?

RS: They think the NFL players deliberately try to get away with things other people don't. You're talking about young kids, young kids who do dumb things like everybody else. If your neighbor gets arrested for DUI, you might not know about it. But if anybody on an NFL roster gets a DUI, it's front-page news. I think the problems—legal issues, in particular—of athletes get blown out of proportion, but I also recognize it's the nature of the beast.

Joe Thomas, *football*

February 2010

Joe Thomas co-stars with *The Plain Dealer* writer D'Arcy Egan in *Outdoors Ohio*, a popular show on SportsTime Ohio.

Thomas also happens to be a fairly decent offensive tackle in the National Football League.

On draft day 2007, his passions intertwined. The Wisconsin standout opted to go fishing in the Midwest instead of joining other prospects in New York City. He found out by cell phone that the Browns drafted him third overall.

Thomas is charting a course to rank among the Browns'

Joe Thomas
photo by John Kuntz/*The Plain Dealer*

greatest catches ever. He has made the Pro Bowl three times in three seasons.

DM: You played high school basketball. How good were you?

JT: Pretty good—all-conference a couple of times. I was invited to the all-state game as a senior. I enjoy playing and watching the game, but I knew my bread would be buttered in football.

DM: Favorite basketball player?

JT: Being in Cleveland, I'm obviously a big fan of LeBron. We're the same age, and I have a lot of respect for what he's accomplished. I remember watching him play when we were about fourteen years old and going to the same tournaments.

DM: Did you ever play against him?

JT: No, but I remember going out to Las Vegas while playing AAU for a team from Wisconsin. I'd heard about this LeBron James guy. We went to the gym to watch his team, and I was very impressed at how big and athletic he was even at that age.

DM: What did you do the day after the season ended?

JT: Do you mean the day after the last game or the day after meetings-day that followed the last game?

DM: Both.

JT: The day after the last game was pretty uneventful. We reviewed the Jaguars game and had an end-of-year meeting. We talked about the off-season. Obviously, there was uncertainty at that point about the coaching staff, so we didn't have a whole lot of answers for what would happen. Coach [Eric Mangini] thanked us for our effort, especially in the last four games, and said he hoped to see us in the spring.

The next day, I actually went back to northern Wisconsin to do a little ice fishing for a couple of days.

DM: Why is it not surprising that Joe Thomas, in his first day free and clear, would go fishing?

JT: Oh, yeah.

DM: How would you sum up your season?

JT: From a team standpoint, obviously disappointing. It was good for us to finish the way we did, but I had higher expectations. I thought we'd be able to win more games. I felt like we had some pretty good players, a core group of guys.

DM: Individually?

JT: I was pleased with the way I played. I felt like I grew as a player from the year before, which is always my goal. I think this was my best season. I improved in a lot of areas that needed improvement, and I stayed good and even improved in the areas I thought I was already solid.

DM: Main difference between Joe Thomas who broke in and the Joe Thomas of today?

JT: (*Chuckle*) Besides being twenty-five instead of twenty-two?

DM: Touché.

JT: I understand the game a lot better. I understand the offense and I understand defenses. Coming in, you're so concerned about learning your job and the things you need to do to be successful individually. Once that's good, you can start to focus on learning guys around you and learning defenses and what they're trying to do to you.

DM: What can a three-time Pro Bowler improve in year four?

JT: Everything. Even though you strive for perfection, you're never going to play the perfect game. I want to learn more about the game as a whole and about the finer points of technique across the line of scrimmage. I want to learn more about coverages and blitzes so I can kind of see the game before it happens.

DM: Is that occurring?

JT: Yes. Sometimes I feel like I'm out there and everything is in slow motion, which is what you want.

DM: Word association—Eric Mangini?

JT: (*Chuckle*) I don't want to get myself in trouble. ... He's smart.

DM: How would you get yourself in trouble?

JT: (*Laughs*) You never know.

DM: Mike Holmgren?

JT: Leader.

DM: D'Arcy Egan?

JT: Fun.

DM: Is D'Arcy a Pro Bowl angler?

JT: I would say yes.

DM: Take me inside the locker room of the 2009 Browns as they careened toward 1-11. Please live up to your reputation as an honest man.

JT: I thought the locker room was exceptional. We have tremendous people on the team. There was never a point where any of the players were bickering among themselves. We were upset about losing, of course, but we weren't bickering among ourselves. We were basically a team without stars—you can call Josh [Cribbs] a star, but he's not a star in the traditional sense—and that was one of the reasons we were able to turn it around and win the last four. We didn't have anybody give up or point fingers. We were searching for answers at 1-11, but we stayed together.

DM: Do you think most players believed in Mangini from start of camp to end of season?

JT: In the NFL, guys realize the coach is your boss and you've got to do what he says. If you don't, you're going to be gone. Every coach in the NFL is smart and has a good plan. It's just a matter of whether you're able to execute the plan.

DM: Did Mangini at any point work the players too hard?

JT: Every coach does what he feels is necessary. As players, it's not our job to tell a coach what we think about his practices. Some teams barely do any work during the week and win on Sundays. Some teams work for three hours and win. It's hard to say what's too much and not enough. I just try to work hard and do what I'm supposed to do every day.

DM: Did this team need Mangini's discipline after what happened the previous season?

JT: I felt one of the best things Eric did coming in here was to have rules that were enforced. One thing that is certainly important is discipline. Anybody can have rules, but if you don't enforce them, they don't mean anything. I was really happy with him having rules and sticking to them. There was punishment if you broke the rules.

DM: What do you do to relax besides fishing?

JT: Besides hunting and fishing?

DM: My bad. You relax by fishing and hunting.

JT: Exactly.

DM: When did you begin fishing/hunting?

JT: I started fishing at about age two. I started hunting at thirteen or so.

DM: Are you a better left tackle or angler?

JT: I'm a much better left tackle. I pretend to be a professional fisherman and pretend I know what I'm talking about, but I really don't. I'm a good faker when it comes to fishing.

DM: Your favorite catch ever?

JT: A ten-pound walleye I caught last spring on the show with D'Arcy.

DM: What is one fish you'd like to have on your resumé?

JT: A marlin or sailfish.

DM: Wildest thing you've ever witnessed in a fishing boat?

JT: When D'Arcy and I were filming a muskie show in West Branch [Ohio] Reservoir a couple of summers ago, we caught a thirty-pounder. It was unbelievable.

DM: How does a thirty-pound muskie not trump a ten-pound walleye for favorite catch?

JT: Because it technically was D'Arcy's catch. I was holding the rod when the fish hit and I gave it to him. He reeled it in. I don't want to steal D'Arcy's thunder.

DM: How does a Pro Bowl offensive tackle have to give up his line to anybody?

JT: (*Laughs*) We were trolling. When you troll, you alternate who gets to catch the fish. I caught the first, which was eighteen pounds or so. We were both holding rods; whoever's rod got hit next, it would be D'Arcy's fish.

DM: Favorite fishing hole?

JT: I have the most experience on Lake Michigan, but Lake Erie is probably number one because of the diversity of fish.

DM: Smartest person you've ever met?

JT: That's a tough question. ... No, it's not: my wife, Annie. She's the smartest person I've met, no doubt about it.

DM: Least-favorite household chore?

JT: Making my bed.

DM: Now that you're a multimillionaire, do you still need to make it?

JT: I do not make my bed. … My wife makes it … sometimes.

DM: When you came out of college, what were your goals/expectations?

JT: Team goals come first, so I wanted to win the Super Bowl every year. Individually, I had high expectations. First things first: I wanted to be a starter. Once I became a starter, I wanted to make the Pro Bowl. And I wanted to be a Hall of Famer. I'm off to a good start but I've got a long way to go.

DM: What is the key to your success from play to play?

JT: I take great pride in my technique and footwork. It came a little easier for me because I was pretty athletic and I wasn't 370 pounds, but I still work hard every day on footwork and hand placement.

DM: How do you deal with the anonymous nature of your job?

JT: Everyone who plays at this level understands that it is a no-glory position. When things go well, nobody notices you. When things go bad, everybody blames the offensive line. The no-glory aspect of the position is why, I think, a certain type of person is drawn to it and why the brotherhood and fraternity are so strong.

DM: Is it true holding happens on every play?

JT: If you go by the definition of holding from twenty, thirty years ago, which is built into the technique, yes. If you didn't do it, you'd be a poor technician. You've got to look at how the rule has evolved. There's certainly holding on every play, but where the game's rules are today, it's legalized holding.

DM: By all accounts, you are a gentle giant. How do you work up the hostility it takes to play in the NFL trenches?

JT: I look at the offensive line as a bit different than the defensive line. (*Chuckle*) The defensive guys probably would not be too happy to hear me say this, but they're the crazy ones who chase the ball all day and don't have to think about anything, really. On the offensive line, it's sort of a controlled anger. You can't run around like crazy and get off-balance; if you do, you'll fall on your face and your man will beat you.

DM: You and Josh Cribbs are represented by the same agency, All Pro Sports & Entertainment. Within APSE, Peter Schaffer is the point man for you and Josh. Will a problematic outcome of the Cribbs negotiations have any effect on your relationship with the Browns?

JT: I think everybody on the team wants Josh to get a new contract. But when you're dealing with a situation like that, one player should be separate from all other players. Whatever happens with Josh is between Josh and the Browns. Whatever happens with me and the Browns is between me and the Browns. There's not going to be a grudge or anything like that.

DM: So your agents won't use you as the means to get back at the Browns if the new contract for Cribbs is not realized?

JT: You hope you have an agent who is professional enough to understand that it is not his job to leverage different players against each other and use one guy to get a deal for somebody else. If you're an agent, you need to treat each player as his own case.

DM: Has Josh Cribbs outperformed his deal?

JT: I don't really want to get into the specifics of his contract situation, but I will say this: I don't think there is anybody who knows the game of football, and who understands contracts and the way things go in football, who wouldn't say Josh has gone above and beyond the contract he signed however long ago. I feel for him in the respect that, every coach and management that have been here has said, "Let's do a new deal" — only to leave or be forced out. It seems like every year he has to prove himself to new people, and he does. It's only because of the turnover that he hasn't gotten a new deal.

DM: What about the critics who say a contract is a contract, that he signed for six years and needs to play it out?

JT: As far as I know, the NFL is the only sport or business in America where you can sign a contract and they can cut you and tear up your contract and there is nothing. But a player, if he wants to tear up the contract, can't do it. If Josh gets injured at any point in the six years or if the Browns don't want him anymore, they can tear up the contract. It's one of the risks for NFL players associated with the way contracts are.

DM: Why does it have to be that way?

JT: Some people want to change it, but with fifty-three guys, it's hard to have all guaranteed contracts.

DM: What about those who say that if Cribbs gets a new deal, numerous teammates will line up at the door seeking theirs?

JT: I don't think I'd be worried about that, because it's pretty clear that Josh is the only case that has gone so far above what his contract was signed for that he really deserves to be rewarded. I don't know if there's anybody on the team who has done so much better than his contract that he could even with a straight face go to management and say, "Hey, let's redo my contract." The ball's always in management's court, though. If 53 guys say they want more money, it doesn't matter. It's up to management whether they want to do it. Josh getting a new deal would set a precedent for the rest of the group as in: If you do so much better than your contract, we'll be willing to reward you. That's a great incentive for guys.

DM: What is your favorite kill as a hunter?

JT: The first pheasant I shot that my dog, Maddie, retrieved after I trained her to be a bird-dog. It was last winter, the first time I'd taken her out after she was ready. It was the most enjoyable, most gratifying hunt I've been on.

DM: Most dangerous or daring thing you've ever done?

JT: I'm not that dangerous of a guy.

DM: Some would say hunting is dangerous.

JT: Hunting is so safe, though.

DM: Have you ever bungee-jumped or something along those lines?

JT: No, but I did go on a Ferris wheel with my wife once. That's pretty dangerous.

DM: What is one kill you'd like to have on your resumé?

JT: I dream of doing a bow hunt for elk out West.

DM: What is it like to hunt with a bow?

JT: It's exciting. It adds another level of challenge. You need to use different types of skills because you need to get within twenty or thirty yards of the animal without the animal knowing you're there.

DM: What is one thing you can't do no matter how hard you try?

JT: Art. I'm awful at art.

DM: Did you have a football idol growing up?

JT: The closest person to that for me was Brett Favre.

DM: What linemen did you admire?

JT: When I started playing the position toward the end of high school and into college, I watched Walter Jones, Jonathan Ogden and Orlando Pace a lot.

DM: What advice would you give youngsters who want to be offensive linemen at higher levels?

JT: Play as many sports as you can. Develop your all-around athletic ability. It will serve you well in the long run.

DM: Outside of the Browns' locker room, who is your favorite player to watch?

JT: There are so many good ones, but the guy at the top of the list would have to be Peyton Manning because of the way he runs the offense, how intelligent he is and how it's such a chess match with him on the field.

DM: Have you ever looked across the line and been convinced your opponent is taking PEDs?

JT: I'm sure that, during my career, there's been somebody lined up across from me who was taking an illegal substance. But the great part about football is, it's not measured in seconds and inches like track and field [Thomas excelled in shot put and discus in high school]. It's measured in wins and losses. Just because a guy is maybe physically stronger or quicker—whether it's artificial or not—doesn't always mean a guy is going to beat you because a lot of it's related to technique and using your brain. That's why I don't think it's as big of an issue in football as in track and field, where you'll beat somebody if you're bigger and stronger. Having said that, cheating is cheating regardless of what sport you're talking about. It's wrong.

DM: Would you cheat to extend your career?

JT: No. I play by the rules and put in the time. I couldn't look myself in the mirror knowing I was giving myself an unfair advantage.

DM: Do you envision yourself as a Cleveland Brown the rest of your career?

JT: Yes.

DM: Are you saying that because it is expedient or because you really mean it?

JT: I wouldn't say it if I didn't mean it. I want to be a Brown for the rest of my career.

DM: Favorite meal?

JT: Meatloaf and mashed potatoes.

UPDATE: Joe Thomas made the Pro Bowl in each of his first eight NFL seasons (2007–2014)—all with the Cleveland Browns.

Jim Thome, *baseball*

September 2011

Those who think Jim Thome derived his greatest pleasure in baseball from circling the bases 600-plus times nonstop never will have understood him fully.

Yes, the homers were important. Each and every one. But they did not drive him.

The endless hours in the cages did.

Session after session, often in the dank bowels of venues across the country, when no more than one other person was looking.

In search of the perfect power swing.

Thome knew there is no such thing as the perfect swing, but he lived for the chase.

The results Thome got from the callused hands were not too shabby. He will end his career, perhaps at the end of this season, ranked among the game's greatest sluggers.

The Indians, Thome's team from 1991 to 2002 and again this year, will honor his home-run prowess tonight at Progressive Field.

DM: What do 600-plus homers mean to you?

JT: Longevity. When you speak of 600, you speak of longevity. It's a long journey to get there, with a lot of ups and downs along the way. There's a sense of accomplishment. The process is so worth it.

DM: In which of your all-time stats do you take the most pride?

JT: Honestly, it's not the homers. I would say the on-base percentage before anything else. [Career .403 entering last Tuesday.]

DM: You are known as one of the nicest people in the game, a "Gentleman Jim." Does anything get you angry on a ball field?

Jim Thome
photo by Chuck Crow/*The Plain Dealer*

JT: I don't like when people show up the opponent, or even their teammates. I don't have any tolerance for that. It's about competing and respecting the game.

DM: Back in the day as a member of the Indians, you charged Boston pitcher and former teammate Rheal Cormier in Fenway Park. Is that your only career charge of the mound?

JT: Yes. It was a situation where I needed to do it. I got hit, I had to go. I respected what he was doing. I knew him, but when you put on the other uniform, you're competing. It's not about friendship, it's about doing what's best for your team.

DM: I read somewhere that you got in a fight with Chipper Jones in the minors. True?

JT: (*Laughs*) No. No, no, no. Our teams were in a brawl, but, no.

DM: Word association—Phillies manager Charlie Manuel?

JT: Mentor and father.

DM: Former Indians manager Mike Hargrove?

JT: A man who commanded respect.

DM: White Sox manager Ozzie Guillen?

JT: Entertaining.

DM: Twins manager Ron Gardenhire?

JT: (*Long pause*) I want to make sure I use the right term here, because he's so special. The best word for him is respect. Guys truly respect him and enjoy playing for him.

DM: You and Manuel made quite a baseball pair, beginning with your days in the minors, when he was your manager.

JT: For a long time, I think people looked at the outer half of him and didn't give him the credit he was due. But what happened is, he proved over time that he was such a legendary baseball man, and you're seeing it now. The stories from other players, from me, make you realize that Charlie Manuel is one of the greatest baseball men to ever put on a uniform. He's passionate, he's legendary and he cares about the game and his players.

DM: Best baseball advice you ever received?

JT: Don't believe the hype.

DM: Where did it come from?

JT: My father.

DM: You have said you never would take performance-enhancing drugs for any number of reasons, foremost among them, you couldn't look your dad in the eye. Has Chuck Thome ever asked you if you've been at least tempted to do it?

JT: No.

DM: Has the subject of PEDs ever come up between you two?

JT: No. Never.

DM: Does it bother you when select critics opine that your accomplishments might be tainted because of the Steroid Era, even while you are clean?

JT: I've had to answer these types of questions a lot. Look, I was in a time where steroids happened. There's no denying it. But I don't think you can go through life and worry every day about what other people say or think. You go about your business, you do what you do, you believe in what you believe in. Having said that, I don't see why 600 homers—or 400 or 500—ever need to have an asterisk when you did it the right way.

DM: Are you rankled, though, by the cheaters who muddied the waters for the clean ones?

JT: It's not for me to judge people, it's not for me to say this or that. People make decisions and have to live by those decisions. I made my decision to play by the rules and I can feel good about it.

DM: What was the best life lesson your late mother, Joyce, taught you?

JT: Be kind.

DM: Is your son, Landon, going to be a ballplayer?

JT: I have no clue. I really don't. He's three years old.

DM: When you think of Jim Thome, Cleveland Indian, what pops into your head?

JT: Great times. Where it all started.

DM: You hear it said often that baseball is a kids' game, that it's fun to play. But there's also an incredible amount of work needed to perform at this level, let alone excel. How much of the game has been work for you, and how much has been fun?

JT: Obviously, there's been a lot of work. The bottom line is, you're not going to have fun if you don't put the work in. You're going to struggle in this game, and struggling is not fun, but enjoyment comes from getting out of the struggle. That's where "Don't believe the hype" becomes so important: The best way I know of to deal with the ups and downs is to work hard and stay grounded.

DM: On an average day at the ballpark, at any point in your career, what have been the most enjoyable aspects?

JT: Being in the clubhouse with the guys. Talking hitting with your teammates and coaches. The laughter. The dinners on the road.

DM: What is the first lesson you would want a youngster entering the majors to master?

JT: Respect the game. You don't need to add anything to that.

DM: When it comes time to retire, have you thought about what comes next?

JT: Not really. I know this: I want to be the best father and husband I can be. Baseball has taken me on a great journey, but I look forward to being at home.

DM: What do you want your legacy to be?

JT: It's hard for a player to pick his legacy; that's up to others. But I hope I'm remembered, more than anything, as a good teammate, as someone my teammates wanted to play with.

DM: Does one regular-season homer stand out?

JT: That's tough. There's been a few. They're all special. I remember some good ones at the old ballpark [Municipal Stadium], when my parents were there. The 500th—a walk-off. The 600th was great. The 511-footer against Kansas City at Jacobs Field. The flagpole in Minnesota. The Skydome crouton.

DM: The Skydome crouton?

JT: You know, the one in the old Skydome in Toronto. I was with the Indians.

DM: What happened?

JT: (*Laughs*) The ball went into the restaurant and landed on the croutons of a salad. That's what they told me.

DM: Describe the feeling of hitting a walk-off homer, which you've done twelve times.

JT: It's indescribable. That's the ultimate in a regular-season game—to hit a home run and win a game. To have your teammates waiting on you. It really doesn't get any better than that. And you can't script it, you can't try to do it. You have a good at-bat, and if it happens, it happens.

DM: You've always talked about the ultimate goal—to win a World Series ring. It has not happened. How do you summarize that void?

JT: I won't look at my career and say, "If I don't win a World Series, it hasn't been complete." Man, I've been given so much.

The game has given me so much, so many opportunities. I've been very fortunate. So there's no regret about not winning a ring. Do you understand that?

DM: Yes.

JT: Would I love to do it? Absolutely. If it never happens, it would still eat at me every day. I've been close, and I can't imagine what it would be like to actually get there. But again, it's not regret as much as it is disappointment.

DM: Who joins you at your dream power hitters' roundtable?

JT: Babe Ruth, Hank Aaron, Mickey Mantle. It would be pretty cool to talk hitting with those guys, wouldn't it?

DM: What is the highlight of your career? One snapshot that continues to give you goosebumps?

JT: No question: Catching the ball at third base for the last out against the Orioles to clinch the division in 1995. It's my favorite because of what it meant to the city.

DM: Why did you wear No. 25 for all these years?

JT: It was my grandfather's number, a family number. But I only wore it in Cleveland after Buddy Bell left. In my mind, that was Buddy Bell's number in Cleveland.

DM: According to baseball-reference.com, the only other number you've worn is No. 6, when you broke in.

JT: And No. 59.

DM: Fifty-nine? You wore that number in your first spring training?

JT: No, no — that was my number when I debuted. I got my first hit as No. 59. Can you believe that? I was No. 59. I made my debut on the road and got my first hit. Then when we came back to Cleveland from that trip, No. 6 was available. It was a smaller number, so I took it.

DM: Do you realize that, in 1996, you led the Indians with five triples?

JT: Wow. That's awesome. That's a good trivia question.

DM: Even more amazing: Kenny Lofton was among those on that team. You broke his four-year run as triples leader.

JT: (*Laughs*) I'll have to harass him over that one.

Y. A. Tittle, *football*

July 2009

Football legend Y.A. Tittle is scheduled to be at the International Exposition Center in Cleveland Friday to sign autographs as part of the National Sports Collectors Convention.

Tittle, a seven-time Pro Bowl selection and two-time NFL MVP, threw for 33,070 yards and 242 touchdowns in a career that began with the Baltimore Colts of the All-America Football Conference in 1948 and ended with the New York Giants of the National Football League in 1964. He also played for San Francisco. He was inducted into the Pro Football Hall of Fame in Canton in 1971.

Tittle's Giants won division titles in 1961, 1962 and 1963 but lost the NFL Championship Game each year.

On October 28, 1962, Tittle authored one of the greatest single-game performances by a quarterback in NFL history. He completed twenty-seven passes in thirty-nine attempts for 505 yards and seven touchdowns in a 49-34 victory over the Washington Redskins.

The following season, he threw thirty-six TD passes, the NFL record at that time.

DM: Highlight of your career?

YAT: Being inducted into National Football Hall of Fame.

DM: When you began playing pro football, was that a goal?

YAT: Oh, no. Not in my wildest imagination. My goal was just to make the team.

DM: Greatest player of all-time?

YAT: I think that's unfair to say because there are so many candidates with so many different skills. And a lot depends on the team you play for.

DM: Favorite teammate?

YAT: (*Chuckle*) The guy who could block the defensive right end. Over the course of my years in the game, I was blessed to play with a lot of great players and great people.

DM: Did you have a football hero as a youngster?

YAT: Sammy Baugh.

DM: What is the first thing that comes to mind when you think about your football career?

YAT: How much I loved playing. Football was my whole life. Being successful in pro football was such a dream come true, because I never really thought I'd be that good. I didn't grow up cocky, believing I was the best. I was surprised when I made the LSU starting team, I was surprised when I was good at professional football. I knew I could throw, though.

DM: Favorite player to watch today?

YAT: If I had to pick one, it would be Peyton Manning. He's terrific. I identify with him because he's the type of player I was. I wasn't a scrambler, and neither is he.

DM: What was your thought process in the pocket?

YAT: I was first choice, second choice, throw it away into open space to avoid the loss. If I didn't find a receiver on the first or second choice, I got rid of it and hopefully didn't get penalized for intentional grounding. I wasn't any kind of genius back there, trying to survey the whole field. You can't see the whole field, anyway. People talk about that all the time, but you can't. You can only see one side at a time. You look to the right, then to the left. How are you going to look to the left and see the right? Your eyes don't go sideways; they go together.

DM: Talk about the game against the Redskins.

YAT: I had a chance—I'm not trying to brag, now—to throw for eight touchdowns and a record. We had a first down deep in Washington territory in the final minutes. The coach wanted me to throw for number eight. I didn't do it. I wouldn't do it.

DM: Why?

YAT: We already had the game won. It would have just been for personal gain. Anybody in the stands, anybody on the other team, would have said, "Y.A. Tittle was doing his thing for personal glory." That's not why I played football. I didn't want to be remembered as the guy who threw three or four passes in a row so he could get an eighth touchdown.

DM: You were—

YAT: I'll tell you what, though: After all these years, I wish I would have gone for number eight.

DM: Why?

YAT: (*Chuckle*) Because I'm more selfish now than I was then.

DM: One of the most famous sports photos ever is of you on your knees, dazed, bloodied and helmetless, moments after an interception in a loss against Pittsburgh in your final season.

YAT: You had to bring that up, didn't you? I'm kidding. It's no problem.

DM: What do you recall about that moment?

YAT: I really don't remember the ballgame because I was knocked out. I didn't really regain consciousness until the end of the game. I missed a lot of the events. The picture ended up winning awards and getting a lot of attention. At first I didn't care to see it. But as the years have gone by, I'm sort of proud to be in it.

DM: Do you have the photo at home?

YAT: Yes. And they have it around my insurance office, too, to sort of remind me just in case I had forgotten.

DM: The blood trickling down your face from your bald head makes the photo so compelling. Do you have any scars from that game?

YAT: No scars—just pain knowing we didn't win. I have no scars on any part of my body. I've broken every bone everywhere except my leg—ankles, arms, nose, sternum, back, hips, ribs—but scars? No.

DM: How many concussions did you suffer in pro football?

YAT: I can't be sure because, at that time, I didn't know what a concussion was. You played with grogginess. I got knocked out of some games, regained my senses and went back in. Once you collected your thoughts after the smelling salts, you were back on the field. Today they're much more cautious, which is great. They need to do everything they can to keep the players as healthy as possible.

DM: Part of the reason you achieved legendary status in the game was your willingness to play hurt. Why subject yourself to the punishment?

YAT: It goes back to what I said earlier, about loving the game. I never wanted to leave the field.

DM: I read where you signed your first contract with the Cleveland Browns in 1947, when they played in the All-America Football Conference.

YAT: The first professional football game I ever saw, the Browns played in it. Paul Brown had me flown in and the Browns treated me like a king. I watched the game from the sideline. I was overwhelmed. After it was over, coach Brown took me back to the hotel and I signed a contract. He told me the Browns thought Otto Graham would only play one more year, and that I could learn from him for one season. It wasn't true about Otto, of course. He played for many years after that.

DM: You never played for the Browns, instead ending up with the AAFC's Baltimore Colts in 1948. You became the conference's rookie of the year and played with Baltimore through 1950. What happened with Cleveland?

YAT: I was getting ready to report to Cleveland's training camp when the commissioner [Jonas Ingram] notified me I was going to the new Baltimore team. He decided he wanted more balance in the league, so he took several players from the Browns and the New York Yankees and sent them to Baltimore.

DM: What do you think of the football players of today?

YAT: They're bigger, stronger, faster and have better coaching than we did.

DM: So you're not one of the elder statesmen who insists, "We were better."

YAT: They're definitely better than we were. I think we had just as much heart and desire, but we couldn't match their physical skills. I hear some older guys say, "They couldn't have played with us." Well, we were the ones who probably couldn't play with them.

DM: Any regrets about your playing career?

YAT: We never won a world championship. That hurts. I was a bit embarrassed to lose those championship games. I regret the fact that, in all three of the title games with the Giants, we had to play on an icy field. We were a passing team, so it handicapped us. You were forced to wear tennis shoes and you couldn't grip the football. No excuses, though. We got beat.

DM: Even with those losses, you had an amazing career.

YAT: I gave football everything I had. The game was great to me, and I got as much as I could out of it.

Bill White, *baseball*

February 2008

Bill White was a three-career baseball man.

He played in 1,673 major-league games over thirteen seasons (1956, 1958-69).

At a time when pitchers were king, he batted .286 with 202 homers and 870 RBI. He won seven consecutive Gold Gloves at first base.

White moved on to broadcasting, which featured calls of Yankees games in the 1970s and 1980s. The team of White and Phil Rizzuto often was more entertaining than the games themselves.

White also served as president of the National League from 1989 to 1994—the first African-American to hold such a high position in Major League Baseball.

The straight-shooting White graduated from Warren G. Harding High School in Warren, attended Hiram College, and now lives in Bucks County, Pennsylvania.

DM: What do you make of the steroids era?

BW: It's something that happened. I'm not sure, though, what you do with the players who supposedly took steroids before they were banned. I think it's up to the Hall of Fame and the voters to decide whether they get in. Going forward, anybody caught taking steroids—because they know the rules now—probably ought not be able to play baseball anymore. They should find something else to do.

DM: Wow. One strike and you're out.

BW: If you want to get rid of steroids, you've got to say, "Look, if you take them, you can't play Major League Baseball." If you've got a rule, you need to abide by it. But I don't know about other things that can show up as steroids, so that's a problem.

DM: Recognizing the dark cloud created by performance-enhancing drugs, what is your assessment of the game today?

BW: I think it's in good shape, all things considered. Attendance keeps going up, revenue keeps going up. Players are making money, owners are making money.

DM: What is one change you would make to the game in the twenty-first century?

BW: I would try to find a way to equalize the ability for every team to compete.

DM: Is a salary cap in order?

BW: I don't know. The New England Patriots keep winning, and the NFL has a cap.

DM: How do you view Barry Bonds?

BW: Hell of a ballplayer. It will be up to the Hall of Fame voters to decide if he gets in. The way baseball is being played today, with pitchers not being able to throw at anybody, somebody's going to hit 1,000 homers, so his record will go by the boards. The only question will be: Do guys want to play into their forties?

DM: Other than the money being made and lack of brushbacks, what is a major difference in the game from when you played?

BW: The players are better. They've played the game longer. They're bigger, stronger. They have agents.

DM: What is one thing the players of today need to know about the past?

BW: I don't think he needs to know anything about the past, because the game has changed so dramatically. For example: The reserve clause is no longer there; a player can choose where he wants to play.

DM: Favorite moment of your playing career?

BW: The final out of the 1964 World Series [Cardinals beat the Yankees]. A lot of players don't get the chance to win a ring.

DM: Did you get the credit you deserved for being a quality player?

BW: Sure. I'm not a Hall of Famer, but I didn't lose too many games. I could catch the ball and hit a little bit.

DM: Word association — George Steinbrenner?

BW: Misunderstood.

DM: Phil Rizzuto?

BW: Very funny. Great person.

DM: Reggie Jackson?

BW: Mr. October. Somebody called him that, so I will.

DM: Billy Martin?

BW: Very good manager. Underrated.

DM: As National League president, did you feel extra pressure because you were blazing a trail for your race?

BW: Well, I didn't want to make mistakes because I needed to make sure someone of color could follow me. I needed to micromanage, which I did. I had very good people in the league office who made sure we didn't make mistakes.

DM: What was your greatest accomplishment as NL president?

BW: Expansion [Colorado and Florida] and keeping San Francisco in San Francisco without Major League Baseball being sued.

DM: Best player with whom you ever played?

BW: Willie Mays.

DM: Best player against whom you played?

BW: Willie Mays.

DM: Sum up Mays.

BW: He loved the game. He could beat you with the bat, glove and legs. He taught me quite a bit about baseball. He could have managed had he had the opportunity.

DM: Recollections of your days at Hiram?

BW: Greatest time of my life. The teachers were great, the students were great. I had an English class with about six people in it. I played basketball, baseball and football. I was better at basketball and football than I was at baseball.

DM: What position in football?

BW: Halfback and some quarterback.

DM: I read where you are an avid fisherman and traveler. Favorite catch and destination?

BW: I caught a 100-pound halibut off Kodiak Island [Alaska] and a twenty-eight-inch trout in Colorado. Australia is a great place.

Venus & Serena Williams, *tennis*
November 2005

Even when they are not busy, the Williams sisters are busy. Better known simply as Venus and Serena, they have so much to do—books, clothing lines, reality shows, special appearances—and so little time. Oh, by the way, they happen to be pretty good at tennis, too.

DM: What motivates you at this stage, tennis-wise, given what you already have accomplished?

Serena & Venus Williams
photo by Chuck Crow/*The Plain Dealer*

SW: There's soooo much left to be done on the court. We have so many goals, and we're so young. We want to win more Grand Slams.

VW: I'm very happy with the results in my career—it's more than a dream come true—but I love what I do. I love being successful at it. And I know there's only a limited amount of time to do what I do well.

DM: How do you juggle all the off-court activities with the work required to be great on it?

SW: Everyone says we might be distracted, but I've had so many other opportunities I've turned down because I'm at tournaments. Tennis definitely is number one in my life.

VW: Tennis is at the top of my list. I appreciate what I do every month, every year, as I get older. Tennis has allowed us to do everything else.

DM: What do people most misunderstand about each of you?

VW: Nothing, really. I think people do understand me. They see I'm a person who loves what I do, who loves to have fun. I think people feel my joy on the court.

SW: The biggest misunderstanding about me is: Why, with all the other opportunities, would I still want to play tennis? Well, the answer is, I love the game.

DM: What do people most misunderstand about your father?

VW: (*Laughs*) I think it would take a few years to understand him, so probably everything. (*More laughter*) He's a cool guy. I'm glad he's my dad.

SW: They don't realize my father is the nicest guy in the world. When people meet him, they can't believe it. He's so sweet, one of the most genuine people out there.

DM: One characteristic of your sister you wish you had?

SW: Venus has a stone face on the court. She never gets mad. I'm always mad and angry and, like, "Ugghhh." Venus is like "Oh, well, I'll get her next time." That's her attitude in life, as well.

VW: Serena does what she wants to do. She goes for it. She doesn't let the person next to her determine what she's going to do, and she's not going to worry about anybody thinks.

DM: How often do you consult with your sister off the court?

VW: All the time, definitely, all the time. I want to know what she's doing. (*Chuckle*) I want to know if she's going to be where I am.

DM: Have you ever wondered what it would have been like as two distinct solo careers instead of the sister act?

SW: I've never thought about that, but I guess it would have been interesting.

VW: Sure I've wondered about that, but what we have is great. Nobody else has a sister on tour with the relationship Serena and I do. If anything, I wish more of my sisters had played tennis professionally, and if it had been at the same time, even better.

DM: Imagine if you had two dominant players covering two eras instead of one.

SW: That would have been fun. But I like it better this way, because I get to spend time with my sister, laughing and joking and things like that. And you never know what the results would have been without us pushing each other.

DM: Any resentment toward those who get a lot of notoriety off the court but have not delivered on it?

VW: No. I think everyone has his or her own thing, and whatever you have as your strong point, you should try to capitalize on it as best you can.

SW: I don't resent anyone. It's easy to point fingers and say stuff, but I won't do it. I'm happy for whatever comes to whatever individual, because you never know what people have been through in life.

DM: Can it be assumed, then, that neither one of you is down on Anna Kournikova?

SW: Oh, no. I love her. She's so nice. She's awesome. We love her.

VW: To be honest, I thought she was a great player. I thought the media might have prevented her from being her best.

DM: Seriously, Venus?

VW: Yes, because maybe she wasn't prepared for all the criticism of her play. It's hard to handle that kind of pressure.

DM: If WTA commissioner for a day, what is one change you would make?

VW: Definitely shorten the season.

DM: Venus — one item you could not do without?

VW: My 311 album.

DM: Serena — I read on your Web site that your favorite TV show is *Golden Girls*. Is that actually true?

SW: Yes. Isn't it ridiculous?

DM: Well, as long as you say so, yeah. It seems to be an odd pairing.

SW: I love the *Golden Girls*. I've seen every episode twenty times. I just got an autographed copy of the second season on DVD.

DM: Do you watch reruns?

SW: Yes, but I've moved on to another show — *America's Top Model*. I love Tyra Banks.

DM: Serena — when you broke out the tight black-leather outfit, you knew it would cause a stir ...

SW: I didn't know it would cause so much excitement.

DM: Are you saying that with a straight face?

SW: Yes. I was just thinking, This is comfortable, so I'll wear it. I was surprised by the reaction. It didn't seem like a big deal to me.

DM: You have worn other sexy outfits in becoming a woman of style on the court. Are you concerned it might take attention away from your tennis skills?

SW: No. I think people understand I'm a true athlete. It hasn't distracted, it's added.

DM: The Williams sisters have dominated in a predominantly Caucasian sport, and done so on their own terms. I would imagine both of you have been subjected to pockets of ugliness, yet you never seem to rail against it or otherwise complain about it. How have you managed such restraint?

SW: We've definitely kept a lot of it in. We understand that you have to roll with the punches. Everything isn't always going to be good. You have to take the bad with the good.

DM: Because of how easy you both made it look when you arrived as pros, do you think those on the outside took for granted how hard you worked to get there?

VW: I don't expect everyone to see the deeper side of things, and what it took and what it takes. I've been a working girl since I was four. I have the results, so it's been worth it.

DM: Serena—one thing in which you can't beat Venus, and vice versa?

SW: Venus runs much faster than I do, but I'm a better swimmer.

DM: The Williams sisters endorse McDonald's and do good work for its charitable arm. But how can such tremendous athletes consume fast food and remain in top form?

VW: Well, it's all about having a balanced diet, and, actually, McDonald's has introduced a lot of great things for its menu.

UPDATE: Venus and Serena Williams have been a women's tennis dynasty. Serena has won nineteen Grand Slam singles titles, including the 2015 Australian Open; Venus has won seven. Each sister has won four gold medals at the Summer Olympics: one in singles and three in doubles. Both sisters have been ranked No. 1 by the Women's Tennis Association. During the 2010 French Open, they became the co-world No.1 players in women's doubles, in addition to holding the top two positions in singles.

Kristi Yamaguchi, *skating*
January 2009

Kristi Yamaguchi is a big deal, and not just because of her prowess on ice. Among her figure skating accomplishments: two women's singles world championships (1991–92); two pairs national championships with Rudy Galindo (1989–90); one women's singles national championship (1992); and one women's singles Olympic gold medal (Albertville, France, 1992).

Yamaguchi is a member of multiple halls of fame because of her skating.

She also is a big deal because she can dance.

In May 2008, Yamaguchi teamed with professional Mark Ballas to win the sixth season of *Dancing With the Stars* on ABC. Yamaguchi and Ballas capped a string of consistently fine performances with perfection in the final round to defeat Jason Taylor and Edyta Sliwinska.

A gold medal is nice, to be sure, but so is the *DWTS* mirror-ball trophy. Those with both to their credit have mass appeal.

Yamaguchi is married to NHL player Bret Hedican and is the mother of two.

DM: Be honest: Do you get more questions about *DWTS* than about skating?

KY: Lately, *Dancing With The Stars*.

DM: How were you able to be flawless in the *DWTS* final?

KY: Ten hours of studio time a day going into the final. The competitive side of me clicked in and I knew what I had to do. I was so close to the end and gave it my all. I do feel the athletes can manage their skills in that competition because they know their bodies, they know how to train, they know how to be ready for performances. They know how to turn it on when it counts.

DM: With which other professional dancer from the show could you guarantee a title?

KY: I can't do that for Mark's sake. I won't do that.

DM: You helped write the book, *Figure Skating For Dummies*. I'm a figure skating dummy. What's my first lesson?

KY: The first thing people say is their ankles flop on the ice because of improper fit of skates. In any sport, the equipment, obviously, is No. 1. If you don't have the right-sized skate, if you don't have the right support, you're going to have problems.

KY: Hmmm. Let's get back to that one.

DM: Favorite athlete other than your husband?

KY: That's a good one, because I usually say my husband. Tiger Woods.

DM: After three straight women's singles seconds at nationals (1989–91), did you have any doubts?

KY: Absolutely. I almost gave up trying to win nationals, because even as a novice and junior I was second. My philosophy finally was: Just make the world team and show them what you can do internationally.

DM: What drove you to reach skating's summit?

KY: Fear of failure, fear of not realizing my potential. I didn't want to have any regrets. I wanted to make sure to put in the time, and if it wasn't good enough, I would have been fine. The worst would have been to be second or third and say, "Maybe I could have worked a little harder." Dream big, believe in yourself and work hard.

DM: If not a skater, what would you be?

KY: Performing somewhere, maybe on Broadway.

DM: Word association—Nancy Kerrigan, Olympic silver medalist in 1994.

KY: Friend.

DM: Tonya Harding, who edged you at 1991 nationals?

KY: (*Pause*) Uh, scared. (*Laughter*).

DM: Do you mean scared or scary?

KY: I'm scared of her. (*Laughter*)

DM: Favorite dance?

KY: Hard to pick one, but I'll say the cha-cha. It's fun, but there's technique in it. I think people enjoy watching it.

KY: Triple Lutz.

DM: Greatest athletic feat you've seen on TV or in-person?

KY: Michael Phelps at the Beijing Olympics.

DM: Favorite character from history?

KY: Princess Diana. There's so much history about her, but I also love the compassion she had and her dedication to helping others.

DM: How does the body absorb so many falls during years of figure skating training?

KY: No one in the sport is immune to injury and you do see it happen, but obviously age is on your side when you're competing. As a skater, you almost know how to fall.

DM: Were you more nervous before the 1992 Olympic free skate or the 2008 *DWTS* final?

KY: Olympic free skate, by far.

DM: Was that a stupid question?

KY: No. I know what you're driving at, because skating was my comfort zone and dancing wasn't. Nothing against *Dancing With The Stars*, but there's no comparison.

DM: Who sits at your dream figure skating roundtable?

KY: There are so many to pick from, and I don't want to leave people out. Scott Hamilton definitely would be there.

DM: You have a five-star reputation for integrity, generosity and amiability. In sum, you are good people. Do you have any vices?

KY: Well, thank you. Not obvious vices. I am a procrastinator, though.

DM: Do you ever get mad?

KY: Oh, yeah. I think that, when you become a mother, you realize a threshold of frustration. At the same time, my children have taught me unbelievably unconditional love.

DM: What is one thing about Kristi Yamaguchi that people don't know?

KY: Sometimes I'm not sure there's anything, because I feel like my life has been out there so much, especially lately. Besides, if I tell you, it wouldn't be unknown anymore.

Dave Zastudil, *football*

December 2006

One of the smartest moves the Browns made last off-season was to sign punter Dave Zastudil. He played the previous four seasons with Baltimore.

Zastudil from Bay Village High School and Ohio University, has been outstanding as the successor to Kyle Richardson. When combining gross average, net average, highest percentage of punts inside the twenty and lowest percentage of touchbacks, Zastudil ranks among the NFL's best.

DM: Toughest part of being a punter?

DZ: Knowing that you don't have much margin for error. You only get a handful of punts per game, so you almost need to be perfect. A quarterback can throw a number of incompletions and still have a good game. Our bad punts have to be good, bad punts. If not, we'll be replaced fairly quickly.

DM: Easiest part of being a punter?

DZ: Compared to the other guys, it's the fact that the body's not taking such a beating every day. We have little things that might go wrong, but we're able to take care of our bodies better, because we're not getting hit all the time.

DM: What's hurting you now?

DZ: I've got nagging inflammation issues, but that's normal at this time of year.

DM: What body parts break down for a punter?

DZ: Back, hamstrings, the plant knee.

DM: How does a punter, or kicker, fit in as a teammate?

DZ: You have to know your role. You're a specialist. You can't be

Dave Zastudil
photo by John Kuntz/*The Plain Dealer*

running your mouth, bouncing around. If you work hard and produce on the field, the respect will come over time. Only then will you start to feel like one of the guys.

DM: How do you get some of your punts to dart basically ninety degrees to the right?

DZ: Part of it is luck, no question. But you also can do some things to increase your chances. If I put the nose up, for example, it will give me a side-winding spin. The ball comes down, hits and bounces right.

DM: Why is this, your fifth year in the NFL, clearly your best across the board?

DZ: Consistency. I've always had the strong leg, but my first few years, I was inconsistent. It wasn't until last year that I began to feel like a true pro, because I took the next step mentally. And playing for the Browns, it's no secret that special teams coach Jerry Rosburg is one of the best in the league. When you combine a great coach with a terrific coverage unit, you're going to look good.

DM: Did you make any physical adjustments last year that have carried into this year?

DZ: I used to hold my hand inside the ball, and when I went to drop, the ball spun. Now my thumb is more on top, so the ball is already turned where I need it to be.

DM: In Baltimore, did you have any conversations with Ray Lewis?

DZ: Yes. He's very down to earth, and he's one of the best leaders I've seen.

DM: How did you become a punter?

DZ: In high school, coach [Tom] Kaiser said they were looking for a punter. I said I thought I could do it, because I had been told I had a strong leg when I played soccer growing up. A few of us went out and kicked across the practice field and into the woods.

I still remember it. Eventually, coach Kaiser said, "You're my guy."

DM: Why left-footed?

DZ: In soccer, I was put on the left side, because they said I had a strong left leg. I've always been a lefty.

DM: Highlight of your multi-sport career at Bay High?

DZ: Winning a conference championship in football. The players on that team always will have the memory of working together, day after day, to accomplish something significant as one. [Zastudil was quarterback, punter, and kicker.]

DM: What are the keys to being a quality punter?

DZ: Athleticism and flexibility; consistent drop; willingness to study film and seek out somebody who has proven himself in order to learn as much as possible.

DM: Who was an invaluable mentor for you?

DZ: Sean Reali, a Bay grad who kicked at Syracuse. He helped me a ton.

DM: Punts per week?

DZ: I average 40-45 per day, three days per week, then game day. As the season goes on, I tend to kick a little less during the week.

DM: As a punter in Cleveland, are your Pro Bowl chances automatically sabotaged by the elements?

DZ: Brian Moorman's a Pro Bowler, and he plays for Buffalo, so it can be done. I love the challenge of kicking in tough conditions, when it's cold and the wind is blowing.

DM: Favorite part of NFL game day?

DZ: Running out of the tunnel this year, obviously, has been even more special. When you grew up here and had season tickets, when you dreamed of playing for the Browns, there's no feeling like coming out of that tunnel and hearing the cheers.

DM: When you get a chance to reflect on realizing the dream that so few do, what comes to mind?

DZ: The support I've received along the way. I've been very fortunate to have such great family members, friends, coaches, teammates.

DM: Longest punt in a game?

DZ: Seventy-five yards in college.

DM: How do you respond to those who maintain that punting is easy?

DZ: (*Silence*)

DM: You do hear that, don't you?

DZ: Yeah. I've heard it a lot. I guess the best response is: "If it's so easy, why are you sitting at home watching the game on TV and not out here?"

Acknowledgments

Thanks to *The Plain Dealer* for employing me since 1990 and allowing me to be a sportswriter; to bosses Roy Hewitt (former sports editor), Mike Starkey (sports editor) and Thom Fladung (managing editor) for facilitating the pursuit of the Q-and-A's for the paper; to Mary Schmitt Boyer, Bones Bennett, Chuck Murr, and Rick Noland, foremost among the group of colleagues and former colleagues who supported the book project; to Bill Gugliotta for providing most of the photos; to Kara Johanson and Team Johanson for helping decide which Q-and-A's belong in the book and for tireless editing; to David Wiesenberg and the great people at Wooster Book for making the project possible; to my indefatigable girlfriend, Denise Polverine, for her encouragement and optimism in this endeavor and others; to my daughter Grace for being amazing; and to my late parents, Sam and Linda, who gave me every opportunity to pursue my dreams.

About the Author

Dennis Manoloff has been a sportswriter at *The Plain Dealer* since August 1990. He covers primarily pro sports. He has written on more than fifteen sports/activities, including cricket and curling. He has covered two World Series, several PGA and LPGA championship events, the NBA Finals, MLB and NBA All-Star Games, and the NFL playoffs. He was on the field and hit by a bottle during the Bottlegate game at Cleveland Browns Stadium in 2001.

Among his beats was professional indoor soccer; the Crunch won three NPSL titles in the 1990s. Because pro indoor soccer does not count as a major sport, Dennis, who grew up in Bay Village, Oho, and graduated from Bay High School, has not seen a Cleveland team win a championship in his lifetime. He once coached former Browns punter Dave Zastudil, a Bay High graduate, in baseball.

In 2001, Dennis, a Northwestern University graduate, wrote a twenty-five-piece "Talkin' Baseball" series that ran weekly during the season. *The Plain Dealer* nominated it for a Pulitzer Prize in explanatory journalism.

In 1998, he attempted to break the Guinness world record for most bowling pins knocked down in twenty-four hours. He fell woefully short but still managed 29,000 in twelve hours while raising several hundred dollars for charity. email: *dmanoloff@plaind. com* twitter: *@dmansworld474*